MW01298347

Information Science and Technology
An Introduction for Librarians
(Course Pack)

By

Dr. Yan Quan Liu

2017

Pubished by Yan Quan Liu

Liu, Yan Quan

Information Science and Technology, An Introduction for Librarians / Authored by Dr. Yan Quan Liu – Course Pack Edition.

Including bibliographical references and appendices.

Size 6" x 9" (15.24 x 22.86 cm)

ISBN-13: 978-1530170777 (pbk)

1. Information science. 2. Information Technology. 3 Information and Library Science.

ISBN-13: 978-1974521555

ISBN-10: 1974521559

This book is also available on Kindle.

This book is published on CreateSpace, Amazon's independent publishing service. Printed in the United States of America.

Table of Contents

Appendices: Bibliographic Essay Examples

Unit 01: Introduction and Housekeeping

Welcome to the course: Information Science and Technology!

This course is an overview of the ways information technology and evolving philosophies of service are changing the information professions.

We take a practical perspective. We are interested in information users and the ways that services can be improved for the communities we serve. Most of our focus is directed toward the application of information technologies to libraries and other information centers.

Important things are happening. As Maureen Sullivan has said, change is all around us. We see change everywhere, in the papers, on TV, in all aspects of our lives. We should not be surprised that libraries are also changing.

So we will look at that change, examine trends, try to anticipate the future, and consider implications for our communities. And we'll try to remember that technology is not a goal in itself but rather a means to an end.

I'm looking forward to a fun and productive semester.

Class Discussion Participation and Contribution

- The first assignment you need to do is to introduce yourself to the class by posting your introduction to the "Discussion Board" (Discussion Question 1). It doesn't have to be long, but you might want to share a bit of your background, describe your goals and aspirations, tell why your are taking the course, and so forth. In addition, you should include **your email address** in your introduction. Please attach your picture to your introduction post.

- The next assignment is for you to read the Syllabus and pose questions (Discussion Question 3 [Not Required]) if anything is unclear. You'll find a lot of information on the syllabus. You will note that there is "Discussion" where you can respond to a discussion question given by the instructor, and also read and respond to answers and comments posted by other students. In a typical discussion for a unit, the instructor will pose a series of threaded discussion questions. You are required to participate in all the discussion questions in each unit. To participate in the threaded discussions, click the "Discussion Board" button on the Action Menu located at the left. And select a topic (or question) in the current unit. For detailed information about the Discussion Board tool within the course web page, please refer to the BB Learn 9 online Help that is available at site http://www.southernct.edu/faculty-staff/teaching-learning/learnfactutorialnew.html

- For the Bib Essay work as described in the course syllabus you should review most current literature (traditional and electronic), and the focus should be directed toward major issues and practical applications pertaining to the information profession, information centers and libraries. In other words, the essay should emphasize real-world concerns and issues as they affect professional practitioners on the topics your assigned unit work. Page numbers can be limited but quality is much more important than quantity!

- Go to the Buley Library website and set up your account to access online serials and journals. You will need this in order to do research and to succeed in this course and this program. Go to the following web page titled "Accessing Databases From Off-Campus": http://www.consuls.org/screens/accesshelp.html and follow the instructions.

- Subscribe to the Southern Connecticut Student ALA chapter listserv. This is a great place to learn about the program and the profession from the perspective of your fellow students. You can also join the chapter of ALA, if you want, at a very low, low price. To subscribe to scsu_scala, send an email to "scsu_scala-subscribe@lists.southernct.edu" with a blank message body. If it doesn't work, go to the following web site and fill out the form http://lists.southernct.edu/mailman/listinfo/scsu_scala. After you sent a subscription email to the scsu_scala listserv, you should receive a confirmation email from the listserv in a few hours. Unless you reply to the confirmation email, you will not be added to the scsu_scala listserv. To confirm that you want to be added the scsu_scala listserv, simply reply to the confirmation email message, keeping the Subject: header intact. If your email system uses a Spam Guard (or filter), the automatic confirmation email from the listserv may be filtered by a Spam Guard. In this case, you will have to check a "Bulk" folder in your email system in order to find the filtered automatic confirmation email from the listserv.

Reading

- Currás, E. (2014). Brief Communication: The Nature of Information and Its Influence in Human Cultures. Knowledge Organization, 41(1), 92-96. An electronic copy (PDF file format) of this article is available on the server area called "Class Library" within the course web page.

Lecture Note

The great thing about librarianship or the information professions is that we're in one of the most interesting and arguably one of the most influential places in the world.

We are ideally located between the accumulated wisdom of the millennia and, on the other side, humanity.
Wisdom <--> US <--> Humanity

On one side is all this intelligence, these books, magazines, motion pictures, Websites, slides, clay etchings, databases. On the other side of us is the people who need that information to enlighten their day, solve a problem, make a buck, or to change their lives.
What could be better than to be strategically placed between these two? We're the link, the bridge, the connection, the switching point, the transfer agent, the translator bringing these infinitely interesting entities together.

And of course the work of the information professional requires that we know both. We must understand the techniques and tricks of retrieving useful information, we must know the structure and nuance of indexes and databases and how to use them efficiently.
But we also need to know and understand those communities we serve. We need to understand and anticipate their needs even before they do. We need to relate to them on their level, understand their perspective, and always work to get information to them in a way that makes sense to them, our clients/patrons/users.

So in this course we talk about and consider the structure of technologies. But we always try to remember the human element, because our job is to link these two fascinating and incredibly important elements in the equation.

This linking role is important. I think it was John Steely Brown who said that innovation comes from the interstices, the white spaces between fields. So how do we (society or individual researchers or questors for truth) find those interstices?

Fortunately, there is a profession and there are institutions whose purpose is to provide the critical linkages. And, again, those linking units must know the reservoir of information and the people who might be wandering out of their fields and into unfamiliar territory in the pursuit of innovation.

What do we do, then, in the information professions?

Think CPOD.

CPOD is an acronym from Alan Pratt of the University of Arizona. Ken Dowlin, late of the San Francisco Public Library, cited Pratt's CPOD as a great way to remind yourself what we do. It is also a good way to explain librarianship to people sitting in the seat next to us on that cross country flight.

Collect
Preserve
Organize
Disseminate = CPOD

You'll sometimes see variations on this theme, but this is the heart of it. It's what we do.
Many of us would argue, however, that the first three elements (collect, preserve, organize) are less central today.

This is because of changes in the economics and technology of information systems. Books are no longer rare or breathlessly expensive. Computers make organizing easier and faster and more comprehensive. The mantra of the librarian is no longer ownership but access (meaning that if we can get a customer what he/she needs anyway possible, we don't have to physically own and hold that item).

But dissemination, the D in CPOD, is still very important. And some would argue that it is more important given the range of cheap information services that people might use.

Said another way, successful libraries and information provision depends on service. Great service is critical. We are not the only game in town anymore and our service has to be "knock your socks off" terrific.

The traditional role of the librarian was to understand the reservoir of knowledge, which consisted of a relatively small number of books and other print materials. We thrived for centuries on the basis of that knowledge.

Today, however, the reservoir is huge and expanding at an accelerating rate. If anything, there is too much information out there, it's a fire hose of excessive information. How can the researcher, the child, the student, the library user, find the interstices or indeed anything useful in this avalanche of print materials, electronic materials, mutating formats, and increasing complex finding tools?

Is technology the answer? Not completely. The cold edge of technology is off-putting to many and the expanding complexity of information retrieval tools is a barrier to some. This is especially true for people new to the evolving systems or people moving out of their field of primary expertise.
Good, warm and fuzzy, human service is the key.

As John Updike said, " . . . the problem . . . is not getting more information, it's dodging information and keeping some kind of space in your head."

We can do that, we can provide access to information or reformat information so that it is in a form that makes sense to our customers. The information explosion makes our skills more valuable than ever to assist in retrieval but also to design systems that are more than technical wizardry but rather that remember and hold prominent the needs of users.

Discussion

Discussion Question 1: Introduce yourself to the class. Don't forget to include your email address in your introduction. Please attach your picture to your introduction post.
Discussion Question 2: What do you think about Calle O'Donnell's article (The Nature of Information and Its Influence in Human Cultures)?

Discussion Question 3 [Not Required]: Does the "Course Information" make sense? Do you have any questions or comments with regard to the process, content, or assignments?

Unit 02: Definition of Information and Information Science

Reading

- Williams and Sawyer, Chapter One
- Rowley, J. (2007). The wisdom hierarchy: representations of the DIKW hierarchy. Journal of Information Science, 33(2) 2007, 163–180. An electronic copy (PDF file format) of this article is available on the server area called "Class Library" within the course web page.

Lecture Note

Information

Do you have a sense of what information is?
Is it a book? Something in a book or magazine? A Computer? A database?
Is it a zero or a one, as in a binary computer system?

Perhaps. The presence or absence of a light in the Old North Church was certain valuable information to Paul Revere.

But many think that zeros and ones or streams of zeros and ones is just data.
So we have a definition that works off that notion:
"Information is that data which results from a process upon data."

In other words, information is processed data, not raw data.

Herbert Brinberg said that information "represents the resulting intellectual work product when data elements are organized and communicated in a useful form."

So it is processed, organized, communicated, and useful.
Shannon and Weaver argued that any signal is potentially information. They developed a communication model of information transfer that looks like this

encoder --> channel --> decoder

This is important; this model contains some important elements. For example, it notes that information is a process that involves transference or communication. Information and communication are two distinctly different things but are intertwined. It notes that the channel or format is important. And it observes that coding and decoding is a strong element between the sender and receiver and suggests that there might be problems associated with that process that causes some loss as noise.

Where is information? Is it in the mind of the sender or in the mind of the receiver? Or somewhere else? Does it have to be in a mind? Can it be in a machine? Can information be machine generated? Is it still information if no one sees or reads the information? Or if all human memory has forgotten the supposed information?

SI Hayakawa said that information, like a poem, is not just marks on a piece of paper, but rather an event which occurs when a reader and the marks on the paper interact in some way.

Yu Shreider said that information is data that changes the state of a system that perceives it, whether a computer or a brain; hence, a stream of data that does not change the state of its receiver is not information.

Getting dizzy? There is more.
Jason Farradane said that
"Information is a physical form or representative or surrogate of knowledge."

A surrogate? A substitute? Sure, because the real thing, the knowledge, may not be what is communicated. Information is only the physical form of that knowledge.

You have all been in this kind of argument: "I know that is what I said but that is not what I meant."
This epitomizes information as surrogate and the weakness of information and the communication of information. Farradane goes on to argue that the writer/sender/encoder may not be aware of the discrepancy, perhaps because the writer may not be aware of the truth that lies beneath what they articulate.

Brenda Dervin argued that there are two types of information:

- Information sub one: reality, the innate structure or pattern of reality
- Information sub two: ideas, the structure or pictures imputed to reality by people. "Meanings are in people."

This puts a lot of weight on the receiver.

As do we. As noted earlier, our users or the community we serve are the critical elements in library work. If we focus only on the technology or the books, we are lost. We must always hold foremost the perspective and needs of those users.

Is there a single, widely accepted definition of information? Of course not. There are many useful definitions. The value of each depends on the field, the specialty and the reason for creating a particular definition. How you define information depends on your background, your motivation, and perspective. We can simplify the relationship as this way, my fond of metaphor. The five senses collect data, the brain processes the data and it becomes information, the mind uses the information to develop knowledge, and the soul, hopefully, uses that knowledge to acquire wisdom. Would this be a simple and great way to describe the DIKW hierarchy? (Rowley, J., 2007).

Information Science

So what then is information science? The term "information science" has been with us for some time. Robert Taylor defined it as

" . . . that discipline that investigates properties and behavior of information, the forces governing it's flow, and the means of processing information for optimal accessibility and usability.

It is concerned with that body of knowledge relating to the
origination
collection
organization
storage
retrieval
interpretation
transmission
transformation
and utilization of information."

Another similar definition by Harold Borko is "[Information science] is an interdisciplinary science that investigates the properties and behavior of information, the forces that govern the flow and use of information, and the techniques, both manual and mechanical, of processing information for optimal storage, retrieval, and dissemination."

Vickery and Vickery (2004) defined information science as the study of communications and information in society. In their development of information science, they identify six major points of focus of the science:

1. The behavior of people as generators, sources recipients, and users of information, and as channel agents
2. The quantitative study of the population of messages — its size, growth, rate, distribution, patterns of production, and use
3. The semantic organization of messages and of channels that facilitate their identification by sources and recipients
4. Programs particularly associated with the function of information storage, analysis, and retrieval
5. The overall organization of information systems and their performance and transfer

6. The social context of information transfer, in particular, its economics and politics.

If these definitions seem complicated, it is because the subject matter is complex and multidimensional, and the definition is intended to be all-encompassing. Obviously information science is not the exclusive domain of any one organization. Traditionally, the Association for Information Science and Technology (ASIS&T), founded in 1937 as the American Document Institute, has been concerned with the study of recorded, that is, documentary, information. This is still our main emphasis; however, the work is now embedded in a larger context.

Librarianship and documentation are applied aspects of information science. The techniques and procedures used by librarians and documentarists are based on the theoretical findings of information science, and conversely the theoretician should study the time-tested techniques of the practitioner. Information science as a discipline has as its goal to provide a body of information that will lead to improvements in the various institutions and procedures dedicated to the accumulation and transmission of knowledge (Norton, 2010).

There are people who call themselves information scientists who do research into information flows and trends using a variety of techniques, including citation analysis, bibliometrics, and methods often associated with computer science and engineering. That is not our primary focus in this class. As noted earlier, ILS 507 is practice-based and concerned with practical matters of information use by people.

Discussion

Discussion Question 1: Is it important to think of information as a process rather than a static entity? If so, why?
Discussion Question 2: In your own words, describe the relationship between data, information, knowledge, and wisdom.

Discussion Question 3: Many library schools are changing their names to incorporate the concept of information and are becoming Schools of Information Science or Information Studies. Many, perhaps most, are even dropping the word library from their title. Is this a good or bad thing? Does it matter?

Discussion Question 4 [Not Required]: Do you have any questions or comments with regard to the content, readings, or assignments?

Unit 03: Hardware Issues

Reading

- Ngo, D. (April 24, 2014). Digital storage basics, Part 1: Internal storage vs. memory, CNET http://www.cnet.com/how-to/digital-storage-basics-part-1-internal-storage-vs-memory/
- Ngo, D. (November 16, 2012). Digital storage basics, Part 2: External drive vs. NAS server, CNET http://www.cnet.com/how-to/digital-storage-basics-part-2-external-drive-vs-nas-server/
- Stephanie Buck, "Libraries in the Cloud: Making a Case for Google and Amazon," Computers in Libraries, 29(8) (September 2009), 6-10. An electronic copy (PDF file format) of this article is available on the server area called "Class Library" within the course web page.
- [Use the following Website for definitions and for updates on cutting/bleeding edge technologies. Note: this is for reference only] http://www.webopedia.com/
- Williams and Sawyer, Chapters Four and Five.

Lecture Note

There are three mega trends with respect to hardware: Smaller, faster and cheaper.

Smaller

Compare to ENIAC with 17,468 tubes
vs Pentium with 3.2 million transistors
vs Pentium Pro with 7 million transistors
vs Pentium 4 with 55 million transistors
vs G5 with 58 million transistors
vs Intel Core 2 Quad with 820 million transistors
vs AMD Orochi with 1.2 billion transistors

vs Intel Quad-Core Itanium Tukwila with 2 billion transistors
vs Intel 8-Core Xeon Nehalem-EX with 2.3 billion transistors
vs Intel 15-Core Xeon IvyBVridge-EX with 4.3 billion transistors (as of January 2015)
vs Inter ???? (2016)

An integrated circuit is a single, miniature circuit with many electronically connected components etched onto a small piece of silicon or some other semiconductive material. Integrated circuits are more commonly known as microchips.

The components etched onto a microchip include transistors, capacitors, and resistors. A transistor is a device capable of amplifying and switching electrical signals. A capacitor temporarily stores electrical charges, while a resistor controls current by providing resistance. The complete closed path through which an electric current travels is called a circuit.

At first, only a few transistors could be etched on a microchip. By 1964, the number grew to 10. Ten years later, the number had reached 32,000. Today, a chip can carry more than 4 billion transistors.
The same miniaturization is taking place in secondary storage (hard drives), telecom systems, and most other computer-related technologies. Research is leading us to devices that store information at the molecular level. See http://www.webopedia.com/TERM/N/nanotechnology.html

Faster

Moore's Law: Capacity and speed doubles every 18-24 months.

ENIAC @ 1K calculations per second
8086 @ 4.77 MHz or 4,770,000 per second
Pentium Pro @ 350 MHz
G3 @ 450 MHz
Pentium III @ 800 MHz

G4 @ 1 GHz
G5 @ 2 GHz
Pentium 4 @ 3.8 GHz
AMD FX @ 8.4 GHz
IBM silicon-germanium chips @ 200 GHz
??? (2017)

New microprocessors from Intel and AMD achieve speed over 10 GHz. IBM has recently announced the availability of its fourth generation of chips based on silicon germanium (or SiGe) technology. The new semiconductors, named 8HP and 8WL, are twice as fast as the previous generation of chips. The previous generation chip ran at 100 GHz, while this new generation of chips will run at a maximum speed of 200 GHz.

Supercomputers are used to study quantum physics, nuclear explosions, weather trends, molecular modeling, and air flow over Pringles chips (no kidding), are breathtaking.

As of November 2015, for the sixth consecutive time, Tianhe-2, a supercomputer developed by China's National University of Defense Technology, has retained its position as the world's No. 1 system with a performance of 33.86 petaflop/s (quadrillions of calculations per second) on the Linpack benchmark, according to the 46th edition of the twice-yearly TOP500 list of the world's most powerful supercomputers. [Source: http://www.top500.org/lists/2015/11/]

Note: all these speeds are changing moment to moment as research continues to improve chip capacity and speed. Moore's Law has been expected to "hit the wall" of physical limitation for years. Thus far however, innovation continues and the Law holds it's own even in the face of the Laws of Physics and the skyrocketing cost of constructing fabrication plants (so-called Fabs).

Cheaper

Academic studies seem to show computer prices falling at roughly 20 percent annual rates of decline since the early 1950s. That rate of decline is still holding.

The cost of buying a gigabyte of hard disk storage has declined was dramatic effect.

1988	$11,000
1998	$40
1999	$20
2001	$5
2005	20¢
2007	14¢
2009	6¢
2013	3¢
2015	2¢
2017	?

The progress in hard drives is quite phenomenal over the last decade or so. They are certainly smaller in absolute size while hugely monstrous in their storage capacity. At the same time, they are cheaper and much more reliable.

Data storage

Similarly, data centers are now faster, cheaper, and more efficient to manage—thanks to cloud computing and virtualization. But these new technologies come with new security vulnerabilities. The issues and challenges to libraries can be the following:

- Why the network security challenge needs to be solved.
- How the current digital transformation is making library databases infinitely more difficult.
- How traditional physical security technology falls short of protecting virtual data center assets.
- Why security policies and updates can't keep pace with changes in workloads and virtual reference services.

- Where new security strategies such as containerization and micro-segmentation are required to protect patrons information.

Accounting for this progress

1. Improved Microprocessors: CISC to RISC, copper replacing aluminum, and stackable gates mean we can get more and faster 0s/1s per integrated circuit. "Stackable" gates means that the information can be stored vertically on a chip, much as a building has floors or levels.

2. More Microprocessors are being used -- lots more. Parallel processors, perhaps 9,000 or more in one machine; thus heralding the shift from MHz to MIPS. New Intel's Core i7 Extreme Edition 3960X can execute 53 instructions per clock cycle. As of 2012, dual-core and quad-core processors are widely used in home PCs and laptops, while quad, six, eight, ten, twelve, and sixteen-core processors are common in the professional and enterprise markets with workstations and servers.

3. Faster memory and more of it.
a. RAM (random-access memory). It takes the form of integrated circuits. RAM is normally associated with volatile types of memory (such as DRAM memory modules), where stored information is lost if power is removed, although many efforts have been made to develop non-volatile RAM chips. Several new types of non-volatile RAM, which will preserve data while powered down, are under development. The technologies used include carbon nanotubes and approaches utilizing the magnetic tunnel effect. Recently "solid-state drives" (based on flash memory) with capacities exceeding 256 gigabytes and performance far exceeding traditional disks have become available. This development has started to blur the definition between traditional random-access memory and "disks", dramatically reducing the difference in performance.
b. Cache (Backside, Pipeline, Level 1, Level 2, and Level 3). Today's CPU chips contain two or three caches, with L1 being the fastest. Each subsequent cache is slower and larger than L1, and instructions and data are staged from

main memory to L3 to L2 to L1 to the processor. On multicore chips, the L3 cache is generally shared among all the processing cores.

4. Faster secondary storage and more of it.
a. Hard disk drives (HDD). An HDD records data by magnetizing a thin film of ferromagnetic material on a disk. HDD areal density's long term exponential growth has been similar to a 41% per year Moore's law rate; the rate was 60–100% per year beginning in the early 1990s and continuing until about 2005, an increase which Gordon Moore (1997) called "flabbergasting" and he speculated that HDDs had "moved at least as fast as the semiconductor complexity." However, the rate decreased dramatically around 2006 and, during 2011–2014, growth was in the annual range of 5–10%. Several new magnetic storage technologies are being developed to overcome or at least abate this trilemma and thereby maintain the competitiveness of HDDs with respect to products such as flash memory-based solid-state drives (SSDs). Solid-state drives (SSDs), which is installed in my current MacBook Pro, will gain capacity and get cheaper, but SSDs will not surpass hard disk drives (HDDs) in either price or capacity any time soon.
b. Removable disks (Jaz and Zip and more). Of course, these are dead or dying technologies.
c. Optical disks (CDs and DVDs)
d. Magnetic tapes (LTO, DLT, and DAT/DDC). Magnetic Tape remains a viable alternative to disk in some situations due to its lower cost per bit. This is a large advantage when dealing with large amounts of data. In 2014 Sony and IBM announced that they had been able to record 148 gigabits per square inch with magnetic tape media developed using a new vacuum thin-film forming technology able to form extremely fine crystal particles, allowing true tape capacity of 185 TB.
e. Flash drives. A USB flash drive, also known under a variety of other names, is a data storage device that includes flash memory with an integrated Universal Serial Bus (USB) interface. USB flash drives are typically removable and rewritable, and physically much smaller than an optical disc. As of 2014, drives of up to a one-terabyte (TB) were available. Some predict

flash drives will one day replace hard drives because their lack of moving parts make them potentially faster and more rigorous.

5. Faster telecom and linkages

a. Buses and ports (USB 3.0 and Firewire). USB 3.0 is the third major version of the Universal Serial Bus (USB) standard for computer connectivity. Among other improvements, USB 3.0 adds a new transfer mode called "SuperSpeed" (SS) that can transfer data at up to 5 Gbit/s (625 MB/s), which is over ten times faster than the USB 2.0's highest speed (480 Mbit/s, or 60 MB/s). FireWire is Apple Computer's version of a standard, IEEE 1394, High Performance Serial Bus, for connecting devices to your personal computer. FireWire provides a single plug-and-socket connection on which up to 63 devices can be attached with data transfer speeds up to 400 MB/s (megabits per second).

b. LANs (Gigabit ethernet)

c. Faster modems and broadband modems. Cable modems use a range of radio frequencies originally intended to carry television signals. A single cable can carry radio and television signals at the same time as broadband internet service without interference. Newer types of broadband modems are available, including satellite and power line modems.

d. Fiber optics, satellites, and general bandwidth

Implications for libraries? Give it some thought and answer the following threaded discussion questions.

Discussion

Discussion Question 1: What do the trends toward smaller, faster, cheaper technologies mean for libraries?

Discussion Question 2: Find and share what you learn of the latest technologies for Smaller, Faster and Cheaper in computing devices?

Discussion Question 3: What are the implications for libraries when funding authorities (town comptroller, V.P. for Finance, etc) see these numbers, and what you like to purchase if you have $1000 for computing devices for your library if you are the director?

Discussion Question 4 [Not Required]: Do you have any questions or comments with regard to the content, readings, or assignments?

Unit 04: Software Issues

Reading

- What is a MARC record, and why is it important? http://lcweb.loc.gov/marc/umb/um01to06.html
- What You Need To Know About Peer-to-Peer File Sharing [Blog]. http://www.zonealarm.com/blog/2014/06/what-you-need-to-know-about-peer-to-peer-file-sharing/
- Carl Grant, "Gone Open Yet?," Public Library Quarterly, 27(3) (2008), 223-241.
  An electronic copy (PDF file format) of this article is available on the server area called "Class Library" within the course web page.
- Sharon Yang and Melissa Hofmann, "The Next Generation Library Catalog: A Comparative Study of the OPACs of Koha, Evergreen, and Voyager," Information Technology and Libraries, 29(3) (September 2010), 141-150.
  An electronic copy (PDF file format) of this article is available on the server area called "Class Library" within the course web page.
- Williams and Sawyer, Chapters Three and Ten (lightly).

Lecture Note

Here's a definition of Software: "A program; a set of instructions to complete some task."

Types of software: applications software and system software (operating systems, device drivers, and utility programs).

Problems endemic to modern software

- Bloatware. Critics suggest that much of the software on the market is just too big; too loaded down with seldom used bells and whistles; too inefficiently and inelegantly constructed.
- Flakey, bugs, crashes, instability. This is especially a problem in modern multitasking environments where one software product or utility conflicts with another resulting in freezes and crashes.
- Lack of Usability testing; software designed for engineers by engineers; user hostile software. (Anything come to mind? I have one: TK20.)
- Cross platform incompatibility; lack of standards (as in conflict between MS Explorer and Mozilla Firefox) Websites can look radically different depending on browser. It has even been suggested that some firms design for lack of compatibility in order to expand monopolies. One Very Large Company is said to use the E cubed strategy: embrace, extend, eliminate.
- Cost: out of pocket for updates, "fiddle-factor" or time lost updating, revising setting and otherwise fooling with newly installed software.

Philosophical orientation

Traditional Model:

Centralized, mainframe-oriented systems, all the software was on the central computer resource. This was the age of dumb terminals and later terminal emulators.

More recent models: Decentralized, distributed systems (recall that smaller computers give better value)
Client-server software Peer to Peer (as with file sharing systems like BitTorrent and uTorrent)

Peer-to-Peer or PtoP or P2P is really quite amazing. And it's a bigger deal than most of us may have noticed. Try a Google search on P2P -- January 2015 returns over 59 million hits.

It is used effectively on LANs and over the Internet -- if you have used a napspter-like PtoP system (BitTorrent, uTorrent etc.) you know about the power. In a matter of seconds a world-wide survey is completed and delivered to your desktop, all with NO central database.

PtoP development is taking some interesting turns. One thrust is called smart dust and consists of thousands or more very small (one cubic mm) processors with sensors, batteries and radio/laser connections on each. The particle processors connect to each other as with other PtoP systems and ultimately to larger systems and networks.

The lure of the inTRAnet: it's robust, cheap, works on many platforms, inexpensive, familiar and comfortable to users, and it doesn't cost much. Reason? Intense competition, new revenue models, and open source philosophy. Thus we see what looks like the internet on closed, library systems and on the Online Public Access Catalogs (OPACs) which are renamed WEBPACs.

Middleware. There are many kinds of middleware but one of the prime uses is to link the new internet or intranet-based system with the library's older "legacy" software. The middleware gives new life to those older databases and applications.

When we get to search engines, we'll discuss the so-called deep web or invisible web. Many times the deep web is caused by systems behind middleware, databases that the webcrawlers such as Yahoo and Google do not or cannot index. More later.

Benefits and disadvantages of client-server architecture: While client-server systems save money on hardware, they often require much more training and support. More complex systems mean that more things can go wrong. More hardware, more diverse hardware and the potential for a mishmash of software, coupled with exponential expansion of telecom issues, all contribute to a complex situation where more can go wrong. Managers and funding authorities who see a lower hardware cost and overlook this reality invite serious problems.

Libraries and library software developers have an interest in thin clients, Network PCs and NCs (which are linked PCs with dumb-down hardware). Forester Research has estimated that 80 percent of the cost of operating and supporting PC systems can be cut by moving to thin clients and limited function desktop computers.

All these hardware issues seem to point to more reliance on small computers. But the future is of course very uncertain. Will the calculations hold? Or will we cycle back to centralized systems? Clearly, we see forces in favor of decentralized systems and other forces pushing us back toward centralized systems. Time will tell which will out.

New Model:

Cloud computing

Cloud computing is a paradigm shift following the shift from mainframe to client–server in the early 1980s. Cloud computing is a technology that uses the internet and central remote servers to maintain data and applications. Cloud computing allows consumers and businesses to use applications without installation and access their personal files at any computer with internet access. This technology allows for much more efficient computing by centralizing storage, memory, processing and bandwidth.

A simple example of cloud computing is Yahoo email or Gmail etc. You don't need a software or a server to use them. All a consumer would need is just an internet connection and you can start sending emails. The server and email management software is all on the cloud (Internet) and is totally managed by the cloud service provider Yahoo , Google etc. The consumer gets to use the software alone and enjoy the benefits. The analogy is , 'If you only need milk, would you buy a cow?' All the users or consumers need is to get the benefits of

using the software or hardware of the computer like sending emails etc. Just to get this benefit (milk) why should a consumer buy a (cow) software/hardware? [Source: http://www.wikinvest.com/concept/Cloud_Computing]
The concept of cloud computing is also well described in the following video http://www.salesforce.com/cloudcomputing/. See it.

Operating Systems

What they do: Quotidian tasks like format disks and put data on disks, serve as context under which the application software can perform routine tasks like copying data, showing directories, moving files, etc. There are standard tasks that need to be performed by most applications and it is more efficient to have one piece of software to do them rather than have each application create its own individual sets of code.

Brief outline of OS lineages:

CP/M -> MS-DOS and PC-DOS -> OS/2 & Windows 3.x -> Windows NT -> Windows 95 -> Windows 98 -> Windows 2000 -> Windows XP -> Windows Vista -> Windows 7 -> Windows 8 -> Windows 10

- UNIX and UNIX-based operating systems like LINUX, AIX, etc. The X in the name of an OS name often indicates a Unix derivative; even the labeling of the new Macintosh OS as OS X (for ten) is probably an attempt to refer to the software's Unix roots. And the expanding interest in the various flavors of Unix also (to a large extent) gave rise to the Open Source software movement (along with the excesses of several large software houses, of course)
  Why is Unix (and its flavors) so much in the news? Because it is great for telecom (it was developed at Bell Labs of AT&T) and is the software at the heart of the internet. But is is also very robust, works on many platforms, has great security (compared to other dominant software), and is sometimes free. The downside of Unix/Linux is that it is command driven, not user friendly, and doesn't have much end-

user application software as yet. There are some that suggest, however, that Mac OS X will provide the GUI interface that will overcome the so-called geek factor and will make Unix available to the masses.

- Macintosh OS X (ten)

The stuff of new operating systems?

1. GUIs, user friendliness and windows
2. Multi-tasking and parallel processing
3. Multithreading (partitioning)
4. Object oriented programming
5. Hot links, "events," open-document systems, OLE, OOPs, etc.
6. Networking facilities
7. Security

Open Source Software

With constant upgrades in technology, it can be very expensive and time consuming to keep public computers up-to-date. With licensing fees, costly upgrades to software, and constant patches and updates, the costs can rise very quickly for libraries to keep public machines current and in good working order.

Open source software would be a possible alternative for libraries looking to save money and frustration. Open source alternatives offer the ability to run both free and proprietary software on the same machine. This means that although one may find an open source web browser like Mozilla Firefox useful for library patrons, Internet Explorer could still be used on the same machine. Likewise, Open Office is a possible alternative for patrons, but Microsoft Office could be kept on the same machines for those patrons who feel more comfortable using more traditional office software.

There is a movement of libraries currently operating on open source ILS (integrated library system) programs. Two front-runners for ILS software are Koha and Evergreen. It looks like they seem to gain ground.

Strategies for Evaluation of software

Read and study; be critical of reviews! Check out the exhibits at conferences (can be extremely valuable, even worth the price of a trip to ALA) Consider self promotional lit? Sure, but be skeptical.

Ask for referrals and then really visit with referrals; invest time, ask hard questions.

Should you hire a consultant? Many librarians lay out six figure sums for library automation systems. The cost of a consultant is quite high; but so are the potential losses if a tragic mistake in made in ignorance. What I have noticed about consultants: They all have biases.

Examine the track record of parent organization; will the company survive? Are they growing or contracting? Is an integrated system offered? (acquisition, circulation, OPAC, cataloging, serials control, MIS modules?)

Place high value on service, training and support. Are they over extended? Don't buy on cost alone.

Always make certain that library software has Full MARC capacity, even if your small library is shopping for "affordable" software. MARC records are large, perhaps 5,000 characters per record. Even today some small systems can handle too many of these. And yet the software vendors will often argue that they have "near" MARC or a "better" form of MARC. Which of course is nonsense. It's either MARC or it isn't.

Why invest the time and money in MARC? The main reason is because someday, perhaps quite soon, your library will move to a new hardware platform or new software system. And when that happens you will want to be able to easily migrate to that system. Lack of MARC records will bring your staff and library into very unhappy and very expensive situation.

Discussion [Participation in the unit discussion is worth 5 points]

Discussion Question 1: Why librarians need to know coding? Which library or library school offers coding course and what its content?
Discussion Question 2: Is Open Source a viable alternative for libraries? What are the advantages and disadvantages?
Discussion Question 3: What do libraries do with big data and cloud computing, any examples?
Discussion Question 4 [Not Required]: Do you have any questions or comments with regard to the content, readings, or assignments?

Unit 05: Searching

Reading

- University of California Berkeley Library. "Invisible Web or Deep Web: What it is. How to Find it, and Its Inherent Ambiguity," 2012. [Web Document] http://www.lib.berkeley.edu/TeachingLib/Guides/Internet/InvisibleWeb.html

Lecture Note

Why can't you just go to Yahoo, throw in a few terms, and run with the 137,000 Web sites Yahoo returns to you?

Maybe you can. Maybe finding 'something' or anything is just the ticket. It may be all that is needed for a middle school student working on a report for Monday's Social Studies class. Perhaps a site or two is all you need if you are looking for a restaurant in Newport.

But often this approach is not enough. If you are working on a Master's thesis, you probably want to find all relevant documents and not just some of them. If you are working for a law office, you want to find all the precedents and current standing, not just a mention of relevant cases. If you are working for a doctor, you want to find current treatment for a condition in Medline, not just what Ralphs' Pretty Good Webpage thinks about the medical prognosis.

Good searching technique applies to a variety of situations: web search engines, for sure, but also major databases like Dialog, Medline, or ERIC, for example. It applies to databases, online journal aggregators and online public access catalogs (OPACs). As an information professional, you will want to find all the relevant documents or sites and you want to do it in timely, efficient manner.

It makes a difference. Research has shown that expert searchers find as many as three-times the number of relevant records that regular folks find.

- Experts know how to find and use alternative terms. Rather than searching for records that have some mention of pigs, they know to search for pigs OR hogs OR pork OR swine. This is because many databases (most certainly the internet) do not use what we call a controlled vocabulary system: the sites or articles are indexed under the terms used by the author and he or she could have used any of many alternative terms. Library systems often have a controlled vocabulary system that permits easier access to alternatives terms (See for example the Library of Congress List of Subject Headings.) Over time, search engines will develop automated systems to assist in identifying terms.
- Experts know how to use Boolean operators efficiently. They know that OR expands the size of a set (in the case above, the use of OR finds more relevant postings) and that AND reduces the size of the set (because both terms link by the AND must be included). "Pigs AND smell" means that you want articles or websites or postings that have to do the intersection of those two concepts. (And where both terms, pigs and smell, are used.)
- They know how to read the results of a search. If, for example, a search for "Dolphin-safe tuna fishing" turns up surprisingly few hits, they know to consider other terms, like ORing the word porpoise to dolphin, for example.
- Experts also know the nuance and power of the advanced search. They don't just randomly pound in terms and then sit back. They know and can effectively use the full range of tools and resources the search engine or index provides. Web search engines increasingly have many of these powerful features making it possible to limit results by date, by language, by domain (.edu, .com, .org, for example), or how to better rank the output to suit your needs.
- They also know what's in the database and how it is organized. They know how often a database is updated and how often the spiders ply

their trade; they know how deep the indexing goes; and they know how to best exploit the differences in the varying indexes.

A few comments on searching

Becoming a good, professional searcher doesn't come easily. It takes study, careful analysis of your results, and it takes practice.

- Take the time to read the documentation. On search engines, it might be called the Help page, or Tips, or something else. Read it, there are differences among the indexes and this is how you can learn about them.
- Be very careful using the NOT Boolean operator. In fact, most of the time it probably should be avoided. Example: If I am interested in finding documents or postings on the Mustang automobile, I might find that many documents I retrieve are about the mustang horse. So I might be tempted to search for "Mustang NOT horse."

What's the problem? This search strategy would reject articles or websites that mentioned the term "horse power" or documents that said "The Mustang automobile was named after the wild horse," even though they might have been perfect for our interest.

- Be sure to note whether the default Boolean operator is AND or OR. It makes a huge difference and currently most of the web search engines use AND and the other have use OR.
- Know how to nest your search strategy and how each engine handles compound a search string.

The order in which a particular engine handles terms in a compound search varies. For example, if I do a search

Ale OR beer AND brew OR brewing, depending on the index, the Boolean operators might be implemented from left to right or the Boolean operators

AND might be done before the operator OR. In either instance, the search would yield low precision because the search would also retrieve postings on brewing tea or storms a-brewing. To avoid this problem, use nesting.

Nesting refers to the use of parentheses to relate the various terms. For example, consider this search: (Buddleia OR "butterfly bush") AND prun* In this case, the searcher is interested in documents/sites that discuss techniques for pruning or tell how to prune the bush that is known as the Buddleia or more commonly the buttterfly bush. In the first example, (Ale OR beer) AND (brew OR brewing) uses parenthesis to make larger sets (Yellow things you drink) and combines them with the second concept (terms to describe how you make them).

For a better understanding of using Boolean operators and parentheses, see the following web page:
http://libguides.mit.edu/content.php?pid=36863&sid=271372

- Understand recall and precision and how to use it to improve your search results. This concept is so important it has it's own section below.
- Be careful of truncation and stemming. This is the ability of many (not all) indexes and search engines to search for parts of terms. For example, you might use the truncated term "dog*" to retrieve documents that are singular or plural, dog or dogs. The danger is that you might also retrieve unwanted postings on dogma
- Beware the false drop. These occur when everything you do apparently fine and the index works as designed, but nonetheless irrelevant documents are retrieved. For example, doing a search for "fruit AND fly" could yield postings about shipping mangoes from Jamaica.

Recall and Precision

Both are expressed as ratios or percentages. There is normally an inverse relationship between recall and precision.

Recall is a measure of the proportion of relevant documents that are captured by a search formulation. If for example you are searching a database with 100 articles dealing with dolphins caught by tuna fishermen and you only retrieve ten of the 100 because you only searched for the terms dolphin AND tuna, your recall would be ten percent. You can improve your recall by finding more relevant terms and using the Boolean OR to increase the set. Thus Porpoise OR dolphin would have better recall.

Precision assesses the purity of the output: the extent to which retrieved documents are relevant. For example, if half the articles you retrieve are relevant, your precision is fifty percent.

$$\text{recall} = \frac{\text{N of relevant retrieved docs}}{\text{N of relevant docs}}$$

$$\text{precision} = \frac{\text{N of relevant retrieved docs}}{\text{N of retrieved docs}}$$

There is normally an inverse relationship between recall and precision. This means as you increase one, the other declines. For example, when you start ORing terms together in order to improve recall (trying to get more hits), it often happens that this broadening causes more false drops and other unintended retrievals.

As you read about the search engines, think about recall and precision and how you might expand one or minimize the other to get the kind of results you want. What for example do the Boolean operators do to recall and precision? What about phrase searching (using quote marks)?

The searcher must often walk a fine line between recall and precision, although the best searches have both relatively high recall and precision. It is believed that in general librarians like higher precision while the masses are completely happy with higher recall. So it goes.

Why are there so many Web search engines?

For good reasons.

- They have different tools and capabilities. Some have NEAR as an operator, some can search by different parameters, and so forth.

- They vary in coverage. In fact, coverage is very much incomplete, with the largest search engine providing access to only a minor portion of the web.

- They have different spider or crawlers indexing the web. They go out at different intervals, they crawl to different depths (only the first page, the first three pages, or perhaps all pages), and the spiders differ in indexing techniques.
- They differ in how they rank items for display after they have been retrieved. Most rank on the basis of how many times the terms you search for are found or where they are found (more weight to higher placement) in the target websites.

Some have different protocols. Google, for example, uses an algorithm that ranks output on the basis of the number of other websites that have linked to the websites your search retrieves. The logic is that if lots of people have linked to a site, it must be pretty good and therefore deserves more weight and will appear high on your list.

The Invisible Web AKA the Deep Web

Web search engines usually create their databases by sending out automated software programs called spiders or crawlers or bots to follow the links within and between websites. This software visits the websites at different intervals and thus indexes the linked web, crawling from one site to another.

But the spiders/crawlers/bots can only go so far. They are normally limited to simple WWW sites and therefore don't get into databases that are searched through websites but are not part of a website. For example, a great deal of the reports collected by the Securities and Exchange Commission (SEC) are not normally crawled. Similarly, the vast collection of information maintained by the Census Bureau is in separate databases that the spiders do not normally get to. These data are in totally distinct and separate systems that are only searchable on the web through middleware. Thus they are not written in HTML and they are not part of the WWW. In fact they may be on some creaky old "legacy" system which has found new life through the middleware connection to the internet.

The Deep Web is huge. Some is proprietary but much of it is publicly accessible. If Google is about 50 billion Web pages (as of January 2015, Source: http://www.worldwidewebsize.com/) and as many experts estimate only covers 20 percent of the WWW, the total number of pages on the WWW is 250 billion pages or so (50 x 5 = 250 billion). But wait, there's more! Some estimates put the size of the deep web at up to 500 times the size of the indexed web. So the total size is roughly 125 trillion pages (250 billion x 500). Yikes.

Can you get to this massive collection? Yes, but again it requires some special insights and techniques. And it may require some specialized search tools.

Specialized search engines in narrow subject fields can take the time to prowl below the surface of a limited number of websites. The emphasis is on depth rather than breadth. These specialized search engines look at many fewer sources of information but take the time to develop tools that more completely index the few sites it covers.

Discussion

Discussion Question 1: In the lecture I give an example of expanding a set by ORing pig to hog to pork to swine. If I worked for a law office and was building a case against a hog operation for creating a public nuisance, what terms would I use to build the size of the set for the second concept? Hint: it has to do with "smell."

Discussion Question 2: In the lecture I pointed out that recall and precision are usually inversely related. Give some examples of how that might happen in a search.

Discussion Question 3: Give an example of a false drop.

Discussion Question 4 [Not Required]: Do you have any questions or comments with regard to the content, readings, or assignments?

Unit 06: Management Issues

Reading

- Bengtson, J. & Bunnett, B. (2012). Across the Table: Competing Perspectives for Managing Technology in a Library Setting, Journal of Library Administration, 52(8), 699-715. An electronic copy (PDF file format) of this article is available on the server area called "Class Library" within the course web page.
- Williams and Sawyer, Chapter Eight (lightly).

Lecture Note

Why do we need to know this stuff? Why would a librarian be a manager of technology? Won't there always be technical support and specialists to worry about these arcane details of equipment and technology? And why should we have to think about emerging technologies and (heavens!) the price of a meg of storage?

There are a number of reasons this is important and why you should know what's what with technology.

- There's not always tech help around. Sometimes it is remotely located, slow to arrive and expensive to call upon. One public library I know pays $150 an hour for tech support and the personnel must drive 30-40 minutes to get to the library, and travel time is charged to the library. On occasion, simple troubleshooting costs this library several hundreds of dollars.
- It is likely you will be a decision maker or at least play a role in decisions regarding technologies for your library. It's like this: many of the people now working in libraries are mature incumbents. They've been there for some years and may not be completely comfortable with non-traditional information systems. At library school they studied

"the library hand" at a time when computers were new, rare or unheard of. Consequently, they look to the new graduate for advice, insight, and involvement. You are expected to know this stuff because you are new and your studies are recent. Perhaps a score or more times I've heard stories of new grads making $50,000 or $100,000 decisions for their library. That's lots of pressure on someone six months out of library school.

- Your employer will expect this expertise. Merrily Taylor, University Librarian at Washington & Lee University, analyzed job advertisements and found that the two most common attributes sought by hiring libraries were tech skill and management skills. Another survey of 900 job ads appearing found that 81 percent of the Public Service jobs required or preferred technical/computer skills. The remaining 19 percent of the ads didn't state a requirement or preference but it probably that some of those positions assume tech skills.
- Resources are scarce. Libraries are too important to throw money around or spend it foolishly. A real-world anecdote: I once talked to a librarian who told me her library spent $10,000 for a system component that was widely available for under $2,000. Why? Ignorance or laziness come to mind. Perhaps both.
- Libraries are too important to squander cash this way. How much better to be a little savvy and spent the revenue on more books, a special program for kids, or some part time staff? Or raises for the staff, or incentives for excellent service? How common are gross errors and negligence like this? If you are willing, there are people who will gladly take your money, thank you very much. If you want to pay $10,000 for a used Pinto automobile, someone will sell it to you.
- Good stewardship of these scarce resources demands that you know what is what, that you stay up with technologies, and know what is a reasonable price for standard products.
- You will be working with techies and vendors. You have to be able to communicate effectively with them in order to get service for your library and the community you serve. See the cartoon below.

Anecdote: A man comes up to the reference desk and asks you, the new intern, for The Book.

"What book is that?" you ask
"You know, the book," he responds.
"Could you be more specific? Could you tell me the title of the book you want?" you politely ask.
"Can't remember. Now can you please give me the book?"
"Wait," you say. "Can you tell me the author?"
"No, darn it" an edge coming to this voice. "Sure it had an author but I didn't notice who it was. That's not my job. I thought you were the book expert."
"Can you tell me anything about this book?"
"No, I'm depending on you to give me the book since it's your job. Now please give me the book I need."
How would you, the intern, feel in this situation?

A common reaction is to try to lose this whack-o. Push them off, direct them to the catalog, anything to get away from this unsolvable problem. After all, there are lots of people you might actually help waiting for your attention.

Is this outrageous? Or is it what some of us do to tech support staff? Something goes wrong with our system, we call tech support or the vendor and perhaps vacate all additional responsibility. It's as though a computer breakdown is viewed as an excuse to take an extended break.

Some Notes on Management of Technology

These notes are somewhat telegraphic; ask if any points should be amplified

Your role -- you will be considered the library expert

Be informed, be skeptical.
Translate user and library needs into language the techie can understand

Keep the user in mind
Learn and study.
Know the language. Demand information and communication

You must play a role in Needs Assessment, Design, Creation, Integration
Techies play the preeminent role in Installation, Maintenance, and Operations

Reporting problems:

Don't panic
Check the obvious
Report with details
Saying "the printer doesn't work" is like asking the reference librarian to Give me The Book. Note in detail what led up to a failure or problem, what the error message was, and whether the problem is continual or intermittent. Staff fears maybe be behind some of our weakness in this regard. (Sarah Fine estimates that 20% of staff will resist technology).

Source of fear includes:

Technology itself
Damaging hardware or files
Not being able to learn new system
Loss of job Loss of socialization
Health hazards

Working with techies (including salespeople, vendors and support staff):

Everyone has preferences and biases; we are all blind in one eye
Everyone has their own motivations and goals (and they may conflict with yours)
They may test you
Inadequate documentation
Preeminence of the technical solution

They may not always tell the whole truth in the interest of making their jobs easier. As one vendor put it, "Librarians demand that we lie to them because of their unrealistic expectations."
They don't understand library work and badly underestimate it's complexity and nuance.
Limited/poor communication
Poor people skills

Management role in security:

Hardware and workstation security: tradeoff between security and ease of use
Proprietary and sensitive Information
Data Loss and need for back-ups. 90% of users store personal information on their computer. However, only 57% back up their data. About 70% of business people have experienced data loss due to accidental deletion, disk or system failure, viruses, fire or some other disaster.
Data losses cost U.S. businesses an estimated $18.2 billion dollars annually, taking into account technical services, lost productivity and the value of the lost data.

Backing up filesStrategies: Multiple backups, off-site, regular schedule, test the backups, choose right hardware system for your library

Automatic systems: tape, hard drives, RAID, optical, store on LAN servers, Cloud, or Internet (Backup, Retrospect, Backjack)

Copyright Issues:

According to the 2014 Business Software Alliance Global Software Piracy Study, 43 percent of the software installed on computers worldwide was pirated in 2013. The industry loses nearly $62.7 billion a year to pirated software. Emerging economies where unlicensed software use is most prevalent continued to account for a growing majority of all PCs in service. Surveys of IT managers indicate that only 35 percent of companies have written policies requiring them to use properly licensed software.

Library Perspective:

Need to continue work productivity: backup copies are fair use
We always want to buy as few copies as possible and thus reduce costs
Be smart: read, study, learn
Know what you want before: talk to people, see the equipment and/or systems
Shop around: prices vary greatly
Find out if the product is actually in stock
Beware of partial orders and back orders: a crucial part of the equipment may not be available and thus the whole system could be non-functional
Do the products come in factory seal cartons?
If you get a price that seems too low to you, ask them to fax you a price guarantee.
Don't pay by check or money order
Use a credit card but find out when the card will be billed and if there is a surcharge
Get references or ask around for local experience
Don't order on price alone
Keep your first order small
Ask about product support
Support lines?
On site repairs? Overnight replacement?
Is there a 30 day money back guarantee? Seven day? Any day?

Computer SuperStores: take along competitive ads, may be able to negotiate price.

The "gray" market

Unauthorized dealers?

Factory sealed boxes?

No serial number, no warranty! ASK about service and warranties! Support!

Maintenance jobs: LANs, drives, or upgrades requires staff hired and trained for the role.
Schlepping: don't ask someone to volunteer to do computer maintenance or training "in their spare time." Make certain that someone is hired, paid and evaluated for this extremely important function. Training!

Lancaster says some experts estimate that half of systems cost should be in training.

Traditional ratio is third hardware, third software, third training and support. In recent years, telecom costs have changed this equation and could run to significant percent of tech costs for some libraries.

Some experts argue that unless 25% of the total technology budget is set aside for professional development, the plan is doomed. On top of that, don't forget to plan for staff to maintain and support the machines!

According to Computer Economics' "IT Spending and Staffing Benchmarks 2015/20," IT operational spending categories include personnel, business applications, data center hardware/software, energy/utilities, IT facilities/floorspace, network infrastructure, IT security, voice/data carrier expense, PCs/smartphones (end-user devices), printers/printing, and other expenses. The largest category of IT spending is personnel, which includes personnel compensation (for both employees and contractors/temps), employee training expense, and recruiting expense.

But we often don't train. People who ought to know better (school and colleges, for example) sometimes spend all their tech budgets on hardware and give little or nothing to training. They like seeing the flashy equipment and see training and support as being wasted on staff. There's no hard evidence of the training expenditure and, well, sometimes they just have low appraisal of their staffs. The administrators may feel that if they spend for training, the staff will just leave for better jobs.

A wise woman once said, "The question should not be, what if we train them and they leave? It should be, what if we don't train them and they stay?!"

Discussion

Discussion Question 1: What are common major tech supports a middle size library may need? Give some detailed explanations.
Discussion Question 2: What are your personal responsibilities with regard to keep up with technological changes?
Discussion Question 3: In the Bengtson & Bunnett article (2012), the authors invite the readers to decide for themselves where they fall on those issues such as Innovation and equipment. Choose one of the issues and discuss where and why you fall on the issue.
Discussion Question 6 [Not Required]: Do you have any questions or comments with regard to the content, readings, or assignments?

Unit 07: Internet

Reading

- Williams and Sawyer, Chapter Two
- Miorandi, D., Sicari, S., Pellegrini, F. D., & Chlamtac, I. (2012). Internet of things: Vision, applications and research challenges. Ad Hoc Networks, 10(7), 1497-1516. An electronic copy (PDF file format) of this article is available on the server area called "Class Library" within the course web page.
- Schermer, B. W. & Lodder, A. R. (2014). Internet Governance: an Introduction. In the Handbook on ICT Law (pp. 1-23). An electronic copy (PDF file format) of this article is available on the server area called "Class Library" within the course web page.

Lecture Note

Ithiel de Sola Pool called it the World's Largest Machine.

In 1996 the New York Times said that only The Pill, the automobile and television have had more immediate impact on people's lives.

It is quite a thing and it surely has captured our attention. Even discounting the hype and the enthusiasm (and maybe even the delusions), it is still a pretty impressive phenomenon. And it is certainly affecting the way we do things in libraries.

How so?

The ubiquity of TCP/IP and internet software, coupled with the robustness and low, low cost make it very attractive.

The downside of the internet is quite well established.

Walt Crawford called it a "stuff swamp."

Paul Saffo said it's more a global yarn ball than a data highway.

John Perry Barlow said it's more like slime mold than a super highway.

Karen Schneider called it a garbage scow, a huge pile of bilge. But then she added that "we need people who are adept at diving into dumpsters and finding the gems."

Karen's point is worth considering. There is a lot of good information as well as stuff that is not so good on the net. Sometimes the good is hard to find or hard to separate from the bad. Sometimes the apparent ease of using Google or a search engine leads people to think they have identified everything of value or perhaps to give up in frustration.

Skilled professionals have a role here, as guides, as trainers, as designers, translators, intermediaries and filters. Stepping forward and taking leadership is important, however.

Things you can do on the Internet

- Email, of course. The raison d'etre for many. It is asynchronous, fast (usually) and very inexpensive. Listservs are wonderful ways to create communities or quickly spread the word.

  The downside of email, as I'm sure you recognize, is the ubiquity of spam, the potential for email attachments to harbor viruses and other destructive software, and the seeming inability of both government and industry (thank you Bill Gates) to effectively deal with these problems. If email is the primary benefit of the internet, then these threats are potential seeds of its destruction.

It is interesting to note that some libraries try to disable or forbid email on (some?) library workstations because they interpret email as personal and frivolous. You can imagine what these misguided folks think of IM and internet chat.

- Chat and Instant Messaging (IM). Seems to have some age-specific appeal. Can be use for serious library applications like online reference service.

- File Sharing. The practice of distributing or providing access to digital media, such as computer programs, multimedia files (audio, images and video), documents or electronic books. Peer to Peer file sharing allows users to use software that connects in to a peer-to-peer (P2P) network to search for shared files on the computers of other users connected to the network. Files of interest can then be shared by downloading directly from other users on the network. P2P technology was used by popular services like Napster and is currently used by Infinit and BitTorrent which are the most popular Peer to Peer network products. Cloud-based file syncing and sharing services allow users to create special folders on each of their computers or mobile devices, which the service then synchronizes so that it appears to be the same folder regardless of which computer is used to view it. Files placed in this folder also are typically accessible through a website and mobile app, and can be easily shared with other users for viewing or collaboration. Dropbox and Google Drive are examples of such Cloud-based file syncing and sharing services.

- Voice over IP (VoIP), which is also known as "Internet telephony" is a methodology and group of technologies for the delivery of voice communications and multimedia sessions over Internet Protocol (IP) networks, such as the Internet. The term Internet telephony specifically refers to the provisioning of communications services (voice, fax, SMS, voice-messaging) over the public Internet, rather than via the public switched telephone network (PSTN). Skype and Google Hangouts are popular VoIP service providers.

- World Wide Web. Invented by Tim Berners-Lee at the Cern in Switzerland in one month, December 1990. He made a tour of the U.S., including M.I.T., Stanford and other hot spots in the summer of 1992 and the world was changed. Many people use the terms Internet and World Wide Web (or just the Web) interchangeably, but the two terms are not synonymous. The World Wide Web is only one of hundreds of services used on the Internet. The Web is a global set of documents, images and other resources, logically interrelated by hyperlinks and referenced with Uniform Resource Identifiers (URIs). URIs symbolically identify services, servers, and other databases, and the documents and resources that they can provide. Hypertext Transfer Protocol (HTTP) is the main access protocol of the World Wide Web. World Wide Web browser software, such as Microsoft's Internet Explorer, Mozilla Firefox, Opera, Apple's Safari, and Google Chrome, lets users navigate from one web page to another via hyperlinks embedded in the documents.

  There are also many other web-based technologies: Blogs, Wikis, RSS, and Social Networking Services such as Twitter and Facebook. For more detailed information about Blogs, Wikis, and RSS, check out the following great flash video at Meredith Farkas' Homepage entitled "New Technologies and Their Applications for Information Literacy Instruction (Flash movie)" at http://meredith.wolfwater.com/portfolio.html. For more detailed information about Social Media, check out the following YouTube video at http://www.youtube.com/watch?v=QUCfFcchw1w&safe=active. It's about the social media revolution and how society is transforming.

We sometimes seem to take the internet for granted and perhaps assume it's use and availability as a natural right. According to "the Internet Usage and

World Population Statistics for November 30, 2015" by www.internetworldstats.com, however, only 46.4% of the world population uses the Internet. Global access to the Internet has grown more than 832% since 2000. Nonetheless, there's still a long way to go. While 87.7% of North Americans and 73.5% of Europeans use the Internet, the majority of people in other areas of the world (Africa: 28.6%, Asia: 40.2%, Middle East: 52.2%) do not use the Internet.

Changing of the Internet

Of course, the Internet has changed the way we do things in libraries. Its force has been felt on both sides of the desk, in public service and in technical service. Most of you are familiar with the many of the public service facilities that use the Internet.

Libraries use web software, servers and browsers as the platform for providing access to the online catalog and other online services. The so-called webpac or webcat is very popular with libraries and automation vendors alike. It provides a uniform interface for users whether are at home, in their offices, classrooms, dorms or in the library itself.

The library portal also provides access to other databases and services in the same familiar format. Aggregators (vendors of fulltext magazines, journals and other serials and the indexes that provide access to these wares) connect to libraries or library portals via the Internet. This is usually achieved seamlessly and transparently through the library webpac or portal.

A range of databases might be accessed this way whereas a few decades ago the only access was through dial-up or proprietary common carrier. Dialog, for example, is a large, international collection of databases that once provided its own telecommunication network for users or required those users to access common carrier systems in order to search the databases. Today, almost all of searching is done through the familiar, inexpensive Internet.

Cooperative reference using Chat technologies is used by many libraries to offer 24-7 reference service. In fact big players like OCLC are involved. Of course, simple email or webforms are also used to provide independent service to local clientele. See http://www.oclc.org/questionpoint/default.htm
Libraries also use the Internet and the web in technical services (behind the public desk) for a range of normal communication purposes just as other organizations or individuals. Libraries have their own listservs (sometimes a handful of them) and provide social network services and access to files and databases on web servers. Announcements, policy documents, planning agendas, organizational history and much more can be available to staff and others.

The internet is also affecting libraries in subtler ways. The model of web search engines like Google and Yahoo have caused us to rethink our standards and the way we do things. We have tried to incorporate websites into catalogs and bend cataloging standards to the new environment. We are considering the possible abandonment of one of librarianship's seminal technical standards, the MARC record, in favor of the upstart XML.

Discussion

Discussion Question 1: The lecture mentioned a few problems with the internet. What other problems have you read about? What is the library's role in controlling or dealing with these problems?
Discussion Question 2: One of the terms bantered about with respect to the internet is Disintermediation. What is disintermediation and what does it mean for library service?
Discussion Question 3: What is Internet of Things related to libraries?
Discussion Question 4 [Not Required]: Do you have any questions or comments with regard to the content, readings, or assignments?

Unit 08: Local Area Networks (LANs)

Reading

- M. Krishnamurthy and H.M. Rajashekara, "Current Trends in Wireless Technologies in Academic Libraries," DESIDOC Journal of Library & Information Technology 31(1) (January 2011), 41-48. http://publications.drdo.gov.in/ojs/index.php/djlit/article/viewFile/763/341
  An electronic copy (PDF file format) of this article is available on the server area called "Class Library" within the course web page.

Lecture Note

Purpose of a LAN: to share things within a fairly small area, perhaps 100 - 500 meters. You might set up a LAN in order to share hardware, software, or information:

1. Hardware

(Laser printer, hard disk, plotter, modem, fax, etc.)
Hardware sharing might extend to creation of a SAN (Storage Area Network). See for example http://www.webopedia.com/TERM/S/SAN.html

2. Software

First, application software might be stored on the server and downloaded to workstations as needed.
"Groupware" is another type of software that can facilitate group work. See http://www.webopedia.com/TERM/G/groupware.html

3. Information
(access to common database, electronic mail, etc.)

Advantages of a LAN

Cheaper than mainframes.
More efficient than mainframes: Note evolution toward client-server systems, distributed/decentralized processing
Administrative advantages:
Easier to update software that is used by staff at their workstations
Encourages use of common application software
Saves disk space: one copy of application on LAN server vs. scores on each PC
Control issues improved
Security is easier to maintain
Backups can be made on the server
Intranets
Cheap, tough, ready-made system for distribution of internal information
Not platform specific
Might have access To (but not BY) outsiders, ie, the internet

Type of networks

Server based: this is the model that most often comes to mind
Peer to peer: You may not need a server, especially for smaller LANs. Peer to peer is simpler, cheaper, and easier to maintain. Go with peer to peer if you can.
Peer to peer has no server, although all PC can act as a server. Can share hard drive, printer, modem, etc.

Disadvantages of a LAN

Can be troublesome to install and maintain

Components/aspects of system may conflict with other components/aspects; it can be hard to pin down cause of problems

Complex systems may suffer from Murphy's Law

Managers don't always recognize the problems that come with this complexity: they expect LANs to run themselves or for some suffering staff to administer the LAN in their "spare time."
Possible components:

In order to set up a LAN you might need workstations/nodes, a server, peripherals (see Hardware above), networking facilities like a Network Interface Card (NIC).
You will also need Network Operating System (NOS). These might include Unix/Linux, Windows NT and Novell Netware.

LAN hardware protocols are also important. Hardware protocols are blueprints or standards that define how the nodes recognize each other, how messages are sent so they don't collide, and such. They are not software or hardware or even wires: they are the blueprint for defining elements of the LAN. There are a number of hardware protocols but you are most likely to see Ethernet and possibly token ring.

Ethernet. It's the standard. It's fast, cheap, rigorous, and everywhere. Over the course of its history, Ethernet data transfer rates have been increased from the original 2.94 Mbit/s to the latest 100 Gbit/s, with 400 Gbit/s expected by late 2017. Ethernet avoids conflicts by sending node broadcasting over network, other nodes listen for messages intended for them.

Connecting one LAN to other LANs:

Bridges. connect networks with the same OS
Gateways. connect networks with different OSs, and/or mainframes
Routers. Know the exact address of messages and thus can choose the best

route. Can serve as a firewall.
Cabling. This is often the most expensive component of a LAN, can run to 50 or even 75 percent of the LAN cost. Most LANs consist of a combination of wire types.
Twisted pair. Copper telephone wiring, cheaper and slower.
Unshielded is around 16 cents a foot in bulk
Shielded TP is around 20 cents per foot
10baseT runs 100 meters without a repeater using 4 pairs
Deciphering 10baseT: 10 means a signaling rate of 10 Mbps, base means baseband, (only a single signal is sent), T is 100 meters, 2 is 200 meters, etc.

Coaxial cable. Seldom seen today except in old LANs.

Fiber optics Fast but expensive, can be tricky to install. No electrical interference, can transmit long distances, does not corrode or spark. Difficult to tap. Often used between buildings or even between floors with copper wire used within a building or floor.
Alternatives to Cabling:

Because pulling cable is expensive, libraries and other organizations sometimes look for ways to set up LANs without physically installing wires. These alternatives include:

Installed phone wires, Home PNA, Tut Homerun for example.
Building's electrical grid, the electrical wires in the building. See Homeplug, for example. The major benefit of powerline networking is that users can easily establish a network using a home's existing electrical wiring as the communication medium.

Wireless: this is the hot technology, based on IEEE 802.11 standard, also called Wi-Fi (for Wireless Fidelity).

There are currently three standards. 802.11b offers up to 11Mbps on a 2.4GHz frequency. A disadvantage with operating on the 2.4GHz band is the interference from cordless phones and microwave ovens.

The next protocol developed is standard 802.11a. It is rarely used and not compatible with other protocols as it operates on a 5 GHz frequency. 802.11a is capable of speeds up to 54Mbps, yet the distance is short: approximately 100 feet as against 300 feet for 802.11b.

The third standard is 802.11g.
Like its predecessor, it can also run at a speed of 54Mbps, but in addition can maintain a range of 100-150 feet and is compatible with standard 802.11b. Since it runs on 2.4GHz, interference with household appliances remains a problem.

The fourth standard is 802.11n. 802.11n builds upon previous 802.11 standards by adding multiple-input multiple-output (MIMO).

The additional transmitter and receiver antennas allow for increased data throughput through spatial multiplexing and increased range by exploiting the spatial diversity through coding schemes like Alamouti coding. The speed is 100 Mbps (even 250 Mbps in PHY level), and so up to 4-5 times faster than 802.11g. 802.11n also offers a better operating distance than current networks.

And other wireless technologies (e.g., Bluetooth and RFID).

WiMAX is an IP based, wireless broadband access technology that provides performance similar to 802.11/Wi-Fi networks with the coverage and QOS (quality of service) of cellular networks. WiMAX is also an acronym meaning "Worldwide Interoperability for Microwave Access (WiMAX). WiMAX is a wireless digital communications system, also known as IEEE 802.16, that is intended for wireless "metropolitan area networks". WiMAX can provide broadband wireless access (BWA) up to 30 miles (50 km) for fixed stations, and 3 - 10 miles (5 - 15 km) for mobile stations. In contrast, the WiFi/802.11

wireless local area network standard is limited in most cases to only 100 - 300 feet (30 - 100m).

LTE (Long Term Evolution) is a 4G wireless communications standard developed by the 3rd Generation Partnership Project (3GPP) that's designed to provide up to 10x the speeds of 3G networks for mobile devices such as smartphones, tablets, netbooks, notebooks and wireless hotspots. 4G technologies are designed to provide IP-based voice, data and multimedia streaming at speeds of at least 100 Mbit per second and up to as fast as 1 GBit per second.

4G LTE is one of several competing 4G standards along with Ultra Mobile Broadband (UMB) and WiMax (IEEE 802.16).

The leading cellular providers have started to deploy 4G technologies, with Verizon and AT&T launching 4G LTE networks and Sprint utilizing its new 4G WiMax network.

LTE has the ability to manage fast-moving mobiles and supports multi-cast and broadcast streams.

Topologies

- Bus: Rarely installed today. Tough to troubleshoot
- Ring and token ring
- Star: Most common topology today. Easy to troubleshoot. Can piggyback on existing phone wiring system
- Combinations/hybrids

Security issues: Can be overdone to detriment of library operations.

I've heard a network administrator for a library consortium rail against libraries that find themselves tied into town/city-wide LANs. He says that he was able to serve the library and troubleshoot library LANs without trouble until the library became part of the town LAN. The heavy security and layers of protection made much of his work difficult or impossible. As always, there is a delicate balance between security and effective use of a system.

Staffing! [Perhaps the most important but most overlooked component of a LAN. Some authorities recommend one LAN administrator for every 50 Workstations installed]

Non LAN Alternatives for sharing peripherals
Selector switch, a little box that allows two PCs to share a printer
Modem: useful for sharing files between two PCs
Addidas-net, also known as sneaker-net

Discussion

Discussion Question 1: LANs are widely used by library staff. But what are the advantages of LAN connectivity for library users?
Discussion Question 2: What are your thoughts on wireless LANs and their potential use in libraries?
Discussion Question 3: What, if any, security implications, does a library encounter in regards to the use of LANs (e.g., sensitivity of data accessible on the LAN)?
Discussion Question 4 [Not Required]: Do you have any questions or comments with regard to the content, readings, or assignments?

Unit 09: Web 2.0 & Library 2.0

Reading

- Anttiroiko, A. and Savolainen, R. (2011). Towards Library 2.0: The Adoption of Web 2.0 Technologies in Public Libraries. Libri, 61, 87-99. An electronic copy (PDF file format) of this article is available on the server area called "Class Library" within the course web page.

Lecture Note

Web 2.0

The World Wide Web (or Web 1.0) has changed the way that people share information, communicate and do business. Since its inception in the early 1990s, the World Wide Web has evolved from a collection of Websites containing pages of static or infrequently changing text, images, and hyperlinks to support interactive Web applications for sharing documents, photos and videos, chatting, collaborating, and doing business. In the beginning, static Web pages were being created for one way of communication and these pages were read-only for visitors. Online activities are a growing part of many people's lives, both engaging in interactive and social events on the Web and, increasingly become active partners creating new contents.

Web 2.0 is the unifying term for these kinds of new technologies that enable users to interact and personalize Web sites (Holmberg et al. 2009). Web 2.0 is the name given to the shift in how people have come to use the World Wide Web, from a tool for sharing documents to a platform for linking people and running Web applications. Web 2.0, which is characterized by interactive applications that allow users to participate in contributing, organizing, and creating their content, promotes a culture of participation, interaction, and collaboration. Examples of Web 2.0 include social networking (e.g., Facebook, Instagram, LinkedIn, Twitter), blogging, RSS, YouTube, Podcasting, Instant Messaging (IM), and wikis.

Web 3.0 is the name that is being used to describe emerging trends that allow people and machines to link information in new ways. Web 3.0 proposes a Web where both people and ideas are connected with each other and where personal Web assistants, called agents, can make decisions and take actions based on a user's preferences and past behaviors (Shelly & Frydenberg, 2011).

Whereas Web 2.0 was about participation, Web 3.0 is about anticipation. Many describe Web 3.0 as the rise of the "Semantic Web", where intelligent software tools can read Web pages and discern useful information from them, much as people do, in order to anticipate a user's needs and to perform tasks on a user's behalf.

See the major differences between Web 1.0, 2.0, and 3.0 (Shelly & Frydenberg, 2011):

Web 1.0	**Web 2.0**	**Web 3.0**
The early Web (Web 1.0) was read-only. Most people consumed Web content.	Web 2.0 is a read-write Web where users can interact with each other.	Web 3.0 suggests agents that can make intelligent decisions on behalf of a user.

Library 2.0

The application of Web 2.0 thinking and technologies to library services and collections has been widely framed as "Library 2.0". However, an established definition of Library 2.0 does not yet exist, despite numerous attempts to define it. Some examples of the different definitions of Library 2.0 are as follows:

- Library 2.0 is the application of interactive, collaborative, and multimedia Web-based technologies to Web-based library services and collection (Maness, 2006).

- Library 2.0 is all about rethinking library services in light of re-evaluating user needs and the opportunities produced by new technologies (Chowdhury, 2006).
- Library 2.0 refers to a growing area of interactive and social tools on the Web with which to create and share dynamic content (Connor, 2007).
- Library 2.0 is a change in interaction between users and libraries in a new culture of participation catalyzed by social Web technologies (Holmberg et al. 2009).

These definitions focus on different parts of Library 2.0. Some chose to focus on Web 2.0 technologies, while others emphasize library services or user interaction and participation.

Maness (2006) suggests the following four essential elements of Library 2.0, which capture the different components of the notion Library 2.0:

- **It is user-centered**. Users participate in the creation of the content and services they view within the library's web-presence, OPAC, etc. The consumption and creation of content is dynamic, and thus the roles of librarian and user are not always clear.
- **It provides a multi-media experience**. Both the collections and services of Library 2.0 contain video and audio components. While this is not often cited as a function of Library 2.0, it is here suggested that it should be.
- **It is socially rich**. The library's web-presence includes users' presences. There are both synchronous (e.g. IM) and asynchronous (e.g. wikis) ways for users to communicate with one another and with librarians.
- **It is communally innovative**. This is perhaps the single most important aspect of Library 2.0. It rests on the foundation of libraries as a community service, but understands that as community's change, libraries must not only change with them, they must allow users to change the library. It seeks to continually change its services, to find

new ways to allow communities, not just individuals to seek, find, and utilize information.

See the major differences between Library 1.0 vs. Library 2.0 (Cho, 2013):

Library 1.0	Library 2.0
- References with traditional means - Cataloging - Online communities via mailing lists - Text-based tutorials	- References with Blogs, IM (Instance Messages), RSS, Tagging, Wikis - Tagging in OPACs - Online Communities via Social Networks - Podcast-based tutorials - Digital collection via YouTube

More info can be seen from this resource:
http://www.library20.com/?xg_source=msg_mes_network

Discussion

Discussion Question 1: What might be benefits of using Twitter or Pinterest to connect with your library patrons?
Discussion Question 2: What is your experience in using Wikipedia? Do you recommend it (or recommend against it) to library users?
Discussion Question 3: What services can school libraries provide through their Websites?
Discussion Question 4 [Not Required]: Do you have any questions or comments with regard to the content, readings, or assignments?

Unit 10: Telecommunication Issues

Reading

- Williams and Sawyer, Chapter Six.

Lecture Note

This is one of the fastest changing environments with cheaper/faster technologies always emerging. Lust for bandwidth (a measurement of information transmitted over time) seems to exceed technology developments.

[Note: for purposes of this class we are breaking out Local Area Networks, although LANs are most certainly forms of telecom.]

Telecommunication can be defined as the ability to connect one computer with another. Simple enough. But computers (or integrated circuits) are everywhere including telephones, TVs, automobiles, door locks, etc., and in the telecom system itself. There is even a British professor who has had chips implanted in this body.

Convergence is a big buzzword of the day. It refers to digitalization blending and blurring technologies, as Internet access, digital telephony, HD television, text/graphic messaging, cellular services, etc. Telecom and computerization are becoming central to many different technologies and applications.

There are many examples. You can watch TV or listen to distant radio stations on a computer or surf the Web and get email while watching your TV. Email and other net services are available through smartphones. Global Positioning Satellite (GPS) systems make it possible to unlock your car if you lose your key; wireless Internet services mean that you can listen to Samba broadcasts live on Brazilian radio while driving across Montana at 3 am.

Modems

The zeroes and ones inside the computer need to be converted or processed so they can be sent to some distant device. Often this is accomplished by a modem.

- Traditional (56K and slower): modulators/demodulators, converts digital signals to analog and back again. Probably dead end technology, although many libraries are in late 2000 getting access to the internet through 56K modems. The traditional 56K modem has been losing popularity. However, the dial up modem is still widely used by customers in rural areas, where DSL, Cable or Fiber Optic Service is not available, or they are unwilling to pay what these companies charge.
- High speed (most commonly 20 meg per second): ISDN modems, Cable modems, DSL modems, etc. (After having fast Ethernet at 100 Mbps in your dorm room to download MP3 files, how can you ever accept 56K?) Slowly and surely, the U.S. is inching towards the 100 million broadband subscriber milestones. Latest figures compiled by Leichtman Research Group (December 3, 2015) show that 81% of US households get a broadband Internet service at home, an increase from 26% in 2005. Broadband now accounts for 97% of all households with Internet service at home -- an increase from 91% in 2010, and 40% in 2005.
- And actually, the modem is only one piece of hardware that is needed to connect to the system that brings you the telecom service. That system is made up of servers, proxy servers, switches and more to make the system work.

Compression software.

Works on text, graphics, video, audio

- Text compress to one-quarter the volume (DOC, PDF)
- Graphic compresses by 60 to 100 times (JPEG)

- Video compresses up to ~ 100 times (MPEG-2)

Z39.50

Transparent interfaces and translators like Z39.50. This is a standard that makes it possible to search different databases or library catalogs using search protocols and syntax the searcher is familiar with. See http://www.niso.org/standards/resources/Z39.50_Resources

Here in Connecticut there have been proposals, including one by the State Library some years ago, to use Z39.50 interfaces to link library cooperatives, systems, and individual libraries to create a virtual union catalog. The proposal would mean that library users could search a bunch of library holdings from their home library (or home library Webpage) without having to learn or use the protocols and syntaxes of those different systems. In essence, the software would do the translation for them.

The problem is that not all library software is Z39.50 yet, although it should be in coming years. The translation may also be a bit slow and clunky for some speed-added tastes, although improvements in processor capacity and telecom links could alleviate this potential problem.

Mode of Switching

- Continuous/constant: circuit switching. It's traditional phone service or POTS.
- Burst or Packet switching (as in the internet, LANs, etc.)

One of the great things to come out of the cold war was packet switching. The Rand Corporation was hired by the U.S. Department of Defense in the 1960s to design a telecommunication scheme that could survive nuclear war. Their invention became the Internet, of all things, but the concept was so great it is now used in LANs, in frame relay systems, in digital cellular phones, in wire-based telephony, you name it.

Telecom connections:

Connection may involve satellites, radio, infrared technologies, microwaves, lasers or a host of wiring technologies, including copper wire, fiber optics, or coaxial cables.

Fiber Optics technology is the workhorse: it uses laser light flashing down fiberglass threads. Each cable may have up to a thousand fiber threads bundled together.

Dark Fiber: Nationwide maybe only one percent of capacity is being used. Example, some service providers light only four percent of fibers and run one channel per fiber. Will fiber optics bandwidth become too cheap to meter as some suggest?

The once high-flying fiber optics companies have hit on hard times in recent years. The collapse of the dot-com empires and hyper-energetic installation of fiber has led to serious devaluation of many of these firms. The bankruptcy of Global Crossing is just one of the noteworthy examples.

So the fiber infrastructure is probably overbuilt for current demand. But besides this mileage, recent improvements include:

- Repeaters now every 50-60 miles; formerly had to have repeater ~30 miles. In the future, erbium doped fiber could function with no repeaters.
- Dense Wavelength Division Multiplexers (DWDM. Prism-like splitting of wavelength of fiber (like different colors. DWDM can yield 80 channels (i.e., messages) per strand and 10 gigabits per channel. (Qwest runs 48 fibers per cable.) Research has gotten up to 1,000 channels in the laboratory.
- Faster routers: routers transmit 10 gig per second or faster.
- "Opto-chip" modulator converts electrical signals to optical at 100 Gbps.

Two decades ago, Nicholas Negroponte predicted that fiber speed would top out at 1,000 Gbps (1,000 Gigabit per second or 1 Terabit per second) [Source: Negroponte, Being Digital 1995]. This was seen as outrageous optimism in 1995. But 9.6 Tbps speed is available with today's commercial systems.

In October, 2012 Nokia Siemens Networks, and a consortium of R&D partners, successfully demonstrated a capacity record using light to transmit information down commercially deployed multi-mode optical fiber. The demonstration achieved a 6-fold increase in optical data speed to 57.6 Terabit per second (Tbps), compared to 9.6 Tbps speed.

The developers said: With this record data rate we can transmit, over a single fiber, double the capacity required for 7 billion people "the world's population"to be connected over simultaneous phone calls... But this is only the beginning. By 2020, we will be able to support 100 times this capacity, which means that a single fiber would have enough capacity to deliver 40 million different TV streams for example one for every household in Germany simultaneously. [Source: News Wire Feed, October 17, 2012]

Frame Relay

Digital, packet switching WAN technology
Non-dedicated circuits, bandwidth on demand
56K to T-3 speed (45 Mbps)

Once used by library consortia to provide WAN and Internet service. Permits the vendor (SBC for example) to maximize their infrastructure since communication is achieved through the frame relay 'cloud' which is similar to the way internet packets are dispersed over a national web network (i.e., there is no dedicated line or circuit; messages find their way to a destination through routers). This should be less expensive than with a dedicated, leased line.

Satellite systems

Primarily used in remote areas where cable and DSL service is not available or is prohibitively expensive.

ISDN (Integrated Services Digital Network) Being replaced by DSL in most areas although area in Europe may have important ISDN services; both run on POTS copper wires

ADSL, xDSL, or just DSL (Asymmetric Digital Subscriber Line) Like ISDN uses existing twisted pair phone lines Broadband downstream, narrowband upstream Cost "comparable to regular phone rates." DSL ~ $30-60 mo. Speed varies w/ distance; 384Kbps or as fast as 52 Mbps.

ATM (Asynchronous Transfer Mode)
Small Cells, work like packets although smaller than TCP/IP
Creates fixed channels, unlike TCP/IP, making it easier to track and bill.
Less adaptable than TCP/IP to surges in traffic.
Currently 25 - 622 Mbps.
Works on LANs and WANs, although the latter seems to be more viable.

Cable

The cable companies typically offer 105 Mbps.
Some cable companies are boosting bandwidth speed but reports are that U.S. speeds are still much lower than in places like Europe, Japan and Korea.
Some so-called phone companies like Verizon are rolling out fiber to desktop services with very large bandwidth -- 500 Mbps for less than $285 per month. http://www22.verizon.com/residential/fiosinternet/Plans/Plans.htm

Wireless Broadband service.

Wireless cable, once thought to have huge potential has effectively died. In its place is Advanced Wireless Services, which is also known as AWS-1. Can be used for mobile data services, video, and messaging.

Most people use cable or DSL for high-speed Internet access at home. In fact, 50% of all broadband customers use cable, 42% use DSL, and 8% use fiber-optic cable, satellite, or a wireless system. However, DSL dominates in Europe and the rest of the world. (Electric Design, February 19, 2013).

Municipal wireless network (Muni Wi-Fi) is the concept of turning an entire city into a Wireless Access Zone, with the ultimate goal of making wireless access to the Internet a universal service. This is usually done by providing municipal broadband via Wi-Fi to large parts or all of a municipal area by deploying a wireless mesh network. Some cities like Philadelphia and many smaller towns have offered or promised to offer wireless service to the entire community at low cost. You can only imagine what the for-profit ISPs think of these plans.
http://www.peninsuladailynews.com/article/20111222/news/312229989/wireless-internet-for-whole-city-port-angeles-city-council-decides

Mobile Revolution: Challenges and Opportunities

According to the recent survey results (see below) by PEW Research Center (2015), 68% of U.S. adults have a smartphone, up from 35% in 2011, and tablet computer ownership has edged up to 45% among adults. Smartphone ownership is nearing the saturation point with some groups: 86% of those ages 18-29 have a smartphone, as do 83% of those ages 30-49 and 87% of those living in households earning $75,000 and up annually. At the same time, the surveys suggest the adoption of some digital devices has slowed and even declined in recent years. This mobile revolution has clearly presented challenges and opportunities for libraries.

In order to serve mobile (particularly smartphone) users, libraries should also prepare for the followings:

1.Text message reference: Short Message Service (SMS): SMS is a service for sending short messages of up to 160 characters to mobile devices, including cell phones and smartphones. For more information about library SMS, see the following online slides http://www.slideshare.net/chadmairn/using-text-messaging-to-enhance-library-services

2.QR Code (Quick Response Code): A QR code is a two-dimensional barcode, so it can contain more data than a standard barcode, such as contact information or a link to a website, audio file, image, or video. It can be scanned with a mobile device that has a camera. For more information about using QR codes in the school library, go to the following website http://eduscapes.com/sessions/qrcodes/

3. Mobile Website and Mobile OPAC
For more information about library mobile websites and OPACs, see the following online slides http://www.slideshare.net/ellyssa/libraries-to-go-mobile-tech-in-libraries-presentation

Discussion

Discussion Question 1: The power of telecommunication means that libraries are no longer institutional islands. What are the good aspects of this? What are the bad things that derive from this technology?
Discussion Question 2: What mobile services does your local library provide? Do you frequently use the mobile services? If not, why?
Discussion Question 3: How do you connect to the internet at home and at work (if available) and are you happy/satisfied/displeased with the the speed and reliability of the connection? What do you think will be the most common and speediest Internet channel -- cable, DSL, fiberoptic, or something new?
Discussion Question 4: [Not Required]: Do you have any questions or comments with regard to the content, readings, or assignments?

Unit 11: Media Formats

Reading

- David R. O'Brien, Urs Gasser, and John Palfrey, "E-Books in Libraries: A Briefing Document Developed in Preparation for a Workshop on E-Lending in Libraries," Berkman Center Research Publication No. 2012-15 (July 1, 2012). http://papers.ssrn.com/sol3/papers.cfm?abstract_id=2111396##. An electronic copy (PDF file format) of this article is also available on the server area called "Class Library" within the course web page.

Lecture Note

Many argue that we can publish indexes, serials, and books cheaper, faster, and store them in less space while providing more searching capabilities.

- Conference Proceedings sold for $190 on paper or $30 on CD ROM
- One Megabyte of info on paper costs $3.50; on CD-ROM it's fractions of a cent.

Acquisition of electronic resources such as e-journals, e-books, and databases would be a major outlay for many libraries. According to the 2014 report by National Center for Education Statistics (NCES), US academic libraries spent, on average, about 58% of their "information resources" budgets on purchasing electronic resources. Information resources include books, serial backfiles, current serial subscriptions, document delivery/interlibrary loan, preservation, and other expenditures for information resources.

Indexes and Abstracts

The OPAC might provide access to a combination of print and electronic formats, including the library's print holdings, locally held electronic databases mounted on a server, consortium holdings, web-accessed commercial databases, and other remote databases. It might also include links to websites for content, reviews of books, and other information. Given the range of data and formats accessible through the OPAC, it is not surprising that web-based catalogs (Webcats) are in high demand.

The choice of format will be influenced by volume of demand as well as costs. Most expensive direct cost could be the most cost effective. For example, the cost of leasing access to a commercial engineering database and mounting it on the OPAC may run into many tens of thousands of dollars a year. But it may be a wise investment for an engineering library where that access is the prime reason for using the library.

Depending on demand and cost issues, other formats (paper or Web access) might make the most sense for one library but prove totally ineffective for another.

The relationship between commercial indexes and those created by .gov or .org enterprises is a complex and often politically difficult one. For example, the striking success of ArXiv http://arxiv.org/ may be giving INSPEC a run for its money.

An aside: The X in arXiv should be thought of and pronounced like the Greek letter Chi. So it's pronounced "Archive."

Serials/Journal Crisis

Cost of serious academic journals can run to thousands of dollars per journal per year. In some libraries, 90 percent of the materials budget is spent on journals, ten percent on books. One study found that the cost per read article may be ~$80.

There are many attempts to reduce costs and provide alternatives using electronic publishing. See for example Directory of Open Access Journals

(DOAJ) http://www.doaj.org/, Public Library of Science http://www.plos.org/ and the SPARC Project http://www.arl.org/sparc/.

The primary means of gaining access to scholarly articles is now through e-journals. E-journals are now the preferred way to access scholarly articles because of its convenience. Moreover, published reports indicate that e-journals are less costly to maintain than paper journals. Because of user preference, cost considerations, and space considerations, the move to electronic journals would be inevitable. There are many refereed scholarly e-journals. Academic libraries offer downloads of articles through subscription access, which is fast, timely, convenient, available to many users simultaneously and no cost to the researcher. Content aggregators such as EBSCO, GALE, and JSTOR provide access to thousands of e-journals in their databases, which are offered by academic and public libraries today.

E-books

As more companies create new eReaders, the market for purchasing e-books has also expanded in the past years. According to the recent numbers from the Association of American Publishers (2015), e-books now account for about 20% of book sales. E-book growth, once in the triple and double digits, has slowed to a crawl in recent years. Users of eReaders now have a number of online options for buying materials compatible with their device. Some of the more popular e-book websites include Amazon.com, oysterbooks.com, ebooks.com, scribd.com, and barnesandnoble.com.

While there are many eReaders on the market that we are all familiar with, such as Kindle, Nook, iPad, JetBook, PocketBook, Sony Reader, etc., there are many more that are less popular. Some of the less popular eReaders that have been on the market including Kobo, Icarus, Cybook Odyssey,
Pyrus, and BOOX. In addition to eReaders, e-book users can access materials on their smartphones, laptops, desktops, and other handheld devices. Users have the ability to access e-book sources via the Internet with the push of a button.

There are commercial services providing e-books to library and library user's workstations or eReaders. See for examples: OverDrive http://www.overdrive.com/, ebrary http://www.ebrary.com/corp/, Questia http://www.questia.com, and Safari Books Online http://www.safaribooksonline.com.

Audiobooks are another item that is easily downloadable. They can especially benefit patrons with literacy challenges, children, blind, visually impaired, dyslexic, and other learning disabilities. Learning Ally https://www.learningally.org offers the world's largest collection of human-narrated audio textbooks and literature.

Project Gutenberg http://www.gutenberg.org/ is the oldest producer of free e-books on the Internet. There are over 100,000 free e-books in the Project Gutenberg Online Book Catalog. The Library of Congress also has major projects underway to digitalize its collections. See http://www.loc.gov/library/about-digital.html.

One of the most intriguing and potentially valuable programs is Google Books. See http://www.google.com/googlebooks/about/index.html. Google has been scanning fulltext books into its database for a number of years with the goal of making them fully searchable -- every word of text -- and available for libraries and readers. This includes books now out of copyright, books owned by the libraries, and whole or partial texts with approval of the copyright holders. Google, if permitted, would scan and make available to searchers basic bibliographic information and other info, such as tables of content or indexes.

To no one's surprise, a number of authors and publishers were not pleased and met with Google's representatives in courts. In October 2015, a federal circuit court made clear that Google Books is legal. A three-judge panel on the Second Circuit ruled decisively for the software giant against the Authors Guild, a professional group of published writers which had alleged Google's scanning of library books and displaying of free “snippets” online violated its members’s copyright. As of October 2015, Google's database encompasses more than 30 million scanned books.

Another issue relates to a trend toward convergence of formats. For example, many libraries are offering downloadable eBooks, audiobooks, music, and videos on computers, eReaders, iPads, iPods, smartphones, and other mobile devices. Major corporations like Apple, Amazon, and Google are heavily into this aspect of delivering content in different formats.

Formats for E-journals, E-books and Other E-publications.

Most e-journals are published in HTML and/or PDF formats, but some are available in only one of the two formats. A small number of e-journals publish in other formats such as DOC, PS, or ASCII text.

A wide variety of file formats (e.g., EPUB, PDF, PDB, HTML, AZW, DJVU, LIT, DOC, DOCX, PS, etc.) have been used in different eReaders. Different eReaders followed different formats, most of them specializing in only one format, thereby fragmenting the e-book market even more. Due to the exclusiveness and limited readerships of e-books, the fractured market of independent publishers and specialty authors lacked consensus regarding a standard for packaging and selling e-books. In the late 1990s, however, a consortium formed to develop the Open eBook format as a way for authors and publishers to provide a single source-document which many book-reading software and hardware platforms could handle. Open eBook Publication Structure (OEBPS), also known as the EPUB format, is an XML-based specification for the content, structure, and presentation of e-books. OEBPS was developed by the Open eBook Forum, a group of organizations involved in electronic publishing and now known as the International Digital Publishing Forum (IDPF). The EPUB format is the most widely supported vendor-independent XML-based (as opposed to PDF) e-book format; that is, it is supported by the largest number of e-Readers. The EPUB format is supported by iBooks, iPhones, iPads, Barnes & Noble Nook, Sony Reader, etc. except the Amazon Kindle that uses its own proprietary file format of AZW.

Discussion

Discussion Question 1: What does this diversity of formats mean for libraries?
Discussion Question 2: How does it affect the look, the feel, the sociology, the economics of libraries?
Discussion Question 3: How should a library determine the best format among these choices?
Discussion Question 4 [Not Required]: Do you have any questions or comments with regard to the content, readings, or assignments?

Unit 12: Future Prospects

Reading

- Williams and Sawyer, Chapters Seven and Nine.
- Agresta, M. (April 2014). What Will Become of the Library? Slate. http://www.slate.com/articles/life/design/2014/04/the_future_of_the_library_how_they_ll_evolve_for_the_digital_age.html
- Barclay, D. (August 2015). Turning a page: downsizing the campus book collections. The Conversation.
- Blakemore, E. (2016). High Tech Shelf Help: Singapore's Library Robot. Retrieved from http://lj.libraryjournal.com/2016/08/industry-news/high-tech-shelf-help-singapores-library-robot/
- Darnton, R. (April 2011). 5 Myths About the 'Information Age. The Chronicle Review. http://chronicle.com/article/5-Myths-About-the-Information/127105/
- Feldheim, Ben. (November 2015). How libraries stay relevant in the digital age. Chicago Magazine. Retrieved from http://www.chicagomag.com/Chicago-Magazine/November-2015/How-Libraries-Stay-Relevant-in-the-Digital-Age/
- Martin, C. (August 2015). Who says libraries are dying? They are evolving into spaces for innovation. The Conversation.
- Matchar, E. (2016). The Future of Libraries, Besides lending books, the local institutions are training young journalists, renting garden plots and more. Smithsonian. Retrieved from http://www.smithsonianmag.com/innovation/future-libraries-180959925/#jAco7FVoOdm4krUO.99
- Spinks, R. (January 2015). The future of libraries has little to do with books. Good. http://magazine.good.is/articles/public-libraries-reimagined

Lecture Note

Future of Libraries

So what is the future of libraries. Is it dark? Or is the future bright and optimistic with hope and potential.
Jeremy Rifkin, writing in The End of Work, said that in the future society will be composed of two groups:

- The Information Elite
- The Unemployed.

Question: where did Rifkin puts librarians?

Answer: the second category, the unemployed. Rifkin doesn't think that we'll be able to respond to the challenge of new technologies and new media formats.

Susan Baerg Epstein, a writer and library automation consultant, is a bit more optimistic. As a library professional, she observes that libraries are essentially the same as they were fifty or sixty years ago. In her view, your grandparents or great grandparents would see the library as similar to the ones they knew as children.

Oh, sure, there's a smattering of computer this and computer that but really it's a library with books and magazines and librarians in sensible shoes.

Here's the scary part:

She says that it is this immutability that attracts students to library school. People want to be librarians, she says, because they like the fact that libraries are unchanged and unchanging.

And, she says, it is no surprise that as professionals they resist serious change in their libraries.

These are not, to my mind, healthy views of the future. As Maureen Sullivan pointed out, change is everywhere. Change is inescapable. So why would library staff not expect change in their libraries, Sullivan asks?

Charles McClure has argued that libraries should not be peripheral to people's lives. They should be central. People should think of libraries as a first resort, not as a last resort.

If libraries are only thought of in passing or as a place "my children used to go to," we are in serious trouble. No matter how strong the warm feelings politicians have for the memory of a library, if it is not central, if it is not timely and up to date, if it is not a part of people's lives, then the funding authorities will have trouble allocating money for the library.

Change is always difficult. It's natural to latch onto the familiar, to be comfortable with the status quo. Change is unsettling. It takes energy and will to change.

Chuck McClure, again, points out that we make excuses for staying with the tried and true. "Oh, we can't do that because (add lame excuse). And besides, it's so expensive! We can't possibly afford that technology/system/service," we whine.

McClure says we can. We can buy the technology or offer the service we want to. If it's a priority, we'll fight for it and find a way. "I'm tired of whiners," McClure says. It's time to stop whining and do something.

Sometimes change means re-examining priorities and spending money in new ways. Sometimes it means recognizing that, as Peter Young put it, the traditional curatorial role is metamorphosing into an interpretive role.

Will these changes signify the end of libraries as we know it?

Not likely, in my view. It is more probable that any demise of libraries will be attributable to a lack of change, a lack of responsiveness to new needs, a perceived irrelevance in the eyes of the public and funding authorities. Not changing could mean that traditional services - including books and magazines - suffer as the price of a general malaise that comes from irrelevancy.

If our job is still to Collect, Preserve, Organize, and Disseminate (CPOD), clearly the emphasis must be on disseminating. We must provide the service that gets the right information to the right person at the time in the right format. If anything, emphasis on the Big D, will increase our importance as the information explosion continues and as the diversity of information and information formats expands. The ubiquity and volume of information requires our services more now than ever.

Umberto Eco, writing in Le Nouvel Obseratveur, said it this way:

"We face, though, dangers from the abundance and the triumph of the written...

The excess of information has become noise. The political powers of our nations now understand this. Censorship no longer is exercised by retention or elimination, but by profusion: to destroy a news event, it is enough today to push forward another just behind it...

A bibliography of twenty titles is useful. But what do we do with one of 10,000 titles obtained by pushing a computer button? Into the wastebasket!

Just so, photocopying kills reading, and therefore understanding. Before, I would have gone to the library and taken notes on the books which interested me. Now, I am content to carry home this reservoir of knowledge which I have photocopied - because it is easy - and which I never again will open. The problem is to filter this information overload."

Libraries are, to be sure, still collections of materials. It just happens that now the physical format of those materials may be changing. But the real soul of the library is the service we provide to make those materials useful. The interpreting, teaching, guiding is the real work of the librarian. The process of linking users with information is central to our mission; it will not cease because of new media. If anything, the complexity and power and coldness of computer-based systems require a human being to interpret, teach and guide much more than the traditional formats ever did. As Kathleen Crea puts it, libraries need to become the midwife of change and the muse of innovation.

Rifkin and Baerg Epstein are wrong. The new technologies do not signify the end of libraries but provide an opportunity for the liberation of library service. The future is bright with hope and potential if we seize the opportunity.

New Developments in Libraries

RFID & Robot

Singapore's Library Robot, Erin Blakemore (2016) reported: "For my news share, I am passing along this article about a library robot created and tested in Singapore. It was interesting to hear the challenges and the trial and error that went into making the robot. When I first started reading, a concern was that robots could be used to replace library staff, but as I continued, I realized this was not the purpose of the robot. The robot is a shelf reader in that it checks to see if items are missing and mis-filed. It sounded like it would run at night to not disrupt patrons and staff in the browsing process. The robot would basically take away the time consuming clipboard/scanner tasks of inventory and shelf reading. In the end, the librarians are happy because the robot removes the need for this task which allows librarians to focus on customer service, planning and programming activities. Interesting!"
http://lj.libraryjournal.com/2016/08/industry-news/high-tech-shelf-help-singapores-library-robot/

Starr (2016, June 6) also reported, "Robotic librarian finds lost books, won't tell you to shush. Retrieved from CNET: http://www.cnet.com/news/robotic-librarian-finds-lost-books-wont-tell-you-to-shush/"

Digital

Feldheim' piece, How libraries stay relevant in the digital age, is very interesting but has many real stories, it is an interesting research paper.

Feldheim, Ben. (November 2015). How libraries stay relevant in the digital age. Chicago Magazine. Retrieved from http://www.chicagomag.com/Chicago-Magazine/November-2015/How-Libraries-Stay-Relevant-in-the-Digital-Age/

Spinks, R. (2015, January 4). The Future of Libraries Has Little to Do with Books. Retrieved from The Daily Good: https://www.good.is/articles/public-libraries-reimagined

Seed libraries

Another program which works well in collaboration with library gardening space is seed sharing. This is becoming increasingly popular, and is even available at libraries throughout Connecticut! Here is some information on Westport's program: http://westportlibrary.org/services/seed-library-exchange. How many public libraries have this Seed Exchange program in CT or US would be an interesting research project.
This is a new development of RFID technology and could be part of a smart library.

Discussion

Discussion Question 1: What will it take for libraries to become central to more people's lives?
Discussion Question 2: I talked a lot about change as always being good. But are

there times and situations when change in libraries is not good for our future prospects?

Discussion Question 3: Will libraries ever become so evolved that, in Susan Baerg Epstein's words, our grandparents and great grandparents won't recognize it?

Discussion Question 4 [Not Required]: Do you have any questions or comments with regard to the content, readings, or assignments?

Unit 13: Final Exam/Wrap-up

Final Exam

The Final exam is worth 20 percent of the grade for the course.

You should consider the final an in-class exam. In fact, you will have no time to consult to the textbook or other reading materials while you are taking the exam (a time limit of 90 minutes). There will be a penalty for turning in the exam late: 10 points for each minute. The exam will be composed of three parts: (1) Multiple Choice, (2) Short Answer, and (3) Essay Question. If you carefully read all the required readings, you should be able to easily answer the questions.

Using the Quiz tool within the course web page, you will take the final exam at any time between Monday, May 9, at 12:01 AM and Friday, May 13, at 11:59 PM. I have made the Quiz tool ("Final Exam") hyperlink unavailable on your course web page. However, I will make it available on your course web page during the period of the final exam.

For information about taking an exam using the Quiz (or Assessment) tool within the course web page, please refer to the online Help that is built in the course web page. The online "Help" link is located at the right top corner of the course web page.

If a Pop-Up Blocker were installed on your computer, you must turn off the Pop-Up Blocker before you take the exam.

When you take the final exam, you should keep in mind that you must save each answer by clicking the "Save Answer" button after you answer each question. Otherwise, your answers will not be saved. I repeat - you must save each answer by clicking the "Save Answer" button after you answer each question. And then you should finish the exam by clicking the "Save and

Submit" button. Once you started to take the exam, you cannot stop taking it. You must finish the exam at one time.
*Reading Days, which are designed to provide time for you to prepare for the final examination, are the last week of this semester.

Appendix - Course Syllabus

Course Description

Principles and applications of computers and information technologies in libraries and information centers.

This course fulfills one of the requirements for the Master of Library and Information Science degree at SCSU.

Enrollment in this course is limited to 20 students.

Prerequisites

The prerequisite for this course is a basic undergraduate or graduate-level computer literacy course, such as CS101. Alternatively, students with extensive experience working with information technologies may elect to waive this prerequisite.

We assume that all students admitted to ILS 507 will have:

(1) An understanding of the concepts underlying computer-based technologies.
(2) Familiarity with the associated vocabulary.
(3) Ability to use a computer in a work setting.
(4) Ability to navigate the WWW, use URLs and the like.

Probable Texts/Readings

Liu, Y. Q. (2017). *Information Science and Technology* (Course Pack).

Recommended Text:

Brian K. Williams and Stacey C. Sawyer (2015). *Using Information Technology: A Practical Introduction to Computers & Communications* (11th Edition, Complete Version). McGraw-Hill. [ISBN-10: 0-07-3516880] [ISBN-13: 9780073516882]

You are also encouraged to find current literature and sharing them with your course work.

TK20 Requirement

All students are required to purchase TK20 accounts. For this course, you will submit a reflection paper on the student learning outcomes through your TK20 accounts. Students who do not submit their assignments in this way will receive an incomplete in the course. For information on the TK20 Assessment System and how to purchase it, please go to the School of Education's website at http://www.southernct.edu/academics/assessing-studentlearning/tk20/

Course Objectives

1) The student will demonstrate mastery of basic terminologies, concepts, and theories related to information science and technology.

2) The student will demonstrate knowledge of technologies used in the library including introductory knowledge of computer hardware, software, telecommunication, networks, and digital formats used by libraries.

3) The student will demonstrate mastery of advanced techniques, skills, and knowledge necessary for searching the Web.

4) The student will demonstrate mastery of skills and knowledge necessary for the development of a Web page.

5) The student will demonstrate proficiency in using MS Office software programs.

Student Learning Outcomes

II. Embrace, utilize and critically assess both current and emerging information technologies to select, organize, manage, facilitate access, and disseminate information.

In accomplishing Goal II, students will:

a. Use professional standards to select, organize, manage, preserve, retrieve, evaluate and deliver information resources in various formats.

b. Identify, analyze, explain, use and evaluate current and evolving information technologies in libraries and information services.

c. Articulate how technology is making a difference in the library and information profession.

d. Adopt and utilize technology to connect, communicate, and collaborate.

e. Explore, develop, promote, and assess information systems and technologies.

Modes of Instruction

Read the assigned readings and participate in the weekly discussions. Complete individual and group assignments.

Evaluation and Methods of Assessment

The final grade for the course will be based on one exam, individual assignments, a group project, and class discussion participation and contribution to the class.

1) Participation/Contribution/Rubric 20%
2) Final Exam 20%
3) Group Bibliographic Essay 20%
4) Web Search Exercise 20%
5) "Menu" Exercise 20%

Final letter grades will be based on total points accumulated through completion of these components. Grades will not be curved. The distribution is

A 95-100 points
A- 90-94 points
B+ 86-89 points
B 82-85 points
B- 79-81 points
C+ 76-78 points
C 72-75 points
C- 69-71 points
D+ 66-68 points
D 62-65 points
D- 59-61 points
F 58 or fewer points

Evaluation Criteria

Expectation: This is a graduate level course and graduate level performance is expected to be demonstrated in exams, papers and projects. Recycled materials from other classes or "seat of trousers" projects are not acceptable.

An "A" project does not just fulfill the assignment: it has something original and important to say, and the points it makes are supported well. It is organized effectively, develops smoothly and is written clearly.

A "B" paper fulfills the assignment well: its general idea is clear, and it is effectively presented. It handles its sources well, with no serious errors of fact or interpretation. Its content, however, may not be very original, agreeing with accepted views without adding anything new, or it may be original but fail to offer sufficient support for the points made. It is based on adequate and appropriate data or literature and refers to it when points need support.

A "C" paper is adequate to fulfill the assignment, and its general idea is clear. Its content may be repetitive or oversimplified, refusing to acknowledge complexity or failing to cover important points. Points may be hard to follow, and the paper may be poorly organized (e.g., literature reviews that summarize what one source after another has to say, instead of making general points supported by reference to a selection of sources). There may be a serious error of fact or interpretation. Sources or data may be poorly chosen -- insufficient in number, of inappropriate types, too old, lacking in authority, etc.

An "F" paper does not fulfill the assignment: it does not do what was required. It may fail to focus on a single topic or subject. It may omit large amounts of data or material lying within its declared scope, or make repeated errors of fact or interpretation.

Course Outline

Unit 1 (Week #)
Introduction and housekeeping
Unit 2 (Week #)
Definition of Information and Information Science
Unit 3 (Week #)
Hardware issues
Unit 4 (Week #)
Software Issues
Unit 5 (Week #)
Searching
Unit 6 (Week #)
Management Issues
Unit 7 (Week #)
Internet
Unit 8 (Week #)
LANs
Unit 9 (Week #)
Web 2.0 and Library 2.0
Unit 10 (Week #)
Telecommunication Issues
Unit 11 (Week #)

Media Formats
Unit 12 (Week #)
Future Prospects.
Unit 13 (Week #) Final Exam

Assignments

1). Participation/Contribution (20 points)

1.1 Attending class “discussion”

You will note that there is "Discussion" where you can respond to discussion question given by the instructor, and also read and respond to answers and comments posted by other students. In a typical discussion for a unit, the instructor will pose a series of threaded discussion questions. You are required to participate in all the discussion questions in each unit.

1.2 This is just an outgoing/continuing exercise that we need to begin now.

The participation/contribution component of your grade is a significant 20 percent. But not to worry, you can do it within the whole week of the unit week.

- We expect you to share news items from professional publications or postings from professional listservs, blogs, RSS (Really Simple Syndication), SNS, or others with the class. They should be somehow relevant to the course, of course. You can post any time during the semester. However, you should post at least once a week. And of course, you can comment on or interact with the information provided by others.
- One good way to find news and another good information is to subscribe to a professionally oriented discussion list. When you find something good, forward a message (or cut and paste) from that list to the class. Can't find a good professional list to subscribe to? Check

out the suggestions at the Library of Congress at http://www.loc.gov/rr/program/bib/libsci/guides.html. Your forwarded message to the class must contain an introduction and comments on why this posting and this list is important or interesting to you.

For a subscription to CNET newsletters, go to
http://www.cnet.com/newsletters/?tag=nl.e404
For a subscription to Computing Update, go to
http://www.technologyreview.com/cust/newsletter.aspx

Then, of course, find a news item of interest and share it with the class. You should also introduce and comment on the item, explaining why the item is important or interesting. Please don't forget to put your full name in your news, professional publications, or postings from the professional listserv, blog, or others.

Again, all this is part of the participation and contribution portion of your grade. There will not be specific grading of your postings but your contribution will be noted as part of the 20 percent component. In other words, I'm not going to comment on or grade specific postings you make but I will monitor your contributions and interactions.

1.3 Reflection Paper on the Rubric Student Learning Outcomes, due on Monday of the last week.

I want you to write a short reflection paper (double spaced one or two pages), which includes your experience and learning with regard to the student learning outcomes based on the course Rubric. You firstly **fill out the Rubric form with grades you think you deserve aligning with each of 5 criteria**, then submit the reflection paper along with the Rubric Form through your TK20 account. This is part of the participation and contribution portion of your grade and you may receive an incomplete grade if you don’t submit it to TK20.

2). Bibliographic Essay (20 points), due at different times during the semester.

The next thing you need to be concerned about is the Individual or Group Bibliographic Essay. Details concerning this exercise (how to do it, etc.) are as follows.

The essential idea is that the student will prepare a bibliographic essay and lead discussion for the assigned unit topics. Primary concern falls immediately to those persons doing Unit 03. The concern is most central because *gosh* they only have a couple of weeks to get on this. Although normally you will be assigned to the various Bib Essays (randomly and capriciously), my heart goes out to this first group. As a result, the odds are that I'll be more generous and understanding of those early pioneers. And I'll accept volunteers for the Unit 03 Bib Essay. If you want to volunteer, you will have to send me an email (liuy1@southernct.edu) immediately. We can't wait long for volunteers. If none appear in a few days, I'll unleash the random and capricious forces previously mentioned.

Students choose the units you like voluntarily by sending me an email, but will be assigned to units by the instructor in an arbitrary and capricious manner if no volunteers. The number of each unit leaders could vary based on the class size which can be one to three people. If it is a group, members of the group should coordinate development of the bibliography to avoid duplication and redundancy.

The Bibliographic Essay should review recent literature (traditional and electronic) for the class. The focus should be directed toward issues and practical applications pertaining to the information profession, information centers, and libraries. In other words, the essay should emphasize real-world concerns and issues as they affect professional practitioners. It should be brief; less than 2,000 words (approximately four single-spaced pages) excluding bibliographies, citing perhaps twelve to twenty articles, books, or electronic documents.

There would be several ways to do a group bib essay. First of all, you will have to discuss with your group member(s) about major issues that should be included in your four-page bib essay. Then you may assign the major issues to your group members. Or you may write your bib essay individually and later you can combine them into one. It is totally up to your group. However, one thing you should keep in mind is that your group should turn in a single, collaborative bib essay. Again, quality is much more important than quantity! An example ("Bib Essay Example") of the bib essay group assignment is available in the server area called "Class Library" within the course web page.

In leading the discussion, each member of the group is to summarize one or two key or important issues contained in items on the bibliography and pose a case where the issue would come into play in practice. Classmates are to problem-solve or advance the case example using the leaders as a resource for additional information.

Only the instructor is allowed to upload a file on to an accessible server area called "Class Library" within the course web page. Therefore, you should email me (liuy1@southernct.edu) your bibliographic essay as an email attachment by a day prior to the beginning of the unit. The file format of your bibliographic essay should be an MS Word file format (".docx"). In order for the entire class to view, I will upload your bibliographic essay file on to the "Class Library" within the course web page. Of course, you can download those uploaded bib essay files for your reading at any time.

Each unit leader/group should also send the instructor unit discussion questions to lead the assigned unit topic. The instructor may also create additional discussion questions within the topic (unit).

3). Web Search Exercise (20 points)

The assignment of all the detailed instructions is in the Lecture note. Submit the Web Search Exercise through the "Assignments" tool within the course Web page.

4). "Menu" Exercise (20 points)

The assignment of all the detailed instructions for the exercise is in the Lecture note.
Submit the Menu Exercise through the "Assignments" tool within the course Web page.

5). Final Exam (20 points)

It consists of multiple choice and short questions.

Library Resources

You are responsible for all materials covered in class. With regard to the journal articles listed in the class reading list, for example, you should be able to find them in the full-text online databases that are available through the SCSU Library homepage. If you have any problems in accessing the full-text online databases of the SCSU library, contact Ms. Rebecca Hedreen, the Distance Education Librarian at the SCSU Library, at "hedreenr1@southernct.edu". She should be able to help you. Rebecca Hedreen's home page is available at http://libguides.southernct.edu/profile/hedreen. Ms. Rebecca Hedreen will be always available if you have questions or problems about library services.

If you have any difficulties or problems in finding reading materials related to this course, please let me know. I can help you.

Accommodation for Disabilities

"Southern Connecticut State University seeks to provide appropriate academic adjustments for all individuals with disabilities. Southern is committed to fully supporting all applicable federal, state, and local laws, regulations, and guidelines with respect to providing appropriate academic adjustments to afford equal educational opportunity. There are a variety of resources available to you through the University's Disability Resources Center located in Engleman Hall, ENC 105A: (203) 392-6828; (203) 392-6131 TDD." The Center for Adaptive Technology can also be reached by email at cat@southernct.edu.

If you are a student with a disability, before you may receive accommodations in this class, you will need to contact Southern's Disability Resource Center (DRC). For Further Information please refer to the DRC website: www.southernct.edu/drc

Academic Honesty Statement

Plagiarism involves taking and using as one's own the writing and/or ideas of another and ranges from outright stealing to inadequate attribution. The department does not tolerate plagiarism in print or online. Violations of plagiarism or the use of commercial organizations or paid individuals to write all or part of work submitted for a class may result in a failing grade for the course or dismissal from the program.

"Academic Standards and Program Regulations" (from Graduate Studies Catalog):

"The integrity of scholarship is the cornerstone of the academic and social structure of the University. It is the expressed policy of the University that every aspect of graduate academic life, related in whatever fashion to the University, shall be conducted in an absolutely and uncompromisingly honest manner. Violations of academic honesty are grounds for a failing grade and may result in dismissal from the School of Graduate Studies."

Proscribed Conduct (from Student Handbook)

"Academic misconduct including all forms of cheating and plagiarism. Academic misconduct includes but is not limited to providing or receiving assistance in a manner not authorized by the instructor in the creation of work to be submitted for academic evaluation including papers, projects and examinations; and presenting, as one's own, the ideas or words of another person or persons for academic evaluation without proper acknowledgment. Disciplinary sanctions which may be imposed by the University include expulsion from all universities within the CSU System. In cases of academic misconduct, the faculty member may fail the student on the work or the course. Ability to take action extends beyond the semester in which the course was taken."

Late Submissions Policy

Any LATE assignments must either (a) be approved by the instructor at least 24 hours before they are due, or (b) be accompanied by a doctor's note; otherwise, there will be a 10% penalty each day for turning in assignments late.

Incompleteness

A final grade of "I" or "Incomplete" will NOT be given except in extremely extenuating circumstances, such as serious illness.

Participation Policy

You can access each unit (lecture note) and its class discussion board only according to the course schedule throughout the semester. You are expected to complete all the units within the assigned time limits, read the assigned articles/documents/chapters and participate in class discussion. I will not accept any early or late participation in class discussions. For example, while we are in Unit 3 (Hardware Issues), you can post your discussion messages only to the discussion board of Unit 3. During the period of Unit 3, you are not allowed to post your discussion messages to any other units except Unit 3.

As the course schedule indicates, each unit (except for Units 1 and 13) runs for seven days from Monday through Sunday. The first and last units run for almost two weeks respectively. The lecture note and discussion board of each unit will automatically appear on the first day of the unit according to the course schedule. Please keep in mind that I will not accept any early or late participation in class discussions.

Your involvement and contribution to the class discussion are very important to your learning and the success of the class. Contribution/participation grade includes appraisals of:

1). *The quality of participation (not just quantity!) in class discussion.* Civility and good manners toward colleagues in "Discussion" and in email communication are important.

You will note that there is "Discussion" where you can respond to a discussion question given by the instructor, and also read and respond to answers and comments posted by other students. In a typical discussion for a unit, the instructor will pose a series of threaded discussion questions. You are required to participate in all the discussion questions in each unit. To participate in the threaded discussions, click the " Discussion Board" button on the Action Menu located at the left. And select a topic (or question) in the current unit. For detailed information about the Discussion Board tool within the course web page, please refer to the BB Learn 9 online Help that is available at site: http://www.southernct.edu/faculty-staff/teachinglearning/learnfactutorialnew.html

2). *E-mails*. Regular reading of your Southern email is very important. In general, you must check your Southern email daily. The instructor will send you an email message from time to time and your conscientiousness will be reflected in this grading component.

Your instructor (liuy1@southernct.edu) often gets hundreds of email messages a day and uses an aggressive deleting style. If the subject line does not grab his attention, it could be inadvertently excised. All your emails must have the course number, section number, and your name in the subject line. For example, "ILS 507, Tiger Woods". If your email address were changed, you must immediately inform me of your new email address.

Technical skills

The instructor will NOT teach you the following things:

- How to navigate the course web page.

- How to use a variety of tools and features (e.g., Discussions, Assignments, etc.) that are available on the course web page.
- How to solve technical problems related to computer and communication technologies.

In order to learn all, the basic tools and features in the Blackboard Learn 9 system, please refer to the online Help that is available at site http://www.southernct.edu/faculty-staff/teachinglearning/learnfactutorialnew.html

In short, you must achieve a mastery of the tools and features available on the course web page in the period of the first unit.

If you have any problems with registration, contact either one of the following two people.

- If your last name begins with the letters A-K: Ms. Hicks at (203) 392-5303 or by email at hicksc3@southernct.edu
- If your last name begins with the letters L-Z: Mr. Benson at (203) 392-5317 or by email at bensonj1@southernct.edu

If you have any problems with your computer and communication technologies or the Blackboard system, contact the SCSU Help Desk.

- SCSU Help Desk phone number (203) 392 - 5123, and an email address "Helpdesk@southernct.edu".
- SCSU Help Desk is staffed internally (on campus) Monday through Thursday, 8 am to 8 pm and Fridays from 8 am to 5 pm.

Instructor Biography

See details in the course website.

On this class site, every effort has been made to acknowledge the work of others. Any omission is unintentional. If anyone finds an oversight, please contact me at "liuy1@southernct.edu" immediately so that any error can be corrected.

Appendix - Course Welcome Message

Dear Students:

Welcome to ILS 507, Introduction to Information Science & Technology, offered by the Department of Information and Library Science, through WebCT Vista. I hope you enjoy this course.

I am Dr. Yan Liu and I have been on the faculty at Southern since 2001, first as an assistant professor and then as a full professor faculty member. I began teaching online as one of the first faculty to try that new way of delivering courses. I think that's about 17 years now.

My terminal degree is in Information Science from the University of Wisconsin-Madison School of Information and Library Studies. My specialty is digital information management. I have written several books on that topic. I also conducted a number of empirical studies and published dozens' peer-reviewed journal articles. They can be found in the Library of Congress catalog at Worldcat.org.

If you need to get in touch with me, I have an email at Southern (liuy1@southernct.edu). While you email me, please identify yourself and the class you're in. I am teaching 3 courses so it can be confusing if students don't identify both the class they're in and who they are.

For the first time, you are attending this course, I ask each of you to post a short note to introduce yourself. Your introduction doesn't need to be long, but it should include your professional and educational background, why you are interested in this course, as well as any other details you would like to share.

For the first and second weeks of the course, I ask you to read through carefully all documents on the course pages, especially course syllabus and unit lectures. Then, complete the assigned readings for the unit week shown on the syllabus and lecture notes.

Each unit starts on Monday mornings, and ends on Sunday nights, so most likely, your assignments and participation in unit discussion are due on Sunday nights by 11:59 pm.

Please note that we will use the WebCT Email tool (internal) for our class communications. Unless there are emergency needs, please contact me with this internal tool for any inquiries and class activities; also feel free to call me or come to my office by appointment.

Your 1st and one of the major assignments is to conduct a Bib Essay paper, which will be a team project. The student forms a group to conduct the Bib Essay work and lead the unit discussion. I will complete the group based on the last name when the course roster is finalized. Please read the instruction in the syllabus, and prepare leading/monitoring questions for which your group is responsible.

I have taught this course both on onground and online. Several professors developed the content of the online materials. For the purpose of this course, there may be changes to better fit the student needs. So although I have opened all units for unit leaders but NO UNIT should be considered as "ready to work on" UNTIL the actual Unit week starts. Do not print and use your print version. Revisions to the unit are possible up while the actual unit begins. Please feel free to contact me if you come across any oversights.

Good luck and have fun in the class. I hope it will be a rewardable one for you.

Dr. Liu

Appendix - Assignment 01

Search Exercise

"Surfing the web" has become an international pastime, perhaps even a fixation. However, here we expect a serious search with near-scholarly analysis and commentary. We are looking for graduate-level, systematic, intelligent searching that uses a range of search engine capabilities and tools. We also expect growth and learning to be manifest.

The goal of this exercise is for you to become an increasingly proficient searcher -- not just a casual user of search engines. You should come to understand the nuances of and variances between the major search engines and, in the process, develop sufficient expertise to assess the strengths and weaknesses of each. To make progress toward this greater mastery and skill, before beginning this exercise you must look at the great resources at http://en.wikipedia.org/wiki/List_of_search_engines

Choose a fairly narrow topic; it should be a non-unitary or compound topic that can be expanded or narrowed as the need arises -- in fact, you should plan on that eventuality. Example of a unitary topic: "Blue Mist Spirea" or "Dachshund." Example of a non-unitary or compound search: (attack OR security) AND dog AND (drugs OR narcotics OR crack). Another example: (coryopteris OR "Blue Mist" OR "Blue Beard") AND (disease OR insects OR fungus). You see the difference? The unitary search is simple and easily targeted, the compound takes some analysis and skill on the part of the searcher.

Choose three Web search engines and one meta search engine. Execute a preliminary or simple search. If the results are in the 1000s, narrow the search. Ideally, you would like to get fewer than 500 hits. Use the advanced or power search and use the range of tools provided at each search engine. Be sure to note whether the default Boolean operator is AND rather than OR.

Evaluate the search engines by comparing the quality of results you find in at least thirty sites or sources retrieved. If the abstracts are good, you may not have to actually look at the sites.

Compare and contrast the results for uniqueness and overlap. Note the value or importance (vs. irrelevance) of sites you find. Compare and contrast the search tools available at each search engine site. Write a summary of what you did and what you found. Evaluate all aspects of the process you find relevant. Analyze both the quality of your search and the performance of the search engine. Include a recommendation or summative evaluation.

One more tip: The annotations are really important. You must demonstrate in your search and analysis that you have achieved a mastery of the tools and features available through the different search engines. You must demonstrate that you understand what happened in the search.

In order to receive full credit, you will have to conduct very thorough and systematic Web searches. Please refer to the Web Search Exercise Rubric below for the evaluation criteria.

Web Search Exercise Rubric:

CRITERIA	UNACCEPTABLE (1)	ACCEPTABLE (2)	TARGET (3)
Appropriateness of Search Formulation for a Compound Search	Search formulation is not for a compound search.	Search formulation is for a compound search, but Boolean operators are not effectively used in the formulation.	Search formulation is for a compound search and Boolean operators are effectively used in the

			formulation.
Capability of Refining the Search Formulations	Get more than 500 search results on all of the search engines	Get fewer than 500 search results on most of the search engines	Get fewer than 500 search results on all of the search engines
Understanding of Major Differences between Web Search Engines	Does not discuss any major differences between Web search engines.	Discusses some major differences between Web search engines.	Discusses all the major differences between Web search engines.
Familiarity with Advanced Search Tools and Features Provided at Each Web Search Engine	Does not demonstrate familiarity with any advanced search tools and features provided at each Web search engine.	Demonstrates familiarity with some advanced search tools and features provided at each Web search engine.	Demonstrates familiarity with the full range of advanced search tools and features provided at each Web search engine.
Assessment of the Strengths and Weaknesses of Each Web Search Engine	Does not provide any assessment of the strengths and weaknesses of each Web search engine.	Provides superficial assessment of the strengths and weaknesses of each Web search engine.	Provides thorough assessment of the strengths and weaknesses of each Web search engine.
Descriptions of the Search Processes	Does not provide any detailed descriptions of the search	Provides somewhat detailed descriptions of the search processes.	Provides very detailed descriptions of the search

	processes.		processes.
Objective Relevance Judgment of the Search Results	The relevance judgment of the search results is not based on an operational definition of relevance.	The relevance judgment of the search results is based on an operational definition of relevance, which is not objective enough.	The relevance judgment of the search results is based on an operational definition of relevance, which is objective enough.
Conclusions	Conclusions are not supported by the findings of the Web search exercise.	Conclusions are insufficiently supported by the findings of the Web search exercise.	Conclusions are fully supported by the search results.

Appendix - Assignment 02

"Menu" Exercise

Submit the Menu Exercise by the due date through the "Assignments" tool within the course Web page. Twenty points total.

You might want to note that date: this exercise is really multipart and is in fact "the" exercise for the latter part of the course. However, multipart does not mean you do all the parts. Rather you choose the pieces that ultimately add up to 20 points. You choose from the menu.

Because students in a class like this frequently have a variety of backgrounds and knowledge, you will choose from among several alternatives for this part of the course.

The goal is to broaden your experience and/or to free you from "learning" things you already know. But because of the nature of the setting and the fact that perhaps only a small portion of the class might elect to do a specific exercise, most instruction is self-administered through tutorials, manuals, and occasionally a brief in class demonstration. The essence of the exercise is to "sharpen skills" that are needed for your future professional career, or "fire for familiarization" rather than to become an expert in any particular application.

Again, even low-level, rudimentary knowledge means you should not do the exercise here. The spreadsheet and presentation software exercises are not designed to give students extensive exposure or detailed experience with an application. They are, rather, quick and minimal introductions to an extremely limited number of features. This exposure will give you entree, a foot in the door that, we hope, will give you enough insight and confidence to explore on your own. Because this level of involvement, even minimal prior experience will merit exclusion from the exercise.

Menu Option 1. Data Analysis. Twenty points

Data analysis is reported as **"one** of the hottest **skill** categories over the past two years for recruiters, and it was the only category and it was the only category that consistently ranked in the top 4 across *all* of the countries" (Dykes, B. (2016). *Data storytelling: The essential data science skill everyone needs*. Forbes.)

This exercise is to provide you an opportunity to conduct a **Data/Text Analysis with a data analysis tool(s)**. This exercise will be creative:

1) find a set of textual data (see samples in Assignment section),
2) analyze relationships of the data that are significant, meaningful, and prominent for you
3) illustrate the relationships by **heading**, groups, charts, figures and/or tables,
4) write a report of the results and/or meaningful findings.

The purpose of this exercise is not knowing how to sort or organize data, but to explore the statistical **relationship** from the mass of collected data and draw meaningful conclusions. Email the instructor if you like to do this option

Here are tutorials available on the web (and elsewhere) on Excel, a common tool for data analysis:

a) Data Analysis in Excel - EASY Excel Tutorial: www.excel-easy.com/data-analysis.html
b) How to easily perform text data content analysis with Excel - YouTube: https://www.youtube.com/watch?v=c_r1eqwBlWM
c) If that's not enough or if you want to triangulate, go to Google and do a search on Excel AND tutorial.

The other data analysis tools:

a) PSPP - a program for statistical analysis of sampled data. It is a free as in freedom replacement for the proprietary program SPSS, should work on most modern computers and most operating systems. More info from PSPP - Wikipedia

b) SPSS - a software package used for statistical analysis. More info from SPSS - Wikipedia

c) SAS - a software suite for advanced analytics. More info from SAS (software) - Wikipedia

Menu Option 2: Enhanced Website Exercise. Twenty points

This project would involve additional work on a homepage. This must go beyond a simple Web page. There is much more to explore and to learn and a "wide variety of bells and whistles" to be added, *including things like graphics, sound and videos, and also features like calendar, contact info, site search engine, links to social media, contact info, comment/feedback, etc*. All hypertext links on your home page should be functioning.

Content of this Web work: you can work on a library home page, or a home page that is in the field of information and library science, or something that can benefit your professional career, all that said, hope this exercise will not only show your skills and capabilities but also be useful to your work or studies in this ILS field. You might even tackle a larger project in collaboration with a classmate. But in the latter instance, of course, higher expectations will prevail.

Develop a website that your instructor can access. You might: (1) sign up a free home page service such as SiteBuilder, Google Sites, Weebly, Wix, Angelfire, or Tripod, or (2) use an ISP that provides home page service to its customer.

Most of these commercial Web page services are easy to construct using canned templates. It's usually just a matter of choosing options from a menu, clicking a mouse, and a Web page is created. This is of course the minimum and you are encouraged to move beyond the templates into more creative realms.

You may also choose to learn an html editor such as Dream Weaver and mount a simple Web page that goes beyond a template. Even a bit of simple HTML can be enough to get a page operating.
I'd like to recommend you the following HTML tutorials:

- http://www.davesite.com/webstation/html/
- http://www.w3schools.com/html/default.asp

To archive your Web page to a CD or a local directory, you may want to use any application that allows you to download a Web site from the Internet to a local directory, building recursively all directories, getting HTML, images, and other files from the server to your computer. One example is HTTrack at http://www.httrack.com/, a free and easy-to-use offline browser utility.

The webpage must have two things: (1) It must work and you should inform me of its URL address so that I can access to it and (2) You must annotate the enhanced Web page development exercise. That is, tell me in a message what you did, what you learned, problems you had, and the like. The annotation might be a part of the Web page or it might be a separate MS Word document. The annotation/commentary is critical for the instructor's evaluation of your efforts. The narrative matters.

Most importantly, the webpage/website must have an acknowledgment that includes your name and the course info on the main page so you can claim this is a project for this course and cannot be used for other courses.

Menu Option 3: Excel Exercise. Five points

For this assignment, you are going to create a monthly budget for yourself spanning a twelve-month time period. Therefore, you will need to start by creating twelve column headings across the top representing the months January through December.

You will then need four row headings for your expenses -- Rent, Food, Utilities, and Insurance. Then create a fifth row heading for the subtotal of your expenses, and a sixth row heading for your income.
Now for the first four rows of your expenses, make up a series of numbers for each of the twelve months, but try to stay within the bounds of reality! Skip filling in the subtotal row for now, and fill in the income row with a fairly large number (something that is larger than the sum of your expenses).

At this point you will be graded on the following instructions:

1. All headings (in both columns and rows) should be boldface. Column headings should be centered within cell, and row headings should be aligned to the left.
2. All cells should be formatted for "currency"
3. Using the Autosum, calculate your four expenses for each month, with the results going in the "Subtotal" row
4. The Subtotal row should be a different background color for emphasis
5. For all of the numbers within the "Income" row, make the text color red
6. Create a new row under "Income" with the heading "Money Leftover". This should be a calculation for each month, subtracting "Subtotal" from "Income". After getting the result for each month, make sure all the numbers in this row are boldfaced, and a text color of blue.
7. Make a graph for the entire chart. The graph should be a column chart (any of the column charts), and the legends should be done "by rows". The chart title should be "My Monthly Budget." The X axis should be titled "Months", and the Y axis should be titled "Dollars". The graph should be created within the SAME sheet, and located below where you've typed in your budget statistics.

There are excellent tutorials available on the web (and elsewhere). See, for example, http://www.fgcu.edu/support/office2007/Excel/index.asp

Menu Option 4. PowerPoint Exercise. Five points

You are to create a PowerPoint presentation, in which you present any topic you are interested in.

You should include the following features in your presentation:

1. The first slide should be a title slide, which should include your name, email address, course and section number, and the topic of your presentation.
2. At least 9 slides
3. Use at least two pictures on your entire slide presentation.
4. At least a hyperlink that connects to a Web page
5. A slide transition effect between all of your slides (e.g., "Box In" and "Wipe Up")
6. A footer on every slide except for the title slide which includes the date, slide number, and the topic for your presentation
7. The use of speaker "notes" on at least two pages
8. Use a design template

Again, there are many good tutorials, such as http://www.fgcu.edu/support/office2007/ppt/index.asp

If that's not enough or if you want to triangulate, go to Google and do a search on Powerpoint AND tutorial.

Menu Option 5. Other Learning. Ten points or more

If you are already proficient with Excel and PowerPoint and you taught Tim Berners Lee everything he knows about HTML or data analysis, you will have to be more creative for your twenty points. You may want to design and develop a database using a database system such as MS Access for a PC or FileMaker Pro for a MAC. Your project could look like a traditional term paper. Or it might involve original research; a survey, perhaps, on some aspect of information science.

Students with very short projects (five or ten points for example) may elect to read and annotate current articles in the field. The rate of exchange is one article/annotation per point. Articles must not have been assigned nor used for projects in other classes.

Students who attempt an especially challenging or new (to them) project will be given more credit than a colleague who elects to pursue a safer, perhaps easier project.

The projects listed here are not inclusive but are intended to give you a few ideas of the range of possible projects. It is probably a good idea write up a proposal and talk to the instructor before beginning the project, however. Email (liuy1@southernct.edu) always works.

How long should the project be? The length of the project will, of course, depend on the nature of the work and quality of effort. Quality is always more important than quantity. There is no hard and fast rule on how long a paper or project should be; but it should always be complete and excellent.

*Please note: you are not to do all these exercises listed under the title "Menu Exercise." Rather, you are to choose exercises from the list that total twenty points. When you submit your Menu exercise, you should use the "Assignments" (Menu Exercise) tool within the course Web page.

Remember to format your files names in this order: yourlast_name First_initial Menu Exercise.html or .ppt or .xlsx or docx

The last note: you should write a short production note after your Menu Exercise, and tell me what and why you do for your twenty points. In particular, you will have to explain and justify why you have chosen those Menu options. If you chose Excel and PowerPoint, for example, you should tell me why you have not had a chance to learn those basic software programs so far.

Appendix – Search Exercise Example

This paper will fully examine the searching technology methods of three search engines and one metasearch engine. In this search exercise, I will explore the various capabilities of each search engine and perform a compound search to compare and contrast the outcomes. In addition, various analyses of the compound search results will be explored to better understand how each of the search engines compiles their results. Also, I will compare and contrast data of the each search engine by evaluating the relevance, overlap and uniqueness of the search results.

Picking the Search Engines

Before starting my compound search, I decided to do further research to give me a better understanding of search engines. The research consisted of three elements: picking my search engines based on what the top most popular search engines of 2017, what is a Meta search engine, and how do search engines work/find web pages?

As of February of 2017, the top 15 search engines are: Google, Bing, Yahoo Search, Ask, Aol Search, Wow, WebCrawler, MyWebSearch, Infospace, Info, DuckDuckGo, Contenko, Dogpile, Alhea, ixQuick ("Top 15 Most Popular", 2017). The ranking was based on the number of monthly visitors using the search engine. After seeing the layout of the ranking, I decided to pick the top most popular search engines to review-Google, Bing, and Yahoo. Upon doing further research, I found that in 2009, Yahoo's search has been powered by Bing. Due to that fact, I thought there would be considerable overlap in the search results, therefore I decided to take out Bing and go to the next most popular search engine –Ask. Thus, the three search engines this review will focus on are Google, Yahoo and Ask.

What is a Meta Search Engine?

Metasearch engines give a great idea of what information is out there across the web by allowing users to search several search engines at the same time. Some examples of Meta Search engines are Yippy!, Dogpile, Mamma, MetaCrawler, and WebCrawler (Williams & Sawyer, 2015). This search exercise with focus on examining the MettaSearch engine Dogpile in addition to the individual search engines- Google, Yahoo, and Ask. I decided on using Dogpile because I had never heard of it or used it before and wanted to explore something new.

How to search engines work?

In general search engine's connects information to a user by gathering its own searchable database on the web. After typing in a word(s) or phrase in the search engine's search bar a list of web pages also known as, "hits" will come up on the screen. The hits that pop up ranked in order from most relevant to lease relevant based on the key words typed in the search bar (William & Sawyer, 2015). In addition, every search engine's ranking system is unique and is determined typically through proprietary ranking algorithms. These algorithms decide the equality and relevance of the webpage's before adding them to their page of index. In addition, search engines consider things like: keyword usage, Title tags, Web page copy, and the amount of relevance of the inbound hyperlink when determining their resulting webpage's in the index (Songire, 2016).

Individual search engines are maintained by special software robot programs called *spiders, crawlers, bots* or *agents*- that retrieve information from web pages. According to the book, *Search Engine Visibility*, by Shari Thurow, "Search engine *spiders* find and fetch web pages, a process called crawling or spidering, and build lists of words and phrases found on each web page" (Thurow, 2003).

ABOUT EACH SEARCH ENGINE

For each search engine, I conducted a thorough analysis of their individual searching characteristics such as: advance search and preference options, how they search, their searching individual searching tips, and any other unique methods/information the search engines uses to perform/analysis their search.

Google

Google follows their links from page to page through the crawling method. Google is not the number one search engine for no reason They uses several different algorithms by continually writing new formulas and programs to better understand what the searcher is specifically looking for. Google ranks its results based in 200 factors.   This search engine's most famous trademarked algorithm is called *PageRank*. In addition, the search engines fights spam 24/7 to make it an easier experience for users and to keep results relevant (How Search Works). After investigating the search engine I found that there are many ways to refine a search to find the answer you are looking for. In addition, there are multiple ways to narrow a search through the various search features and in the advanced search section. My investigation findings are listed below.

<u>Google Search Features</u>

- Specialized search options that narrows your search results
    - Examples: Images, Maps, Videos, News, Shopping , Books, Flights
- Google Scholar- paid search option for scholarly literature (articles, theses, books, abstracts and court opinions, from academic publishers, etc…)
- Shows results in order of most relevant
- "Google Instant Prediction" option- shows you results as you type (can be turned off/on)
- User can program searching settings
    - Search in other languages
    - SafeSearch option- automated filter of pornography and potentially offensive content

- Results per page option
- Private Results-result search connections that only you can see.
- Search History option- receive more relevant results and recommendations based on your search activity (can be turned off at any time).

- Traditional search option and an "I'm feeling lucky" option
  - In the "I'm Feeling Lucky" search option that automatically brings user to a single web page
- Has option for searching time, weather, stock quotes, calculator, unit conversions, movie show times, local search, synonyms, local search, currency conversion, package tracking and area code.
- Asterisk * (Wild Card Option), fills in blanks, used as a place holder for a word or more than one word
- Capitalization use in word search does not matter
- Helps with spelling through a spell check mechanism- "did you mean?" giving you options of similar word choices
- The use of AND is not necessary between terms, Google searches automatically for all typed words
- Has a search within results option
- Under Tools Tab- Search results in various sequences:
  - Anytime, Past hour, Past 24 hours, Past week, Past month, Past year or Custom range
- Under Tools Tab- Search results ranking Verbatim
- Automatically ignores common words- example: is, of, as
  - To include them- a + must be used before the term
- Word Variation-searched for words similar to the ones entered

<u>Google Advance Search Options</u>

- Search option feature to include-"all of these words" "exact words" or "one or more of these words"
- Search Option feature to omit hits that contain an unwanted word

- In the Advance Search section
- Settings for Narrowing results by results per page
- Setting for the language
- Setting to look for a particular file type (example: .pdf or .doc documents only)
- Setting to search within as particular site or domain
- Setting for Time frame in which the page has been undated- by date (24hrs, a week, a month, or year)
- Advance search by adding "quotation marks" and using Boolean operator OR
- Add a – (minus sign) before unwanted word
- Filter explicit results

Yahoo

Yahoo is another crawler based search engine that shares alliances with Google and Bing. Though Yahoo developed its own crawler based algorithm technology called "Yahoo Slurp," it does partially pull search results from Bing and Google. (Madiraju, & Talluri) After investigating how to use Yahoo Search, I found that this search engine has multiple ways to refine a search. In addition, there are options to further narrow a search through the advanced search section by specifying and selecting preferences. My investigation findings are listed below.

Yahoo's Searching Features

- Results are shown in order of most relevant
- Top search filter options: images, news, video, local
- Adding a + sign in front of a word to include the words in a search
- Adding a – sign in front of a word to disregard it
- Boolean operator OR can be used between words
- Quotation Marks can be used to find exact phrases
- Search shortcuts for weather, maps, zip codes and more
- Advertisement and paid sponsored results are shown in results

- Various other filtering options: shopping, autos, recipes, sports, finance, celebrity, dictionary, games

Yahoo Advance Search Options

- Time frame (when hit was last updated)- 3 months, 6 moths, 1yr
- Search within a specific site or domain- example: .gov, .org, .com or just within yahoo.com
- File Format-restrict your search to a specific type of file- example: .html, .pdf, .ppt
- SafeSearch option-blocks inappropriate, and adult-oriented content from Search results
- Country and language settings- filter results to a specific country or language
- Numbers of Results- adjust the results per page anywhere between 10 and 100.
- "Show Results In" filter for searching: "All of these words" "the exact phrase" "any of these words" or "none of these words"

Ask

Ask.com originally called Ask Jeeves, has a simple question and answer type of format. This crawler based search engine uses their own search technology algorithm called the "ExpertRank" formula. According to Ask.com, their top results in searched are determined by expertise rather than popularity (Macmanus, R. 2006). Ask search technology responds best to questions, phrases, or single word searches such as -*"car rentals" Connecticut* or *What is the weather forecast in Miami, FL?* (Boswell, 2016). After investigating how to use Ask I found that this search engine provides multiple options to narrow a search. My investigation findings are listed below.

Ask Search Features

- Search option "Did you mean"-

- Additional; search options-such as: video, images, news, maps, local search, weather, encyclopedia listings, blogs and feeds
- Search Shortcuts- Conversation Calculator, Dictionary, Famous People Search, Product Search
- Smart Answers feature: "Smart Answers" pops up in results page and contain brief information and links for more information
    - Example- quick access to weather, sports scores, movie times, translations and conversions
- "Related search"- appear on right side of results with a list of similar topics
- "Search Suggestions" appear in results with tips on how to have a "better" search
    - Example: "Make sure all words are spelled correctly, Try different keywords or Try more general keywords"
- "Search Tips" link in results bring you to a page with various strategies to getting a more fruitful search
    - Example: Spelling Counts, Use Related Search, One Search or Question at a Time, Try Searching With Synonyms to Improve Results
- Word Order Matters
- "Sponsored Links" (Advertisement) shows up at the top and bottom of the results
    - Search uses- Google AdWords program database (paid ad results)
- The default setting is an AND operator between search terms
- Supports the use of the NOT and OR Boolean operator (must be in upper case)
- Automatically ignores common word and single characters- example: of, the, or
    - By putting a + in front of word will include them in a search
- Sorting- sites are sorted in order of relevance.
    - No option for sorting alphabetically, by site, or by date.

<u>Ask Advance Search Options</u>

- Filter for search results appearing in a specific language,
- Search within a specific domain- example: .gov, .org,
- Options for searching specific Geographic region- such as: continents and subcontinents
- Date Options- Last week, 2 weeks, month, 3 months, 6 months, year, or 2 years.
- Displays 10 Web Pages per result page- Options to change result number per page up to 100 at a time

Dogpile

Dogpile is a metasearch engine that "fetches" or gathers its results from various search engine and directories. Though Dogpile pulls its information from many search engines and directories, the main sites it gets their results form are Google, Yahoo, and Bing (Boswell, 2016). After investigating the search engines, Dogpile had a fair amount of ways to refine a search to get "better" results. In addition, the engine had advanced search options to further narrow ones search. My investigation findings are listed below.

Dogpile Search Features

- Specialized search options that narrows your search results
    - Examples: Image search, Audio and Video Search, News Search
- Meta Search Features...
- Search results are mixed with Ads
- "GoFetch" =Dogpiles term for searching for results
- Provides Suggestion Search "Are You Looking For..." that the sites provides "better" search queries with "better" results
- Search Engine Options within search results: users click on "Google, Yahoo, MSN Search etc. to see search results from that specific search engine
- Download Dogpile Toolbar to get: Joke of the Day, SearchSpy, Web searches, Maps, Weather, and more

Advanced Search Options

- Narrow Search exact word phrases
- Language filters
- Date and Domain Filters
- Adult Filters
- Option to set search preferences-ability to customize default search settings

Search Feature Comparison Chart

	Google	**Yahoo**	**Ask**	**Dogpile**
Crawler Based	Yes	Yes	Yes	No
Filtering	Yes	Yes	Yes	Yes
Result Language Modification	Yes	Yes	Yes	Yes
Result Region Modification	Yes	Yes	Yes	Yes
Domain and Site Specific Search	Yes	Yes	Yes	Yes
Date Specific Results	Yes	Yes	Yes	Yes
Ads within search results	Yes	Yes	Yes	Yes
Search Within Results Option	Yes	No	No	Yes
Explicit Results Filters	Yes	Yes	No	Yes
Spell Checking Mechanism	Yes	Yes	No	Yes

MY SEARCH

Topic Question and Compound Search

In my search, I decided to start out with a very broad question and then work my way into a narrow compound search. For the search settings I decided to keep the date and domain range open without limitation because I wanted to get the largest possible hits. Also, due to the topic of teething, I did not believe it was important to date the materials to a specific timeframe because teething babies is not a new concept. Therefore, any information on baby teething would be beneficial. The only area that I used advanced settings was to control the language results to limit hits in English only.

I played around with the advanced search settings in all of the sites but, decided not to manipulate them in this search experiment to keep the search as similar as I could for all of the search engines. I thought that if I changed the settings for each individual search engine my results would not be reliable because there would be too many outliners that would influence the results and to determine the best search engine without having constants would be too difficult. Therefore to have stronger validity, I knew I should not change the setting too much.

My initial topic search question was: *How do I help my baby get through teething pain?* Knowingly, this would yield large search results as it did with Google having 1,900,000 results, Yahoo 1,850,000 results, Ask was at a 122 and Dogpile was over 300 hits. The second search I conducted I introduced more of a compound search by adding the AND Boolean operator and quotation marks. The second search was *baby AND teething AND "pain relief" AND remedies.* This cut down the search results significantly but was still very large. Google has the most at 597,000 followed by Yahoo at 213,000, Ask interestingly went up 130 and Dogpile was still over 300 hits.. The next search went a step further in a compound search by adding an extra quotation mark expression of “remedies and cures” to the search. This once again cut the results down well for most search engines except for Google. Google had 46,600 followed by Yahoo at 309, Ask had only 27 results and Dogpile was still over 300 hits. In an attempt to lower Google down to under 500 search results I reworked my compound search to add more Boolean operators of AND and OR in :(Baby OR Infant) and “Cutting teeth” OR “Cutting tooth”) and took out “remedies and cures” to just be remedies. In the end, the compound search was *(Baby Or Infant) AND teething ("cutting teeth" OR "cutting tooth") AND Sooth AND "tooth Pain" AND "pain relief" AND remedies.* This search did the trick and lowered Googles results to 491 followed by Yahoo at 41, Ask at 40 and Dogpile lowered to 110 total hits.

As a fun side challenge experiment, I decided to try one more compound search to see if I could get the results even lower by reworking the compound search to: (*Baby Or Infant) AND teething ("cutting teeth" OR "cutting tooth") AND "tooth Pain" AND "pain relief" AND "soothing remedies."* This new search added “Soothing remedies” in quotes to narrow the results. My challenge was fulfilled because I got Google down to 10 results, Yahoo at 2, Ask at 12 and Dogpile at 260. Even though the numbers were low the results were not high quality. For example, in my Google search I got only a few sites on baby teething remedies and the rest were irrelevant tooth issue and remedies that had nothing to do with baby teething such as, topics on adult tooth ache relief.

Search Results

Topic Search	Google	Yahoo	Ask*	Dogpile*
Original Question (Non Compound) “How do I help my baby get through teething pain?”	1,900,000	1,850,000	122	Over 300
Baby AND teething AND "pain relief" AND remedies	597,000	213,000	130	Over 300

Baby and teething and "pain relief" and "remedies and cures"	46,600	309	27	Over 300
(Baby Or Infant) AND teething ("cutting teeth" OR "cutting tooth") AND Sooth AND "tooth Pain" AND "pain relief" AND remedies	491	41	40	110
(Baby Or Infant) AND teething ("cutting teeth" OR "cutting tooth") AND "tooth Pain" AND "pain relief" AND "soothing remedies"	10	2	12	260

*Both Dogpile and Ask results were hand counted due to the fact that these search engines did not give a total results number. Therefore I opted to stop counting if results were over 300 hits.

RESULTS: Overlap/Uniqueness

After collecting the data on the results, I sought to do a comparison of the first thirty sites that came up from each search engine. It seems that there was considerable overlap in the resuting hits. In my overlap comparison data collection, I focused on only reviewing the results from the compound search: *(Baby OR Infant) AND teething ("cutting teeth" OR "cutting tooth") AND Sooth AND "tooth Pain" AND "pain relief" AND remedies.* In Google's first thirty hits, the most overlap came from ASK with 10 sites being the same.

Yahoo and Dogpile had much lower overlap with Yahoo only having 3 sites that were in Google's results and Dogpile only has 2. In Yahoo's search results, Dogpile and Yahoo had the most similar results with a total of 15 hits followed by Google and Ask both having only 3 overlapping sites. ASK's results again were the most similar to Google's with 10 being the same followed by Dogpile at 7 and Yahoo at only 4 of the same results. In Dog pile's first 30 hits, the most overlap was in found in Yahoo at 15 followed by Ask at 7 and Google at only 2 of their hits being the found in the search results.

Therefore, the outcomes show that Google and ASK have the most overlap in the results and Dogpile and Yahoo's results are the most alike. Though in the most overlapping search engines, (Google & Ask and Dog & Yahoo) the results were not listed in the same relevancy order. Thus, in regards to the way the search engines crawls the web and pull information to be put into their index, the difference must be in algorithms or the software that each engine is using. Specifically we know that Dogpile pulls its information many search engines such as Google and Yahoo, however Yahoo must have a stronger influence on Dogpiles results.

****The chart below is the overlap results from the compound Search:** ***(Baby OR Infant) AND teething ("cutting teeth" OR "cutting tooth") AND Sooth AND "tooth Pain" AND "pain relief" AND remedies.***

Overlap Chart

Search Engine	**Number of Overlapping Results Appearing within Each Search Engine**			
Google	Google: N/A	Yahoo: 3	ASK: 10	Dogpile: 2
Yahoo	Google: 3	Yahoo: N/A	ASK: 3	Dogpile: 15
ASK	Google: 10	Yahoo: 4	ASK: N/A	Dogpile: 7

Dogpile	Google: 2	Yahoo: 15	ASK: 7	Dogpile: N/A

*The data highlighted in Red points out the highest number or overlapping results For example, In the Google Search there where 10 results that were found in ASK's results as well.

Uniqueness Chart

Google: Results only appearing in Google	19
Yahoo: Results only appearing in Yahoo	10
ASK: Results only appearing in ASK	14
Dogpile: Results only appearing in Dogpile	9

Though many of the search engines had over lapping results, each had a variety of unique results as well. Google was by far the leader in matchless search outcomes with 19 out of 30 of them being only found in Google. In other words, that is 63% of the hits were found in Google. ASK was next in line with 46% uniqueness by having 14 out of 30 results only in that search engine. Yahoo had 10 unique hits out of their 30 results with 33% exclusivity. Lastly, Dogpile had 9 unique hits in their search results of 30% of them only being found in Dogpile.

RESULTS: Relevancy

The following is an assessment based on the relevancy of the first thirty results from each of the four search engines in this study. The chart below represents a relevancy scale (High, Somewhat, Minimally Relevant, and Irrelevant) based on each web source's results. Below is a description on how the relevancy scale was determined.

1. **Highly Relevant**- Source's specific purpose is to give support on how to help a teething baby. The source nearly exclusively focuses on babies not adults and addresses teething remedies and pain relief during the teething process.

2. **Somewhat Relevant**- Source talks about teething specifically in babies and provides some help in remedies and to help with teething pain to some degree. The sources could include a lot of additional information about other aspects of babies that have nothing to do with teething.
3. **Minimally Relevant**- Source talks about teething, but provides little in support on how to help relieve pain or provide remedies during the teething process.
4. **Irrelevant**- (False Drop)The source has nothing to do with teething and providing pain relief, remedies for babies during the teething process. Source could be focused on advertising a product or company.

Relevancy Search Results Chart

	Google	Yahoo	Ask	Dogpile
Highly Relevant	9	17	4	11
Somewhat Relevant	7	4	3	2
Minimally Relevant	5	8	14	13
Irrelevant	9	0	9	4
Totals-	30	30	30	30

ANALYSIS Overlap/Relevance/Uniqueness

This analysis is based on the relevancy, overlap and uniqueness of the search results provided in the first 30 hits in each search engine. Though this analysis will focus primarily on the relevancy I did take into consideration the uniqueness and overlap of the results to some degree. Overall, the most unique results came from Google, followed by ASK, Yahoo and Dogpile. Google had the most unique result pulling from site that none of the other search engines had. Though at a first glance this seems like a positive thing, many of the unique sites were not the most relevant. For example, many of the hits were either somewhat relevant or irrelevant after the 13th hit. For example, the 20th hit was titled "How You Can Prevent Cavity/Decay and Care for Your Baby's Gums"- this had nothing to do with how to help teething pain. It seemed that ASK did the same thing because though their results were unique but, they were not always highly relevant. ASK in particular has the most advertisement like sites compared to all the other search engine's results. All in all, Yahoo has the most relevant unique hits. For example, one of the sites pulled from webmd.com titled "Teething symptoms and how to soothe a teething baby" that was right on target with the compound search.

As far as overlap goes, Google and ASK had the most overlapping sites. Consequently, Dogpile and Yahoo were the search engines that had the most in common hits. This is an interesting outcome and to a degree, makes sense because of the relationships some of the search engines have with each other as it pertains to them crawling or pulling from the web to add to their index. As stated earlier, Dogpile pulls from various search engines such as Google and Yahoo, so it did not surprise me that it shared so much overlap with Yahoo. I was a bit perplexed how it didn't pull more from Google with only having 2 sites in common. However, I was surprised that Yahoo and Google didn't have more overlap because Yahoo has alliances with Google and Yahoo partially pulls information from Google's search. It was interesting how ASK and Google had a great amount of overlap. This makes me think the ASK uses a similar algorithm as Google in determining and ranking their hits. However, the primary purpose of this analysis was so focus on the relevancy of the search results. Overall, as previously stated, Yahoo provided the most highly relevant hits with none of them being irrelevant. Yahoo had great results that pertained specifically to teething babies and how to help them relive teething pain with minimal advertisement. The runner up is hard for me to decide between Google and Dogpile. Even though Google had many highly relevant and somewhat relevant results they had many irrelevant hits as well. This surprised me because the way Google recognizes Boolean operators such as the ones I used in my search (AND, OR etc), I thought that there would be very minimal irrelevant hits. Also, Dogpile is a contender for 2nd place because they still have a great number of highly relevant hits but, the majority if the results are minimally relevant. It seems that the minimally relevant sites were ones that touched on the topic of teething, but the source didn't really answer the search question.

ANALYSIS: Limitations and Recommendations Of Each Search Engine

Google- I was overall happy with Google as a search engine. However, there were some disappointments as well. The search engine did many things right as far as search engines go. First off, Google was the best at being very easy to use. The labeling of search tabs is fantastic they were easily visible giving me confidence on knowing how to navigate the page. Also, by far the search filtering options and advanced search options were above all of the other search engines. Also, Google provided a wealth of information on the web on how to use the site and gave suggestions for creating a better search to maximize results. This was the only search engine that offered this much support from their company. I watched a simple video right on Google's help page that really helped me understand how their search engine works. Those little details of customer service that Google puts out I believe really makes the difference in user experience. It really is no surprise that Google is the number one search engine. They make users feel confident in their ability to find their answer.

However, as a negative, I was surprised by the amount of advertisement. It was not everywhere but, I did notice more and more of it as I moved to my 3 and fourth page of search results. This was unique because most search engines had them throughout the results. This advertisement didn't bother me but, I it caused many of the sources to be irrelevant and I had to filter through to find better hits. Therefore, as far as relevancy is concerned, Yahoo was better in that category then Google.

Nevertheless, Google is still a shining star in terms of performance capabilities.

I definitely would recommend this search engine to others and will still continue to use it myself. The figures I liked the most was the spellcheck options and the way Google helps fill search queries. It is fast, easy, and provides a multitude of search options (images, news, maps) with a simple click of a button. I would recommend this search for all levels and all ages due to how user friendly it is.

Yahoo- By and large, Yahoo was my favorite search engine! Yahoo has a very clean layout to their search page and tool bar. The search engines various narrowing search tab options were very easy to understand and use. For example, there were 5 tabs below the search bar pertaining to focusing ones search (web, video, images, etc). I also liked and found the various other advance search options to narrow a search to be simple and easy to use. My search results came up in seconds and overall I was very pleased with the list of hits that came up. Compared to the other search engines Yahoo's results had the most relevant hits pertaining to my search. The wealth of information in the results were not only relevant but, I also liked how is had minimal advertisement. In addition Yahoo was great in offering plenty search suggestions after I ran my search on how to narrow it further.

Even though Yahoo was super easy to use and filter results I think it is very close second to the capabilities Google's search engine possess. Yahoo has many search features but, they have a bit more requirements one must follow. For example, in Yahoo you must use capital letters with the Boolean operators AND/OR. Overall, this search engine will now be my go-to search engine. I was simple, easy, found relevant information fast, and didn't have a lot of advertisement.

Ask- Overall, I was not happy with Ask. Though it was easy to type in an answer and get results quickly, I found it not to be as user friendly as Google, Yahoo and Dogpile in terms of filtering results. I was frustrated with the amount of advertisement being forced in my face. When I am searching for something, I want the answers to be relevant and easy for me to filter through. In this case I found it hard to actually find the web results for a few reasons.

One, I had to filter through a mass amount of advertisement on each search results page to find any sort of web results on my topic. Also, I felt bombarded by search related suggestions on each results page that caused even more frustration because all I wanted was to be able to find a relevant answer to my question. Due to the length of time it took to find a real answer it will not be my first search engine pick to use. I do think that ASK is good search source for getting answers to really simple questions. For example, if I needed to know the weather forces in Orlando, FL or an acronym for a world. This would be a great site to get a direct answer fast.

Dogpile- Dogpile really surprised me, I was impressed with many aspects of this search engine. First, it had a very clean, bright, easy to use site and search bar. The simple design of the search engine made it easy to understand how to navigate the site and how to narrow my search. Also, for the most part, the actual relevancies of the search results were overall strong with plenty of hits on pain relief and remedies for teething babies. I also liked how this search engine had their advertisements in sections. The advertisement and web results had their own distinct sections and each were clearly labeled "Ads" or "Web Results", making it really simple for me to navigate to through the advertisement right to the information I wanted.

The only downfalls to this search engine that one, compared to the other search engines Google and Yahoo, Dogpile had limited advanced search settings. Also, even though there were clearly marked areas for advertisement, there still was a significant amount of it. I didn't find it overwhelming but, I did think there was enough of it to make a point of it. ASK definitely had a lot more advertisement to filter through then Dogpile. Overall, I really enjoyed using this search engine. Before this search exercise I never used Dogpile before, and now that I have, I will definitely use it. I think it will be best used for simple questions and for an initial search. I liked how it pulls information from various sites and that is a great way to initiate any search to see what is out there on the web.

Conclusion

This search exercise clearly demonstrated the searching abilities, strengths and weaknesses of the search engines-Google, Yahoo, ASK, and Dogpile. Overall, to my surprise Yahoo was the leader in providing the most relevant information fast, in addition to having many easy to use filtering search options. Google was the leader having the most user-friendly capabilities for searching and advanced searching options. Though it was not the leader in relevancy, it did provide many great hits that would have helped me answer my search question. Dogpile was the big surprising search engine that was not only easy to use, but it gave simple filtering options (not as many as Google or Yahoo) that anyone would be able to use. Also, Dogpile was fantastic at providing direct, relevant hits fast. The only search engine that will not be recommended is ASK. This search engine was not as user-friendly as the other three engines for filtering results and was filled with annoying advertisement making it hard to find relevant information. All in all, if you have never tired Yahoo, now it the time to give it a try because I think you will be pleasantly surprised by what you find.

Reference

Ask.com Search Tips. (n.d.). Retrieved March 01, 2017, from http://sp.ask.com/en/docs/about/search_tips.shtml

Boswell, W. (2016, October 19). Here's What Ask.com Is and How You Can Use It. Retrieved March 01, 2017, from https://www.lifewire.com/ask-com-description-3481610

Boswell, W. (2016, December 18). What to Know about Dogpile Search Engine. Retrieved February 28, 2017, from https://www.lifewire.com/dogpile-search-3482008

Madiraju, L., & Talluri, S. (n.d.). How Do Google, Bing and Yahoo Search Engines Work? Who is Winning the Search War?. Retrieved March 05, 2017, from http://networkedlifeq21.wikia.com

How Search Works. (n.d.). Retrieved February 21, 2017, from https://www.google.com/insidesearch/howsearchworks/thestory

Macmanus, R. (2006, November 15). Ask.com: What differentiates it from

Google? Retrieved March 01, 2017, from http://readwrite.com/2006/11/15/ask_what_differentiates_them_from_google/ _

Top 15 Most Popular Search Engines | February 2017. (2017, February). Retrieved February 19, 2017, from http://www.ebizmba.com/articles/search-engines

Williams, B. K., & Sawyer, S. C. (2015). *Using information technology: a practical introduction to computers & communications* (11th Ed.). New York, NY: McGraw Hill Education.

Appendix – Menu Exercise Example

(Annotation of Enhanced Website Exercise)

Introduction: I have decided to create a website for my menu exercise. The ability to do this is something that will certainly be a benefit to my professional career. I have decided to create a website for the PreK-5 Makerspace that I run in the school where I work. The makerspace, named the Excel-plex (named through a contest) is only a year old, and is still a bit unknown to the parent community in my town. They students talk about it, and I have a Twitter account for the Excel-plex, but I am looking for another way to show parents and the community what we do there and why it is such a worthwhile place/investment/class. Another reason that this is the perfect choice for my menu exercise is that I am in a professional learning group next year that wants to *model* student e-portfolios and one of the very popular options for that is using a website as a portfolio. Hopefully this will help me gain some knowledge into the building of a website so that I might actually be able to go into the next school year with some information/tools on how to best students and my group members how to do this.

I started the process by reviewing of the different web page creators that were mentioned in the exercise description. We use Google classroom and lots of Google tools and apps at our school so I am leaning in that direction although I want to check out all of the options. I also am going to look at Sitebuilder.com and Wix.com.

Enhanced Web Page Process	
Site address https://jensegalla.wixsite.com/ils507	
Deciding on the web page service.	**Google Sites** - This is fairly straightforward and is called the 'new sites' builder. I liked it

	right away because there was a similar feel to it as Google Slides and seems like a good choice due to the fact that all of my photos and documents are in Google Drive. However, I am sad to see after spending some time playing around with Google Sites, it doesn't allow for easy insertion of social media links which to me, seems like a really important feature in a web page. I really want this to hook up to my Twitter in particular because I use Twitter a lot in my makerspace. **Sitebuilder.com** - I love the way this looks after experimenting with it a bit. It has a professional quality that is a bit more polished looking than Google Sites (in my opinion). **Wix.com** This is also a professional looking website builder. It is a little more complicated than Google Sites, but I like it. It has lots of free features, graphics, text options etc. Everything is editable. I am going to go forward at this point using Wix.com because it offers more extensive features and add-ons than Google Sites. I did find Google sites to be too limiting - I couldn't add Twitter Feeds or anything else nonGoogle.
All comments based on Wix.com from this point on.	
Wix.com Getting Started	I found that it was necessary to research several different school websites to see what

	pages I wanted to include in my website. Each of these page heading will be a link to additional information on that topic. So far some of the pages I am considering including are; home, projects, events, blog (not sure) resources and contact. Wix. com offered two options for building the webpage. I have a background in art, so although I started with template - I chose the one where I had the ability to edit and change everything as I have definite design opinions. I also found that although some of the tools were a little tricky, the tutorial options were really helpful. I also found that the undo button was an easy and quick remedy to an inadvertent edit.
Pages	I wanted to make my website have several pages and not just be a homepage. I decided on having four pages: Home, Projects, Events and Contact. I think that will be enough to utilize a lot of the features most websites have. Adding pages was a relatively simple process - clicking add page and then deciding the title for each page. Under the 'projects' page, I added a subpage to use as a gallery for some of my many photos. To add the gallery page I had a choice of many different formats for the gallery. I chose the quilt like option. The gallery menu allowed me to choose the option to add more rows - so although all of the

	photos don't automatically display on the page, the viewer has the option to look at more if they are interested. Note: As the page titles are clicked on at the top of the webpage, the new page appears from the right.
Images	Having an organized system for photos definitely helped in terms of this exercise. Luckily, because I use Twitter in the classroom (in the library makerspace specifically) I have a lot of photos to choose from. It is fairly straightforward process on Wix.com - you have to upload the photos that you want to use and create a saved images folder through Wix.com. I like this option because if I use this web builder done the road, I can easily organize my photos by grade level which is how I do it through Google Photos. I take so many pictures that I really need this option. Organization would be simple within this platform. One other image option that was great - a photo editor tab. Some of the template boxes for the photos are a specific shape - and I can edit my photos to display nicely within the frames. There is also an easy way to rename

	the photo which is very helpful so that when the whole image appears it says "Revolutionary War Diorama" rather than something random such as img 1254. This may seem like a small detail, but I think it will make viewing the pictures more pleasing to someone who accesses the website. It was bothering me when I went into the preview mode after choosing some pictures - so I was happy it was a simple fix/adjustment.
Graphics	Wix.com has a lot of great pre-programmed graphics that you can add in. The toolbar on the left of the editing page has an "add" button and from there you can add pre-stocked graphics which include a variety of arrows, decorative graphics, lines, page dividers etc. I added boxes around some of text to add a color element. There was a slider to make the box transparent (or opaque depending on what you want) so that my text showed through. I used this graphic element on my projects page - adding the purple box around the text. I also used the graphics tool to add in some colorful line break and small graphic elements throughout the website.
Links/ BOE Presentation	On my home page I was able to create a clickable link to a Google slide presentation that I created last year. This was simple to do by following the tutorial instructions. This feature is a great way to keep parents and the public aware of what is going on both inside

	and outside my classroom. I posted it under a heading of events - and I would use this is the future as a place to post about the Makerspace Fair, Ice Cream Social, Parents Night, Open House etc. I could see this as a great way to share videos that I make of special events like the Makerspace Fair or of student explanations of projects. To access the link, you click on the picture that says Board of Ed at the bottom of my home page.
Videos	On the projects page I wanted to add some videos of the projects that the students have completed. I often have them show me their project and then explain their process and if they succeeded on the challenge. I was able to set up the video player and also to upload the videos to my Wix.com media storage page. However, in order to change out the videos from the stock videos on Wix - I had to pay to upgrade from the free service so I didn't. I left the generic Wix video player in place after editing the design of it so that there would be the feature of a video within the website although the subject matter unfortunately is not relevant.
Sound	On the projects page I was able to insert a little music player. To be honest, I would not normally put a music play on this page, but I wanted to experiment with the feature. It

	worked great and was really easy to do. I just found a license free mp3 track that I liked and uploaded it to my Wix.com media storage. Then you add the little music play button and through the setting menu I was able to link the song to the button. Simple and easy. Normally with music, I add it to a slideshow of projects so it would play as the slideshow progressed.
Calendar	I really like this feature. I am able to insert a calendar on my website. I chose to do this on the events page as that makes the most sense. Not only can you design and insert a calendar, I was able to link up a Google calendar titled Excel-plex that I created for this purpose. I could use this calendar to post happenings in the makerspace along with special events at the school and that would help me in my mission to keep parents involved and informed.
Social Media	I was able to add two elements on my webpage involving social media. On all the pages the social media bar runs vertically on the left hand side. I was able to connect my Pinterest page, my Instagram page and my Twitter feed. (My Pinterest and Instagram are my personal accounts and not school or makerspace specific, but I linked them up regardless in order to have it be more finished. My linked Twitter account is my school account, so it is more relevant to the website topic.) This was a really detailed feature and I was able to size the bar, add and subtract the media platforms I

	wanted to utilize and also the design (color scheme and shape) was editable. The other social media element I added required an add-on app to the Wix page. I wanted to display my current Twitter feed on my Events page. On the bottom of the page I added this in and it displays my current feed and updates every 24 hours. There are more feature available for this on the premium paid Wix.com account, but this worked for now.
Contact	This page is pretty basic. I added a textbox inviting people to contact me and some graphic elements to add a bit of design interest to the otherwise simple looking page. There is a box where they can directly email me which makes it simple for the viewer. Also there is a place at the bottom where I was able to insert a Google Map as to the Excel-plex's (general) location.

Conclusion: I enjoyed this exercise immensely and spent more time than I would have planned on tinkering about with the different features and tools that Wix.com allows. It gave me some great information and knowledge to use in my professional career next year. I have never done this before, so it will be really useful to me in the future and I am sure that I can apply it as we move forward with digital portfolios. I know it will be helpful as a Library Media Specialist in time, but I am happy to have a new skill that I can actually put to use next year as well.

Although there were a few features I could not access without a Wix.com premium account, I was pleased with the amount of design features and freedom the free version offered. I am really pleased with the look of the webpage and the fact that it has a lot of images. I find that photos of projects and students working really “sell” the program to the parents. If I were to really use a similar site next year (I am not sure my school would allow an independent website - I don’t think that works with their social media policy.) I would change the gallery subpage on the projects page and make a subpage for each grade level that I teach. That way parents could access their child’s grade and view their specific projects.

Overall, I am pleased with both my learning and the final result of this project. It was time well spent and a positive experience.

Appendix – Course Reflection Paper Example

Reflection/Learning Outcomes

The search exercise gave me the opportunity to use the Meta and subject directory searches for the first time in my academic career. I found the class tutorial on Boolean operators, specifically the concept of precision and recall to be beneficial in my use of commercial search engines. The search assignment gave me the opportunity to conduct a methodical, carefully thought out search due to the fact that sub-500 result searches were required for submission. I was not accustomed to this process as I normally would just impulsively search the first terms that came to mind, but after this exercise, and after utilizing the proper operating terms, I have acquired the necessary skills for finding large quantities of relevant results.

Technology in the library is in fact a major contributing factor in keeping libraries from becoming extinct. Accessible Wi-fi for patrons who don't have access at home, communicating with patrons outside of the library via social media, and providing patrons with resources that can be used from home like online classes and library service tutorials are all ways in which information professionals are encouraging community members to utilize the public library. Advances in technology are making the information professionals job far easier than it once was. For example, before QR codes, a librarian would have to give in-person explanations of a particular service in the library. But now with the help of QR codes, a patron can scan and immediately view the information without needing to enlist the help of the librarian or information professional.

Connecting with patrons outside of the library helps to maintain a regular community of active participants and can potentially attract new patrons who are unsure of the services the library has to offer. Librarians use social media sites like Facebook, Twitter and Instagram to notify the community of upcoming events or upload images of recent events that may interest the public.

To encourage collaboration in the library, information professionals enlist the help of other public and private entities within the community. In some cases, public libraries have partnered with local public school media centers to share IT resources and staff. This collaboration presents an excellent opportunity to weave school curricula in with public library services. I've seen many instances where students have formed "computing clubs", and have devoted their efforts to troubleshooting IT problems within the library and assisting patrons with basic computer literacy. Collaborations like this benefit the student as they are getting first-hand experience in a leadership IT role, and the community as they are receiving legitimate computer instruction from well-trained students. The library has the potential to bring individuals together and make positive contributions to the community. The public library has long been known as a space for collaborative thinking and the current dramatic digital shift will only create more opportunities for individuals and institutions to work together.

Rubric

II. Embrace, utilize and critically assess both current and emerging information technologies to select, organize, manage, facilitate access, and disseminate information.

IIa. Use professional standards to select, organize, manage, preserve, retrieve, evaluate and deliver information resources in various formats.
Score- 3

IIb. Identify, analyze, explain, use and evaluate current and evolving information technologies in libraries and information services.
Score- 2

IIc. Articulate how technology is making a difference in the library and information profession.
Score- 3

IId. Adopt and utilize technology to connect, communicate, and collaborate.
Score- 3

IIe. Explore, develop, promote, and assess information systems and technologies.
Score- 2

Total- 13/15

Appendices - Bibliographic Essay Examples

Bib Essay Unit 03A: Hardware Issues

Introduction

In order to remain effective custodians of information, libraries must keep pace with information technology. Unfortunately, keeping pace with information technology requires a significant investment in hardware. Aside from the obvious difficulties inherent in any major purchase, this investment is complicated by the fact that technology is continually becoming smaller, faster, and cheaper. As new technologies emerge, others become obsolete. One way libraries are beginning to relieve themselves of this burden is by shifting toward cloud computing, in which storage space is rented from outside providers. Libraries are able to use software, and let providers such as Google and Amazon invest in the expensive and evolving storage hardware. No solution is perfect, however. When documents and applications are stored on the internet rather than on a local hard-drive, users are at the mercy of the speed of their bandwidth. In this paper we will explore the complex problems faced when looking at information technology hardware, and also explore some of the more exciting technological innovations that are beginning to appear in school libraries.

Increasing Processing Speed: Implications of Moore's Law

Multiple factors determine how fast a computer will run and the needs it will satisfy: the storage, or capacity of the hard drive or SSD; the memory, or how much random access memory (RAM) the computer is capable of processing; and the capability of the connection interface, which determines the speed at which these can be accessed. (Ngo, 2016) The element that determines the current capability of these separate components is more simple: the evolution of the microchip.

In 1960, Dr. Douglas Englebart theorized that "as electronic circuits were made smaller, their components would get faster, require less power and become cheaper to produce — all at an accelerating pace." (Markoff, 2015) By 1965, Gordon Moore, co-founder of Intel, would take that theory a step further, claiming that "the number of transistors that could be etched on a chip would double annually for at least a decade, leading to astronomical increases in computer power." (Markoff, 2015) This prediction, later known as "Moore's Law" would ring startlingly true. Intel's Markus Weingartner claims, "This simple rule has driven every advancement in the technology revolution for more than half a century and still defines the expanding boundaries of technology today, allowing us to take concepts like artificial intelligence and autonomous vehicles and make them a reality." (Bell, 2015)

Despite the fact that Moore's law would hold true for almost fifty years, five times as long as Moore himself predicted, many now claim chip technology is finally plateauing. "Chip speeds stopped increasing almost a decade ago, the time between new generations is stretching out, and the cost of individual transistors has plateaued." (Markoff, 2015) Last July, Intel announced that it was pushing back the introduction of its 10 nanometer technology until 2017, breaking with its tradition of coming out with smaller chips every two years. Technologists fear that the laws of physics will catch up with technology and that transistors will not be able to both shrink and function reliably. (Markoff, 2015)

It would be foolish to make any assumptions about the demise of Moore's law, however. The industry has been anticipating the expiration of Moore's Law for decades. Intel's CEO, Brian Krazanich, comments, "I have witnessed the advertised death of Moore's Law no less than four times." (Markoff, 2016) Recent advances in quantum computing in a new manufacturing technique known as extreme ultraviolet (or EUV) lithography (Markoff, 2015), in addition to the potential to use gallium nitride in transistors rather than silicon (Markoff, 2016), means Moore's Law may be far from dead, and technology may continue to advance at the same rapid pace for the foreseeable future.

The Problem of Obsolescence

We applaud innovation, but there is a dark side to the astonishing rate that technology advances. As the Financial Times points out, "The economics of microchip production— where factories must operate at enormous scale and only the very latest products make a profit—dictates a relentless pace regardless of what consumers really need." (Hadhazy, 2016) Are libraries trapped in a cycle of hardware obsolescence?

What makes this question worse is the fact that much of our technology goes out-of-date quickly due to "planned obsolescence." The Economist defines "planned obsolescence" as "a business strategy in which the obsolescence (the process of becoming obsolete—that is, unfashionable or no longer usable) of a product is planned and built into it from its conception." (Economist, 2009)

The concept is not limited to computing, but it is certainly found a home there. Intel is a prime example as it begins work on the production of the next generation of PC chips before marketing the last generation. (Economist, 2009) This is especially frustrating when the improvements made in the hardware are not worth cost of buying new technology. It is these cases where planned obsolescence hurts the most, in which "the need to sell more hardware is eclipsing the purpose of any additions or refinements made to the product." (Palmer, 2016)

How do libraries and school media centers deal with this problem? According to the National Center for Educational Statistics (NCES), upgrading hardware must simply be taken into account as an ongoing part of the budget. "Computer hardware follows a life cycle that is perhaps best described as "rapid, planned obsolescence" which refers to the fact that hardware will be overtaken within three years by new models that are better, faster, and (adding insult to injury) cheaper than existing models." (NCES, 2005) Therefore, "it simply has to be recognized and accounted for in long-term technology plans." (NCES, 2005) And although the NCES acknowledges that it is painful to let go of seemingly 'perfectly good' technology after such a short duration, "the pace of change in the computer field is so rapid that three year-old machines are unlikely to be doing their jobs efficiently." (NCES, 2005)

There is a way, however, that libraries are beginning to find a way out of the constant cycle of upgrades— even if only for storage. They are beginning to forsake their own storage hardware for "the cloud."

Cloud Computing, or, Cloud-Based Library Catalogs

Cloud computing entails "storing and accessing data and programs over the Internet instead of your computer's hard drive." (Griffith, 2016) Traditionally, the applications used on computers have been accessed from hard drives or solid-state drives within the computer, or from network attached storage. Utilizing the cloud means accessing applications and documents from a server entirely off premises, where it is essentially rented by the cloud user. In essence, we invest in software and leave the provider to invest in the hardware. (Griffith, 2016) The cloud is used both as a storage device for files and in the context of software-as-a-service; instead of purchasing Microsoft Office, a person might simply use Google docs off of the cloud. (Griffith, 2016)

In "Library in the Clouds: Making a Case for Google and Amazon," Stephanie Buck argues that "there is great potential for cloud computing in libraries and other similar institutions." (Buck, 2009) For one thing, a lot of the software provided for public use in libraries is available on the cloud. "Most everything needed can be found in Google Apps," Buck writes. "If other library-specific software were available through the cloud as a service, software budgets as a whole could be drastically reduced." (Buck, 2009) Even more helpful may be the application of the cloud as a storage device. Many public libraries now offer extensive digital collections. "Storing large digital files can stress local server infrastructures. The files need to be backed up, maintained, and reproduced for patrons. This can strain the data's integrity as well as hog bandwidth." (Buck, 2009)

The New York Public Library began moving to the cloud four years ago. According to Computer World Magazine, the library "has all of its approximately 80 web sites in the cloud. The library has shrunk the number of on-premise servers by 40% and is running those web properties 95% more cheaply than if it had bought the hardware and software to do it all by itself." (Gaudin, 2016) Jay Hague, Director of DevOps and Enterprise computing told Computer World, "We realized very quickly it was going to be cheaper than anything we could do.... It was easier to manage and we realized the benefits of multiple data centers and the repeatability of the platform -- all without increased cost." (Gaudin, 2016)

Research libraries are also a part of the movement to the cloud. Librarians at the University of New Mexico wanted to migrate their catalog to the cloud. The server that hosted UNM's catalog was functionally obsolete, and upgrades were prohibitively "costly, time-consuming, and disruptive of services." (Bordeianu & Kohl, 2015) UNM adopted a cloud-based integrated library system (ILS) developed by OCLC because it was "substantially more versatile and potentially much easier to maintain" than a locally-based server. A cloud-based ILS is also more budget-friendly, another important factor in the librarians' decision. Cloud-based ILS platforms, according to the authors, "have changed the way in which libraries will collect, index, and provide access to their patrons. With more content being acquired electronically and a growing base of patrons that expect the library to come to them, and not the other way around, in order for libraries to remain relevant we must combine discovery and accessibility with the management of library resources." (Bordeianu & Kohl, 2015)

Despite the promise of cloud computing, daunting challenges remain that librarians and school districts must resolve. Offline backup is much faster than cloud storage, however, especially with USB 3.0, SATA, FireWire and Thunderbolt drives. (Saltzman, 2015) What's more, there are a host of intellectual property issues: Who owns the rights to the data you store online—you, or the company storing your data? (Buck, 2009) What right do ILS vendors have to mine the data of users? Do vendors guarantee a right to privacy on the user's part? Finally, and most importantly, access to all the cloud is limited by the speed and reliability of the schools' connection to the server. Ultimately, cloud computing and storage is only as reliable as bandwidth permits.

Inadequate Bandwidth for Schools

In a 2015 tech survey taken by School Library Journal, many librarians indicated that bandwidth was their most significant challenge. Bandwidth is the maximum data transfer rate over an internet or network connection. The lack of bandwidth might well discourage teachers from adopting and "using online materials after a single bad experience." Students trying to access WiFi simultaneously slow down system speed. The result, a New York SMLS explained, is that "pushing teachers to incorporate Web-based activities, plans, and materials . . . can be a hard sell." (Barak, 2013) While almost all schools have wireless access, the speed of their networks are similar to that available for private homes. Such connections work for a family, but what happens when tens of hundreds of students and faculty try to logon at the same time? (Barak, 2015)

As educational technology becomes more ubiquitous, bandwidth must expand to keep pace. "As we move more resources, ebooks, collections, and adaptive reading programs to the cloud, that will increase the need for bandwidth," according to Doug Johnson, the director of technology for a school district in Minnesota. "That pipe has to be bigger and more redundant, too," Johnson contends, because "if someone with a backhoe cuts one piece of fiber, there's a second piece that keeps the connection alive." (Barak, 2015) As attractive as cloud computing can be to school districts looking to maximize access and minimize costs, the lack of bandwidth threatens to stymie the effort to create a more technology-rich environment for students and faculty.

For school administrators willing to write grant proposals, the federal government can be a partner in the quest for expanded bandwidth. The Schools and Libraries program of the Federal Communications Commission is working toward making "telecommunications and information services more affordable for schools and libraries in America." Congress approved the program in 1996, and the FCC fully implemented it in the following year. (FCC, 2010) The FCC recognizes the importance of increasing bandwidth speeds in schools and libraries, since the Internet is a tool that connects "students, teachers, and consumers to jobs, life-long learning, and information." (FCC, 2010) To secure E-Rate Program funding, schools or libraries apply to the FCC. The FCC then connects schools with vendors that offer low-cost telecommunications or internet access and then provides funding for successful applicants. (FCC, 2014) In a 2014 Modernization Order, the FCC set aside funds to support the purchase of bandwidth and increased the spending cap for the E-Rate Program. (FCC, 2014) As schools take advantage of these programs, use of the cloud may be more and more realistic.

Smaller, Cheaper Devices and School Libraries

The ubiquity of smaller and cheaper electronic devices such as laptops, e-readers, and tablets makes it easier for school districts to place one of the new learning tools directly into students' hands. In many cases, districts adopt "one-to-one" programs to issue devices to their students and provide in-house tech support. One-to-one permits school libraries to adopt primarily digital resources for its students and save precious funding in the process. For instance, districts often purchase e-textbooks instead of print textbooks. Moreover, relieved of the need to carve out space for print books, school librarians can redesign physical space to make the library a more user-friendly study environment. (Kuzo, 2015)

Other districts, such as the Quakertown Community School district in Pennsylvania, augment their one-to-one program with a BYOD, or bring-your-own-device, initiative. BYOD programs present real challenges, however. Although BYOD relieves the district of the cost of hardware and software, students still require infrastructure and tech support. What's more, with BYOD, who is ultimately responsible for student technology problems? Can districts afford costly software licenses necessary to install a common software suite on each student's personal computer? Another issue is security: districts have no idea what students have on their devices. Thus, districts need to be very wary of how much access to the network that BYOD students have. (Kuzo, 2015)

A benefit of one-to-one and BYOD programs is that schools can assign e-textbooks rather than traditional print versions. Archbishop Stepinac High School, a private boys school in White Plains, New York, phased out print textbooks and went digital with their entire text collection. In addition to sparing students from carrying an entire backpack full of heavy textbooks, the school's conversion to digital saves each student approximately 75% on cost. (As a private school, the boys pay for their textbooks.) (Barak, 2014) Students at Archbishop Stepinac had the option to buy print textbooks, but only five chose to do so. Another private high school, Archbishop Molloy, converted to digital materials in 2015. In their case, the school paid for e-textbooks rather than pass on the cost to students, and it furnishes all students with an iPad. (Barak, 2014) One challenge remained, aside from cost: Molloy had to build charging stations to accommodate the school's 700 iPads.

Smaller and cheaper also permits school librarians to purchase hardware beyond laptops and tablets that provide hands-on learning experiences for students. Many affluent school districts now furnish their libraries with three-dimensional (3-D) printers. Such printers have been used by third graders in Georgia to create "jewelry" from a variety of "minerals," the point of which was to augment a science lesson on rocks and minerals. (Wapner, 2015) Students in Illinois used the same technology to "design and build models of devices that could solve problems facing residents of an imaginary city—issues related to excessive noise, water pollution, and more." (Wapner, 2015)

Also exciting for libraries are the potential uses for virtual reality (VR) technology. Virtual reality allows library users the opportunity to take part new experiences and explore new places without leaving the library. As the Public Library Association explains, with VR, "visiting museums and national landmarks, once such material is available, becomes quite simple. And since visiting the worlds created by popular authors is not possible, the learner can explore a place outside of our reality." (Lambert, 2016) In addition to learning about different locations on Earth, NASA has developed apps for the Oculus Rift VR system that allows its users to experience riding on a spacecraft. (Lambert, 2016) What is most remarkable about VR technology is the way that it levels the playing field when it comes to the educational experience. While someone who is affluent and able-bodied may travel to Rome or climb the steps of the Great Pyramid, VR would make those experiences possible for those of any ability or economic background. In keeping with library's goals of giving access of information to all, virtual reality may prove to be an enormous asset.

Conclusion

Regardless of the complexities inherent in investing in information technology hardware, it is an extremely exciting time to be involved in equipping a school media center. Long gone is the time when a school's media lab consisted of a handful of computers capable of few programs beyond word processing. Smaller, faster, and cheaper hardware has opened the door for schools to acquire technology unimaginable in the past. And though the difficulties posed by planned obsolescence and limited bandwidth continue to pose challenges, in a world with 3-D printers, cloud-based databases, and schools where every student carries a computer, the solutions must be within our reach.

Discussion Questions

1. Moore's law has driven the speed of technology for the past fifty years. Is the breakneck speed of innovation worth the consequential obsolescence of relatively recent technology?
2. Do you think that shifting to cloud computing is a wise investment for school libraries?

3. Are 3-D printers and VR devices going to be part of school media centers for the forseeable future, or are these fads that will pass? Do you think that funds should be allocated toward this technology?

Works Cited

Barack, L. (2013). Device & Conquer: SLJ's 2013 Tech Survey. School Library Journal. Retrieved September 17, 2016, from http://www.slj.com/2013/12/research/device-conquer-sljs-2013-tech-survey/

Barack, L. (2014). New York High School Goes Entirely Digital. School Library Journal. Retrieved September 17, 2016, from http://www.slj.com/2014/05/standards/digital-textbook-transitions-require-planning-and-charging-stations/

Barack, L. (2015). School Librarians Want More Tech—and Bandwidth: SLJ 2015 Tech Survey. School Library Journal. Retrieved September 17, 2016, from http://www.slj.com/2015/08/technology/school-librarians-want-more-tech-and-bandwidth-slj-2015-tech-survey/

Bell, L. (2015). What is Moore's Law? WIRED explains the theory that defined the tech industry. Wired UK. Retrieved September 17, 2016, from http://www.wired.co.uk/article/wired-explains-moores-law

Bordeianu, S., & Kohl, L. (2015). The Voyage Home: New Mexico Libraries Migrate to WMS, OCLC's Cloud-Based ILS. Technical Services Quarterly, 32(3), 274–293. Retrieved September 17, 2016 from http://0-eds.b.ebscohost.com.www.consuls.org/ehost/detail/detail?vid=3&sid=f4aa7c57-af96-4d44-97f2-8830aaae0a50%40sessionmgr120&hid=111&bdata=JnNpdGU9ZWhvc3QtbGl2ZQ%3d%3d#AN=103244814&db=lxh

Buck, S. (2009). Libraries in the Cloud: Making a Case for Google and Amazon. Computers in Libraries, 29(8), 6–10. Retrieved September 17, 2016 from http://0-search.ebscohost.com.www.consuls.org/login.aspx?direct=true&db=eric&AN=EJ858674&site=ehost-live

Federal Communications Commission. (2010). Universal Service Program for Schools and Libraries (E-Rate). Retrieved September 17, 2016, from https://www.fcc.gov/general/universal-service-program-schools-and-libraries-e-rate

Federal Communications Commission. (2014). Summary of the Second E-Rate Modernization Order. Retrieved September 17, 2016, from https://www.fcc.gov/general/summary-second-e-rate-modernization-order

Gaudin, S. (2016). New York Public Library reads up on the cloud. ComputerWorld. Retrieved September 17, 2016, from http://www.computerworld.com/article/3112207/cloud-computing/new-york-public-library-reads-up-on-the-cloud.html

Griffith, E. (2016). What Is Cloud Computing? PC Magazine. Retrieved September 17, 2016, from http://www.pcmag.com/article2/0,2817,2372163,00.asp

Hadhazy, A. (2016). Here's the truth about the "planned obsolescence" of tech. BBC Future. Retrieved September 17, 2016, from http://www.bbc.com/future/story/20160612-heres-the-truth-about-the-planned-obsolescence-of-tech

Jones, B. (2016). Planned obsolescence has led to ridiculous product cycles, and it's time to say enough is enough. Digital Trends. Retrieved September 17, 2016, from http://www.digitaltrends.com/computing/apple-iphone-7-planned-obsolescence/

Lambert, T. (2016). Virtual Reality in the Library: Creating a New Experience. Public Libraries Online. Retrieved from http://publiclibrariesonline.org/2016/02/virtual-reality-in-the-library-creating-a-new-experience/

Markoff, J. (2015). Smaller, Faster, Cheaper, Over: The Future of Computer Chips. The New York Times. Retrieved from http://www.nytimes.com/2015/09/27/technology/smaller-faster-cheaper-over-the-future-of-computer-chips.html

Markoff, J. (2016). Moore's Law Running Out of Room, Tech Looks for a Successor. The New York Times. Retrieved from http://www.nytimes.com/2016/05/05/technology/moores-law-running-out-of-room-tech-looks-for-a-successor.html

National Council for Education Statistics (NCES). (2005). Forum Unified Education Technology Suite. Retrieved September 17, 2016, from https://nces.ed.gov/pubs2005/tech_suite/

Ngo, D. (2014). Digital storage basics, Part 1: Internal storage vs. memory. CNET. Retrieved September 17, 2016, from https://www.cnet.com/how-to/digital-storage-basics-part-1-internal-storage-vs-memory/

Palmer, M. (2016). New technology is not always a sign of progress. Financial Times. Retrieved from http://www.ft.com/cms/s/2/20f4ecec-6f5a-11e6-9ac1-1055824ca907.html

Planned obsolescence. (2009). The Economist. Retrieved from http://www.economist.com/node/13354332

Saltzman, M. (2015). Hard drive or cloud storage: What's best for backup? USA Today. Retrieved September 17, 2016, from http://www.usatoday.com/story/tech/columnist/saltzman/2015/02/21/hard-drive-cloud-backup/23671659/

Wapner, C. (2015). 3-D Printers: Understanding Copyright, Fair Use, and More. School Library Journal. Retrieved September 17, 2016, from http://www.slj.com/2015/05/technology/3-d-printing-understanding-copyright-fair-use-and-more/

Bib Essay Unit 03B: Hardware Issues

Computers work using three basic concepts. The first is that data must be turned into information (Williams, 2015). The next concept is that the hardware and software components of the computer are responsible for precise activities (Williams, 2015). Finally, the basic operation of a computer is to input, process, store, and output data (Williams, 2015). Computer software and hardware have their specific functions within the processing of data. However, software cannot work without hardware. The hardware is the collection of all machinery and equipment that make up the computer.

Input

The input hardware includes the devices that allow people to enter data. This includes both the keyboard and the mouse. The keyboard converts characters into electrical signals that are readable by the processor. The mouse is used to manipulate objects viewed on the computer display source.

Processing and Memory Hardware

The processing and memory devices are installed inside the computer casing. The computer case contains a power supply element to convert general-purpose electricity into direct current for the other components. The most critical component is the motherboard, a plastic board on which several essential mechanisms are mounted. These components include the central processing unit, or CPU, the main memory and expansions slots for other hardware components. The internal hard disk drive serves as the mass storage device for data files and software applications. An optical disk drive makes it possible to read from and to write to CDs and DVDs. Other components include the sound card, the video card, and some type of cooling fan.

Output Hardware

The output hardware consists of those devices that take the information generated by the computer and put into a form that is recognizable by the operator. This can include video cards that change the information into a video signal that can be sent using a cable to a monitor. The sound card enhances capabilities by allowing sound output into the speakers. The monitor takes electrical signals from the video and creates a display using points of colored lights. Finally, a printer takes the information and creates the image on paper.

Communications Hardware

Communication hardware includes modems which allows the transfer of data using telephone lines or wireless networks between computers.

Moore's Law

Named after Intel cofounder, Gordon Moore, and based on a 1965 magazine article, the theory is that the number of transistors that can be packed onto a silicon chip doubles about every two years (Williams, 2015). At the same time, the price for production remains unchanged. As a result, computer manufacturers are able to decrease the size and cost of hardware while improving their performance. Recent participants in the Fujitsu Laboratories of America Technology Symposium 2015 have declared that Moore's Law has reached its demise (Kishimoto, 2016). Due to the natural limitations of silicon, a new material must be developed in order to continue this process (Templeton, 2016). Some possible considerations include graphene, germanium, and titanium tri-sulfide. However, each comes with its own manufacturing dilemmas which may result in not only delays but may require additional technological creations (Templeton, 2016).

Storage Capabilities

The unit used for storage measurement is a byte. A byte (B) is the smallest form of storage and is considered equal to one character of data. A kilobyte (KB or kB) is equal to 1,024 bytes. Next, a megabyte (MB) equals to

1,024,000 bytes. To imagine the size of a megabyte, it is relatable to two volumes of an encyclopedia (Williams, 2015). Additionally, a gigabyte (GB) has a value of more than one billion characters. A terabyte is more than one trillion characters. Larger forms of storage include petabyte, exabyte, and zettabyte.

Technology Trends

Hardware trends are to continue to allow technology to become smaller, faster, and more affordable. Touch screens and multi-touch screens eliminate need the for a keyboard and mouse. Output trends include 3-D printers and electronic paper (Williams, 2015). In addition, interactive desks and note-taking pens are currently being developed.

Hardware with the Library/School Setting

Laptops allow computer usage to move from classroom to classroom including Chrome Books and touch screen laptops. Most schools maintain designated computer labs including desktops. IPads allow for video streaming. Smartboards have entered the classroom, eliminating overhead projectors. Wireless networks allow for multiple-student access to a network.

Challenges within the School System

Financial constraints are always facing school districts. Buying better quality hardware is expensive and does not allow for affordable student access. In order to purchase larger quantities of merchandise, quality is often sacrificed. Technology is constantly changing and many school districts cannot afford to keep up with current trends. Having a large number of students accessing a networking system at one time can result in delays and other issues.

Questions for Discussion:

What changes have you seen to hardware design, over time? How has this impacted your education?
In what ways do you think modern hardware helps or hinders the education process?

References

Barack, L. (2016, January 30). School Librarians Want More Tech—and Bandwidth SLJ 2015 Tech Survey. Retrieved from School Library Journal: http://www.slj.com/2015/08/technology/school-librarians-want-more-tech-and-bandwidth-slj-2015-tech-survey/

Hardware and Software Essentials. (2016, January 30). Retrieved from Education World: http://www.educationworld.com/a_tech/tech/tech239.shtml

Kishimoto, Z. (2016, January 30). Future Computer Architectures for AI. Retrieved from Tek Tips Forum: http://tek-tips.nethawk.net/future-computer-architectures-for-ai/

Lightfoot, J. M. (2005). Integrating Emerging Technologies into Traditional Classrooms: A Pedagogic Approach. International Journal Of Instructional Media, 32(3), 209.

Maddux, C. D., & Johnson, D. L. (2011). Technology in Education and the Concept of Cultural Momentum. Computers In The Schools, 28(1), 1-4. doi:10.1080/07380569.2011.553150

Romero, A. A. (2012). One Laptop per College Student? Exploring the Links between Access to IT Hardware and Academic Performance in Higher Education e-Learning Programs. Journal Of Distance Education, 26(1), 1-14.

Savitz, E., & Maghsoodnia, M. (2012). Tablets And Education: Why Innovative Hardware Is Not Enough. Forbes.Com, 43.

Templeton, G. (2016, January 31). What is Moore's Law. Retrieved from Extreme Tech: http://www.extremetech.com/extreme/210872-extremetech-explains-what-is-moores-law

Timeline of Computer History. (2016, February 1). Retrieved from Computer History Museum: http://www.computerhistory.org/timeline/memory-storage/

Williams, B. K. (2015). Using Information Technology. New York: McGraw Hill Education.

Zimmermann, K. A. (2016, January 30). History of Computers: A Brief Timeline. Retrieved from LiveScience: http://www.livescience.com/20718-computer-history.html

Bib Essay Unit: 04A Software

Introduction

Software and program applications allow professionals to complete complex tasks with efficiency. From the financial industry to airline industries, professionals utilize a variety of programming software on a daily basis (Kaplan and David, 2014). The easier the software is to use, the larger the number of users (Williams, Sawyer and Clifford, 1999). As global industries rely more heavily on technology, the more important program software reliability, user-friendly interfaces, software version and platform compatibility becomes. This paper will discuss software programs and software application issues which could have significant ramifications for software designers and the everyday user. In addition, this paper will briefly discuss quality assurance test measures, patches and updates after the release of programs applications and softwares. This information could be very useful for those working in information library fields.

Software

By definition software is the instruction that a computer receives to perform a task, as well as the data associated with both the instructions and the outcome. Anything that can be stored electronically is considered data. However the device that it is stored upon, the hard drive, CD or DVD or thumb drive are all considered Hardware. (Beal, 2016)

Software is very important, without it computers would not be able to perform any tasks (Williams, et.al. 1999). Imagine a computer that has absolutely no software, it would be completely useless. There are two types of software: applications and systems software. It is common for users to purchase applications and systems separately, however, Microsoft sells their computers with the latest operating system preinstalled (Horowitz, M., 2015). Users who prefer different operating systems are forced to purchase other computers (Horowitz, M., 2015).

Systems Software

Software systems enable application software to interact with the computer and helps the computer manage its internal resources (Williams, et.al. 1999). It is the interface between the hardware and the system applications (Rouse, 2015). System software makes it possible for a user to run control applications for network devices such as routers, printers and drivers for peripheral devices such as DVD players (PCMag, 2016). Systems software is comprised of three basic types: operating, utility programs, and language translators (Williams, et.al. 1999). Each of these systems software can work independently or dynamically. The user interacts with applications programs through the operating system (Williams, et.al. 1999) i.e. the student uses the keyboard to enter search criteria into the Google search engine. It is the system software that allows the keyboard and the webpage to speak the same language. Applications cannot run without system software (Williams, et.al. 1999).

Operating Systems

Operating systems are perhaps the most important and powerful software, it is the operating system that runs a computer. It is the office manager of the computer, managing everything from memory, to processes being carried out as well as all of the software applications and hardware. Operating systems can connect the user to a word processing application, database program, spreadsheet software, or other types of applications.

There are specific operating systems for single computers, known as stand alone or OS and network applications, known as network operating systems or NOS. Then there are types of operating systems i.e. brand names, the most common types of operating systems are Linux, Windows and Macintosh known as Mac Os (Williams, et.al. 1999). Generally a PC will only run one operating system at a time, however it is possible particularly in the case of Apple, to run more than one OS on a single PC. A user can purchase

Windows from Apple Co. and run it concurrently with the Mac Os system (Apple, 2016).

A stand-alone operating system is a complete operating system that works on a desktop, laptop or tablet computer. A network operating system is an operating system that supports a network. A network is a collection of computers and devices connected together via communications media and devices such as cables, telephone lines, and modems. In some networks, the server is the computer that controls access to the hardware and software on a network and provides a centralized storage area. The other computers on the network, called clients, rely on the server(s) for resources (Lemley, 2005).

On a large network, a public or university library for example, one operating system would most likely be found. Windows is the most common OS found on large (and small area) networks today, primarily due to cost and compatibility, specifically compatibility with servers. Servers are traditionally not Mac Os based. (WhoIsHosting, 2016)

Operating systems are not only found in computers today, most mobile devices now have an OS of their very own, called an embedded OS (Lemley, 2005). Mobile phones, tablet computers and MP3 players are different from the desktop and laptop computers so companies needed to come up with operating systems designed specifically for them. Apple uses its Apple iOS for the iphone, ipod and ipad while Android devices uses Google's Android Operating system. Mobile operating systems are not as extensive as those for traditional computers and they will not run all the same software applications but they are still extremely powerful and enable users to run cloud based software, watch movies, play games and send email (GCF, 2016).

Utility Programs

Utility programs connect the user to external services such as screensavers, data recovery backup, virus protections, file fragmentations, data compressions, and memory management. There are many to choose from.

Each utility program is created specifically to run on a particular operating system and most operating programs have utility programs built in (Williams, et.al. 1999).

Most operating systems include several utility programs that perform specific tasks related to managing a computer, its devices, or its programs. A file viewer is a utility that allows you to display and copy the contents of a file i.e. Windows File Explorer. A file compression utility shrinks the size of a file, a .zip program would be an example of a compression utility. A diagnostic utility compiles technical information about a computer's hardware and certain system software programs and then prepares a report outlining any identified problems, ipconfig is an example, used by software specialists or IT professionals to identify the MAC or IP address of your specific hardware. An uninstaller is a utility that removes an application, as well as any associated entries in the system files. A disk scanner is a utility that (1) detects and corrects both physical and logical problems on a hard disk, and (2) searches for and removes unnecessary files.

A disk defragmenter is a utility that reorganizes files and unused space on a computer's hard disk so data can be accessed more quickly and programs can run faster. A backup utility copies, or backs up, selected files or an entire hard drive onto another disk or tape. A screen saver is a utility that causes the monitor's screen to display a moving image on a blank screen if no keyboard activity occurs for a specified period (Lemley, 2005).

One of the more important utility programs protects a computer against malicious software, or malware, which is a program that acts without a user's knowledge and deliberately alters the computer's operations is known most commonly as anti-virus protection. Operating systems, like Mac Os, purchase utility programs from a third party, relieving the user from having to identify a supplier (Strickland, J., 2008). Convenience and price savings are the largest contributions utility programs offer users.

Language Programs

Programming languages are codes created by programmers that translate computer language to a machine language that the computer understands (Williams, et.al. 1999), (Abraham, N., 2016) while natural language allows interaction between two or more people, a computer language allows interaction between a person or people and a computer. All software is written in a specific programming language which is comprised of a set of instructions or scripts for the computer to execute. (ComputerHope, 2016) Programming languages can often serve more than one purpose for software. An example of a programming language, which also functions as a database management system, is FoxPro. Other examples of language programs are Visual Basic and Java (Reference, 2016). Each operating system has its own language, however it is very possible for an OS to run more than one type of language within its system, for example Windows can run Visual Basic programs and Java programs at the same time.

Viruses are also a language written by programmers that computers understand and are operating system specific (Daniels, B., 1990). A computer virus is a type of malicious software (Difference, 2016), a program or piece of code that is loaded onto your computer without your knowledge and runs against your wishes. Because virus' attack, change and affect the root of the programming language operating system they inherently affect all software applications trying to extract information or instructions from the same OS.

Viruses can cause irreversible damage to user's files, software, and computer operating systems or can silently collect data, personal information or access for others to a single computer or network (Webopedia, 2016).

Quality Assurance Programming Tests

Before programs and software are released to the market, companies conduct a variety of quality assurance (QA) tests. QA is the process by which the software developer makes sure they are delivering the best possible product to its end users. (Guru99, 2016) Each QA test is designed to identify specific "bugs" in the system. A bug is a term used for an error, problem, erroneous logic, or other action that would deviate from the expected result (Techopedia, N.D.). These tests are usually carried out through a system known as the Deming Cycle (Gardler, 2008) The steps of this cycle, described below, are used repeatedly in software development to make sure the end product is working efficiently with product patches, updates and in spite of ever changing virus'. The Deming Cycle involves 1) Plan - Organization should plan and establish the process related objectives and determine the processes that are required to deliver a high Quality end product. 2) Do - Development and testing of Processes and also "do" changes in the processes 3) Check - Monitoring of processes, modify the processes, and check whether it meets the predetermined objectives and 4) Act - Implement actions that are necessary to achieve improvements in the processes. An organization must use quality assurance to ensure that the product is designed and implemented with correct procedures. This helps reduce problems and errors, in the final product (Guru99, 2016).

Every company's goal is to release 'bug-free' software and/or applications. After products are released to the general public for purchase, quality assurance team members continue to identify and provide software updates. When a problem is discovered the developer will release a "patch" which is a record of changes made to a set of resources. Typically, a patch will add a new feature, fix a bug, or add documentation to the project (Oss-watch, 2016).

Software-updates

Software updates, also known as patches, are important and include fixes for known bugs, system application improvements and/or security improvements (Updates and Patches, N.D.). Software updates are usually at no-cost to the user and communicated to the user from the software company. Companies continue QA tests, even after the release of a product. When companies identify areas of improvement, or areas of risk, updates or patches are released for the public to download. This becomes extremely important when it is a security risk (Updates and Patches, N.D.). Two such errors or threats that arise are syntax errors and system application bugs.

Syntax Errors

In English, when words are not arranged properly to create a well-formed sentence, a syntax error occurs (Dictionary, 2016). The same mis-structuring of words can occur in programming languages. When the sentence structure is not properly formed, a programmer and sometimes users, receive a "Syntax Error" message the error code be one small character out of place of something as simple as a typo. Syntax errors block the software from completing the instructions to run the application. But luckily most syntax errors will identify the number of the line of code where it was hung up, making it easy for the programmer to fix pre-release or identify and patch, post release. (Christiansen, 2012)

System Application Bugs

Unlike a syntax error that won't run a software program a system application bug or software bug, is an error or flaw in the program that causes the software to run incorrectly, giving an incorrect or unexpected result. Software bugs can occur at all levels of software, within the operating system, the code, or in components and can often cause a ripple effect, causing an entire network to go down or an e-mail program to send malicious messages that infect the computer of the person who opens them, known as malware. One company that suffered a well-known software bug was Lenovo. Comparative to similar Windows based laptop computers, Lenovo is relatively inexpensive. However, the Lenovo T410 thinkpad has a system's application bug. The thinkpad shuts down randomly with no warning. In order to fix the bug, the user must update five drivers (Lenovo Community, 2010). In an additional, but related issue, Lenovo representatives provide conflicting information regarding the cause and repair of the bug (Lenovo Community, 2010). Just imagine what could happen if Connecticut's electric system was managed using Lenovo's flawed application system.

Conclusion

There is no denying that computers have revolutionized the world we live in, including the world of Library Science. So much so that even the phrase library science has been changed to Library and Information Science. Technology and use of technology is at the heart of any good media center and software is the lifeblood that runs the technology. It's the network operating system that allows computer clients to access the same programs at the same time or find out if titles are available in other libraries nearby. Software is the Utility program that allows library students and patrons to copy, save and print their searches and downloads to thumb drives or printers and it's the systems software that allows all the parts and pieces to speak the same language - the universal translator if you will.

The software industry has turned library use on its head, allowing card catalogs, reference, research and yes even books to be accessed with a few strokes of the keyboard, but software applications are not infallible. Even with strict quality assurance testing throughout the industry, system bugs and errors occur and patches and updates are released to problem solve everyday. But in a world of "a computer" in every pocket, software is here to stay.

References

Software and Patches (n.d.). Science Daily. Retrieved September 19, 2016, from https://www.sciencedaily.com/terms/application_software.htm

Techopedia (n.d.). What is Software Bug? - Definition from Techopedia. Retrieved September 19, 2016, from https://www.techopedia.com/definition/24864/software-bug-

Kaplan, Robert and Norton, David. (2014, August 01). The Balanced Scorecard-Measures that Drive Performance. Retrieved September 19, 2016, from https://hbr.org/1992/01/the-balanced-scorecard-measures-that-drive-performance-2

Abraham, N. (2016). Coding for Dummies. For Dummies.

Updates and Patches (n.d.). Privacy and Information Security | University of Illinois. Retrieved September 19, 2016, from https://security.illinois.edu/content/updates-and-patches

Daniels, B. K. (1990). Safety of computer control systems 1990: Safety, security and reliability related computers for the 1990s ; proceedings of the IFAC/EWICS/SARS symposium, Gatwick, UK, 30 October - 2 November 1990. Oxford: Pergamon Press.

What is a computer language translator? (n.d.). Retrieved September 19, 2016, from https://www.reference.com/technology/computer-language-translator-1c3fb8a9ee90cfde#

Williams, B. K., Sawyer, S. C., & Clifford, S. H. (1999). Using information technology: A practical introduction to computers & communications. Boston: Irwin/McGraw-Hill.

How Utility Computing Works. (2008, April 30)Retrieved September 19, 2016, from http://computer.howstuffworks.com/utility-computing2.htm

T410 Shuts down unexpectedly. (2015, October 22) Retrieved September 19, 2016, from https://forums.lenovo.com/t5/ThinkPad-T400-T500-and-newer-T/T410-Shuts-down-unexpectedly/td-p/275888

Beal, V. (n.d.) What is Software?. Retrieved September 20, 2016 from http://www.webopedia.com/TERM/S/software.html

PCMag (n.d.) System Software. Retrived September 18, 2016 from http://www.pcmag.com/encyclopedia/term/52419/system-software

Rouse, M. (2015) System Software. Retrieved September 18, 2016 from http://whatis.techtarget.com/definition/system-software

Goodwill Community Foundation (2016) Understanding Operating Systems. Retrieved September 18, 2016 from http://www.gcflearnfree.org/computerbasics/understanding-operating-systems/full/

How to Install Windows using Boot Camp. (2016) Retrieved September 20, 2016 from https://support.apple.com/en-us/HT201468

Windows Hosting: Compare Hosting. (2007-2016) Retrieved September 20, 2016 from http://www.whoishostingthis.com/compare/windows/

Difference between Utility Program and Library Program. (2016) Retrieved September 20, 2016 from http://www.differencebetweens.com/difference-between-utility-program-and-library-program/

Lemley, L. (2005). Discovering Computers [Web-published] Retrieved September 18, 2016 from http://uwf.edu/clemley/cgs1570w/notes/Concepts-8.htm

Programming Language. (2016) Retrieved September 19, 2016 from http://www.computerhope.com/jargon/p/proglang.htm

Gregory, Peter (2004) Computer Virus for Dummies [Google Books Version] Retrieved September 22, 2016 from https://books.google.com/books?id=U9diTlQ4erMC&pg=PT61&lpg=PT61&dq=Why+are+computer+viruses+deployed&source=bl&ots=zq_7gQqpnA&sig=r-W-5TQJX0B45qRjV5dsawf7W4A&hl=en&sa=X&ved=0ahUKEwiemveV0aHPAhWDWT4KHcrbClAQ6AEIUzAJ#v=onepage&q=Why%20are%20computer%20viruses%20deployed&f=false

All About Quality Assurance (2016) Retrieved September 20, 2016 from http://www.guru99.com/all-about-quality-assurance.html

Syntax Error (2016) Retrieved September 22, 2016 from http://techterms.com/definition/syntax_error

Christensson, P. (2012, April 27). Syntax Error Definition. Retrieved 2016, Sep 22, from http://techterms.com

What is Defect or bugs or faults in software testing? (n.d.) Retrieved September 20, 2016 from (http://istqbexamcertification.com/what-is-defect-or-bugs-or-faults-in-software-testing/

Bib Essay Unit 04: Software

Software

"Software, or programs, consists of all the electronic instructions that tell the computer how to perform a task" (Williams & Sawyer, 2015). It directly tells the computer's hardware what it needs to do, and there are two basic types of software: application software and system software. "System software enables the computer to perform essential operating tasks and makes it possible for application software to run" (Williams & Sawyer, 2015). Operating systems (OS), device drivers, and utility programs are the three basic types of system software. "Application software enables you to perform specific tasks—solve problems, perform work, or entertain yourself" (Williams & Sawyer, 2015).
Application software must be compatible with your operating system. For example, an app that is only compatible with Android devices will not work on an Apple iPhone because their operating systems differ. Apps can be obtained through system software such as CDs or downloaded from the net (Williams & Sawyer, 2015).

Operating Systems

Operating systems, device drivers and utility programs are the three basic types of system software. The operating system manages the computer, namely controlling the hardware. Different computer brands or mobile devices have different operating systems (e.g., Apple iPhone uses iOS). "An operating system written for one kind of hardware will not be able to run on another kind of machine" (Williams & Sawyer, 2015). Usually one's computer will start up, or boot, from the hard drive which launches the operating system. The OS manages the computer's memory and uses a file management system to keep computer files organized. Additionally, the OS oversees task management of the computer by instructing the processor on how much time to spend performing each program's instructions, especially when multi-tasking. Some security measures are covered by the operating system in that passwords are used to protect personal files on the computer and are even required as part of the log-on process to use the computer.

Device Drivers

"Device drivers are specialized software programs that allow input and output devices to communicate with the rest of the computer system. Each device's brand and model are supported by a different driver that works with only one operating system" (Williams & Sawyer, 2015). These device drivers are responsible for controlling devices such as the mouse, the printer, and etcetera. System software is used to choose and install the drivers needed, if they are not already installed in the first place. When purchasing a new mouse, printer, external storage drive, or any peripheral hardware of that sort to use with your computer, device drivers will be included either through a CD or an Internet download.

Utility Programs

"Utility programs, also known as service programs, perform tasks related to the control, allocation, and maintenance of computer resources" (Williams & Sawyer, 2015). They offer extra functions and services not covered by other system programs. Some are built into the system already, but some can be purchased, too. Examples of utility programs include backup, data defragger, data compression, and antivirus software. However, compression/decompression is now being built into the hardware boards, and the software is on its way out. All of these types of programs will improve the functionality of the computer itself and are geared to users that have more technical knowledge of computers.

Mobile Apps

Mobile devices, like smartphones, are handheld devices smaller than notebook computers that have sophisticated operating systems and provide access to millions of apps. These mobile devices have touchscreens, Internet browsing and Wi-Fi capabilities. Some apps are pre-installed on the device at the time of purchase, while other apps can be downloaded through the device's app store. "Yahoo's Flurry analytics show that 90% of consumer's mobile time is spent on apps" indicating that companies have much to think about when deciding to put time and money into creating mobile websites or mobile apps ("Mobile Marketing Statistics," 2016). Mobile operation systems such as Google's Android and Apple's iOS are the two biggest platforms.

Android versus iOS

The Android operating system was released in 2007, with Apple's iOS released in 2008. Android is used on e-book readers, tablets, and smartphones made by HTC, Motorola, and Samsung (Williams & Sawyer, 2015). iOS is used on Apple products like the iPad tablet and the iPhone, and iOS was the first to utilize gesture inputs (e.g., sliding, tapping, and etcetera). Both Android and iOS have home screens that support apps and widgets, use touch screen input and fingerprint scanning, and have payment platforms: Android Pay and Apple Pay. Android Marshmallow and iOS 9 are the two latest smartphone operating systems from Google and Apple, respectively.

iOS projects simplicity in its use and design and is easy to update. According to Grothaus (2016), "For a pick up and go phone (or tablet), iOS provides the easiest route for many into the world of apps, games and content." In looking at its digital assistant, Apple's Siri has improved its accuracy in cranking out relevant results to its users' queries while also providing a new feature called Proactive, a screen that offers shortcuts to the apps and contacts used most often. iOS is also compatible with older models of iPhones, and "Apple doesn't make any of its bespoke software available on other platforms" (Grothaus, 2016).

Google's Android is highly customizable when compared to iOS. According to Grothaus,(2016), "The combination of detailed drop down menus, ease of sharing and the fact you can use third party apps as primary apps often gives Android the edge over iOS in many users eyes." Google Now is a superior digital assistant to Apple's Siri as the results are more accurate and more relevant because it analyzes what app the users is using and considers that when making sense of what the user wants (Grothaus, 2016). "Google is pretty much platform agnostic with its services, apps and content" which showcases the major difference between iOS and Android.

Bloatware

Bloatware is everywhere. Most people are victims of it; it is the excessive amount of application software that is already downloaded on your mobile device or computer. Hardware makers are paid by the bloatware developers to put this software on devices; everyone is looking to make an extra buck, especially in this competitive industry in which the prices for devices are plummeting. Chacos (2015) says, "Mainstream personal computers are a cut-throat business; prices have been racing to the bottom for years now." On computers and mobile devices, these apps eat into storage space, slow down your processing speed, and eat into your battery life and data usage if using a mobile device. "The preinstalled apps...can lead to specific security vulnerabilities" because "certain app combinations could 'leak' permissions to other apps, which could then be exploited by malicious agents to compromise phone data and user privacy" (Winstead, 2012). The good news is there are ways around being a victim of bloatware. Wipe your computer or device clean by deleting all apps that can be removed and go to pcdecrapifier.com for a software tool to get programs off the computer. Microsoft is the way to go when making a purchase because they circumvent bloatware completely. Microsoft's Surface devices and "Signature Edition" versions of well-known PCs are bloatware-free (Chacos, 2015).

The Cloud and its Concerns

"Cloud computing basically means that instead of storing your software or data on your own PC or your own company's computers, you store it on servers on the internet" (Williams & Sawyer, 2015). Cloud computing is a cheaper alternative for companies because they do not have to run their own servers, microcomputers, and software. They are not only cheaper, but they are faster; however, there are security concerns because "malware is increasingly being detected among the data stored in the cloud. More than 11 percent of companies had malware detected in their sanctioned apps, up from less than 5 percent the year before, according to Netskope" (Lemos, 2016). Lemos notes that Microsoft's offerings are now edging out Google's cloud services according to survey results released in June 2016. Despite these security concerns, more companies are looking to cloud apps because of the benefits and "are increasingly turning to the online versions of more traditional applications" (Lemos, 2016).

The MARC Standard: Software Concerns

"The Library of Congress serves as the official depository of United States publications and is a primary source of cataloging records for US and international publications" and uses MARC 21 as it is "the standard used by most library computer programs" ("What is a MARC," 2009). Utilizing the MARC standard is a wise move for libraries from a software perspective because they are able to share MARC records with other libraries, use system software that is continually updated, and retain bibliographic data when they replace one system with another ("What is a MARC," 2009). However, a library's software's worth comes into question as technologies evolve. Questions librarians must "ask are: Does the library automation system being evaluated make full use of the cataloging information? Does it retain all the data and the MARC 21 content designators?" ("What is a MARC Record," 2009). Even if the full record of information is on the disk, the system may not be capable of downloading all of it, and every bit of the cataloging record is needed to maintain the uniformity of the online public access catalog. Also, are the subfield codes and indicators used accurately? Are the records being stored in the correct format? It is imperative the records be accurate and complete when upgrading the software, and that the records are able to be transferred for communal purposes. If not, it will be quite costly to the library in the long run with both time and money.

Peer-to-Peer Sharing: The Good and the Bad

Peer-to-Peer (P2P) file sharing is "the process of sharing and transferring digital files from one computer to another...without going through an intermediary server." After downloading and installing a program like Dropbox or Frostwire, the user is ready to share music, photos, and other assorted files with those in the network. Dropbox, for example, is an efficient P2P file sharing system because large video files can be sent to another person's computer with ease. However, there is a dark side to using P2P software. The recipient could unknowingly download software meant to harm or incapacitate their OS or computer, or they could download a file with a virus (ZoneAlarm). Also, users should engage in ethical behavior and stay away from illegal sharing services, not share or download copyrighted materials. Users should be aware of the contents of their public share folders when using P2P Sharing because they are putting their privacy, computer, and Internet safety at risk (ZoneAlarm). According to ZoneAlarm "When you close a file-sharing software program's window, your connection to the P2P network may remain active. This could give others access to your shared files, which in turn may increase your security risks." Lastly, kids easily fall prey to these file sharing services as they find their way there looking for a movie or an mp3 of their favorite song and may not realize they are doing anything wrong. There is no question antivirus software is a must when engaging in P2P sharing.

iPads: Popular Choice for Educational Tech Tool

Educational software is a valuable tool for classrooms employing student-centered learning. It is an incredible tech tool for helping all students reach success in the classroom, be it the gifted and talented or special needs students. According to Powell (2014), "Due to the relatively low cost of mobile learning technologies, districts can more easily access these types of tools to provide digital equity among students." Nowadays, the question many districts face is: what device should we purchase for our students to use? Many districts are choosing iPads because of their wealth of educational software. "The iPad's size fits naturally into various learning environments; it can be embedded into the classroom environment; and its content can be customized to meet the individual learning needs of all students" (Powell, 2014). iPads can be supplemental to learning, and educators have the overwhelming task of sifting through millions of educational apps that are right at their fingertips. Educators should collaborate with grade-level colleagues and test out free versions of apps popular on iTunes, evaluate how well they align with the standards, and share their finding with each other to make the most out of using the iPad for educational purposes.

Google Chromebooks and Apps: Another Educational Tool

Web browsers are software applications that have an enormous presence in all informational and educational settings. The sharing features of Google Calendars and Google Docs make it easy for teachers to stay connected with their students, their students' parents, and other teachers, and for students to collaborate with each other on projects. Google even makes it easy for educators to find the best apps for their students with "Chrome App packs, which are groups of popular applications that are tailored to meet different students' needs. Each app pack contains about 20 apps that are categorized by subject. Teachers can easily find and install the apps that meet their classes' needs" (Caputo, 2013). It could not be easier to integrate innovative educational software offered by Google for a 21st century learning experience.

Best Websites and Apps for Teaching and Learning

The American Association of School Librarians (AASL) compiles a list each year of the best free websites and apps available for teaching and learning and sorts them according the to AASL's Standards for the 21st Century Learner. According to "Best Websites" (2016), "The 2016 Best Websites for Teaching & Learning foster the qualities of innovation, creativity, active participation, and collaboration" and are sorted by the following categories: Media Sharing, Digital Storytelling, Managing and Organizing, Social Networking and Communication, Content Resources, and Curriculum Collaboration. For example, Biteable is touted as one of the best websites for Digital Storytelling for grades K-12 and Piktochart is featured as an infographic tool for presentations and posters for grades 3-12. The best apps are again aligned with the AASL's Standards and arranged in these categories: Books, Science, Technology, Engineering, and Math (STEM), Organization and Management, Humanities and Arts, and Content Creation. The site even differentiates which platforms each app is compatible with. For example, OneNote, a digital note-taking app, is compatible with both Android and iOS, but Postit Plus, virtual Post-it Notes, can only be run using iOS. Anyone in the information profession is fortunate to have these software applications evaluated and approved by a credible organization and aligned with learning standards.

Bib Essay Unit 05A: Searching

Introduction

According to Russel (2015), "Looking up pieces of information has never been simpler, thanks to three forces: (1) the growth of content on the world wide web, (2) the increasing competence of search engines to index that content in sophisticated ways, and (3) improvements in the capability to parse queries expressed in question forms. However, without an understanding of the different ways in which to search and places to search, both time and information can be lost.

Web Portals

Web Portals are types of gateway websites that function as "anchor sites," or starting points for users when they connect to the web (Williams & Sawyer, 2015). Examples of portals include Google, Yahoo!, Bing, and Yahoo! Mobile, which is an example of a wireless portal designed for web-enabled portable devices (Williams & Sawyer, 2015). There are also portals designed for specific audiences such as Fool.com for investors and Searchnetworking.techtarget.com for network administrators (Williams & Sawyer, 2015). There are three basic functions of a portal: to find general information such as news and weather, to locate a topic listed by the directory, or to specifically search for a topic using a keyword or subject search (Williams & Sawyer, 2015).

Search Tools

The main, or most popular types of search tools include individual search engines, subject directories, metasearch engines, and specialized search engines (Williams & Sawyer, 2015).

Individual Search Engines

Search Engines are programs that allow a user to find specific information based on a keyword or question. Search Engines vary in what results are provided to the user. For example, some results are based on the popularity of a web page, or in other words, how many users visit the webpage based on the keyword search. Popular examples of search engines include Google and Yahoo!, with Google having the highest statistical rate of performance in retrieving relevant internet resources (Deka & Lahkar, 2010).

Individual search engines, i.e. Google, compile their own databases based on a question or keyword search. Web pages, or "hits" (the sites that a search engine returns after running a keyword search) are listed based on the likelihood that they will contain the information being searched (Williams & Sawyer, 2015). Some search engines provide "one-click" reference answers instead of only a list of search engine links. For example, if a user were to use the search engine, "Google," and type the following question: What is the temperature of the sun?, the first result would be the actual answer to the question, followed by relevant links that explore the question further.

Individual search engines are those maintained by programs called "Spiders" also known as "Crawlers," "Bots" (short for Robots), and "Agents" (Williams & Sawyer, 2015). These programs function by "crawling" through the web, following links from one web page to another and indexing the terms on the websites. Spiders then communicate the web pages to the search engines (Williams & Sawyer, 2015).

Site Search

Site search is an internal search engine that allows users to search a website using keywords. This function allows a website to track how people use the website's internal search. Therefore, it gives the website the ability to track what keywords visitors use, which of those keywords resulted in no results and what webpages visitors went to following the search (Site Search Tracking, 2016). The function of the site search not only helps the user find specific information within a webpage but also provides helpful information to the business or website that can be used to improve the site.

Subject Directories

Subject directories differ from search engines in that they are created and maintained by actual people, not Spiders, and enable a user to search by specific categories within a database. According to Ensor (2016), subject directories cover "… fewer resources but provide more focus and guidance for topics they cover." Subject directories are best for browsing or searching for general information on a topic (Williams & Sawyer, 2015). One such example of a subject directory is "Google Directory."

Metasearch Engines

Metasearch engines search several search engines at once. Since an individual search engine only searches selected databases, a single search does not cover the entire Web and only searches through databases at a certain point in time and are not necessarily searching information in "real time" (Williams & Sawyer, 2015). Most metasearch engines offer excellent an excellent alternative to single search engines in that single search engines can miss substantial pieces of information (Moghaddam, 2006). Metasearch engines enable users to get an overview of what is available across the Web (Williams & Sawyer, 2015). Examples of metasearch engines include MetaCrawler, Dogpile, and WebCrawler.

Specialized Search Engines

Specialized search engines focus on finding information about specific subjects for example: travel, careers, and health. One example of a specialized search engine is Expedia.com, which enables a user to search for topics specific to travel including plane tickets, hotel reservations, car rentals, and restaurants.

Local Search

Local search engines allow users to search for information with a geographic location as a limit (Notess, 2005). A local search can be thought of as a "what" combined with a "where". Examples of local search engines include: Trulia-a local search engine that lists homes/properties for sale and provides general real estate information, Google Maps- where a user can search maps, driving directions or businesses, and Oodle- a local search engine for classified ads.

Multimedia Search Tools

While most searches return text-based results, one can specifically search for non-text resources such as audio, videos and images using multimedia search tools. Examples for multimedia search tools for images, audio, and video respectively, include Google Image Search, Alta-Vista Audio Search, and the Open Video Project. In addition, there are also "Scholarly" search tools, such as Google Scholar, which contain scholarly abstracts, books, peer-reviewed papers, and technical papers intended for academics and scientists (Williams & Sawyer, 2015).

Techniques for Searching

Once the best tool for conducting a search is identified, there are specific techniques for searching that make finding, organizing, and storing the information most efficient. By utilizing these techniques, one can save time and reduce the number of results obtained by an initial search. Williams & Sawyer (2015) identify eight techniques to make searching efficient: "Choose your search terms well, and watch your spelling, type words in lowercase, use phrases with quotation marks rather than separate words, and add a keyword, put unique words first in a phrase, use Boolean operators-AND, OR, and NOT, use wildcards-asterisks (*) and question marks (?), read the Help or Search Tips section and try and alternative general search site or specific search site."

Tagging

Once a user has identified pertinent information while searching, he/she can use the function of "tagging." Tagging allows users to organize their information and retrieve it later with multiple, freely chosen keywords (Gao, 2011). This function allows users to label "...anything found on the Internet, from articles to photos to videos" (Williams & Sawyer, 2015). Tagging also allows users to share their tags with other users via social-bookmarking websites such as Pinterest.com. The difference between using a computer's bookmarking function is that only the user of the computer can access the bookmark. With a tag, information and ideas can be shared with others more easily.

References

American Library Association. (2016). Best Websites for Teaching & Learning 2016.

Retrieved July 1, 2016 from Best Websites for Teaching & Learning: http://www.ala.org/aasl/standards/best/websites/2016

American Library Association. (2016). American Association of School Librarians.

Retrieved July 1, 2016 from Best Apps for Teaching & Learning: http://www.ala.org/aasl/standards/best/apps

Caputo, C., and Teuber, D. (2014, April 1). The Benefits of Google Chromebooks and Apps

for Education. District Administration, 49(7), 40-41.

Chacos, B. (2015, April 1). Bloatware: how, why and goodbye. PC World, 33(4), 36-41.

Chaffey, D. (2016, April 27). Mobile marketing statistics 2016. Retrieved July 09,

2016, from http://www.smartinsights.com/mobile-marketing/mobile-marketing-analytics/mobile-marketing-statistics/

Deka, S. K., & Lahkar, N. (2010, April 28). Performance evaluation and comparison of the five

most used search engines in retrieving web resources. Online Information Review, 34(5),
757-771. doi:10.1108/14684521011084609

Ensor, P. (2016). Toolkit for the Expert Web Searcher. Retrieved July 05, 2016, from http://www.ala.org/

Gao, Q. (2011). An Empirical Study of Tagging for Personal Information Organization: Performance, Workload, Memory, and Consistency. International Journal of Human-Computer Interaction, 27(9), 821-863. doi:10.1080/10447318.2011.555309

Grothaus, M. (2016, February 8). Android Marshmallow vs. iOS 9: The Biggest &
Best Mobile OS' Compared. Retrieved July 09, 2016, from http://www.knowyourmobile.com/mobile-phones/android-marshmallow/23325/google-android-marshmallow-6-vs-apple-ios-9-biggest-
best-software-platform-compared

Lemos, R. (2016). More Companies Trust Cloud Apps, but Security Controls Still Hazy.
Eweek. Retrieved July 2, 2016 from:
http://www.eweek.com/cloud/more-companies-trust-cloud-apps-but-security-controls
-still-hazy.html

Library of Congress. (2009, October 27). What is a MARC record, and why is it important?
Retrieved from http://lcweb.loc.gov/marc/umb/um01to06.html

Moghaddam, A. I. (2007). Web metasearch engines. Online Information Review, 31(3), 300-309. doi:10.1108/14684520710764087

Notess, G. R. (2005). On the net: Locating uses for local search. Online, 29(2), 39-41. Retrieved from http://0-search.proquest.com.www.consuls.org/docview/199930863?accountid=13743

The PC Decrapifier. (2016). The PC Decrapifier. Retrieved from The PC Decrapifier:
https://www.pcdecrapifier.com/

Powell, S. (2014, September 1). Choosing iPad Apps With a Purpose: Aligning Skills and Standards. Teaching Exceptional Children, 47(1), 20-26.

Site Search Tracking and Reporting. (2016). Retrieved July 09, 2016, from https://piwik.org/

What You Need To Know About File Sharing. (2014, June 04). Retrieved from

http://www.zonealarm.com/blog/2014/06/what-you-need-to-know-about-peer-to-peer

-file-sharing/

Williams, B. K., & Sawyer, S. C. (2015). Using information technology: A practical introduction to computers & communications (11th ed.). New York, NY: McGraw-Hill.

Bib Essay Unit 05B: Searching

Introduction

Searching has become a favorite pastime for many people. "Google" has been accepted into the Merriam-Webster dictionary as a verb meaning "to use the Google search engine to obtain information about (as a person) on the World Wide Web" ("Google", n.d.). Although many questions can be answered via a quick google search, librarians are expected to preform expert internet searches retrieving precise data. "Students, teachers and the public turn to their librarians for help researching everything from technology to genealogy to homework help and lesson plans" ("50 Awesome Search Engines Every Librarian Should Know About", 2014). A librarian must be able to perform complex searches on both the "Surface Web" and the "Invisible Web" to gather all relevant information available.

Surface Web

"The Surface Web (also called the Visible Web, Clearnet, Indexed Web, Indexable Web or Lightnet) is that portion of the World Wide Web that is readily available to the general public and searchable with standard web search engines" ("Surface Web", n.d.). This is the portion of the web that is indexed by popular search engines, such as Google, Yahoo!, Bing, etc. These search engines utilize programs called "spider","crawler","robot",or "intelligent agent" that search for and index information on the Web by following links from page to page ("Definition of: spider", n.d.). What these programs are lacking "is the ability to index the vast amount of data that isn't hyperlinked and therefore immediately accessible to a Web crawler" ("The Ultimate Guide to the Invisible Web", 2013). This data can be found through a more in depth search in the Invisible Web.

Invisible Web (aka Deep Web)

Devine and Egger-Sider (2014) state that the "Invisible Web, sometimes referred to as the Deep Web, represented all the rich and valuable resources not found by general-purpose search engines, including government information, journal articles, white papers, special collections of materials, blogs, wikis, social media and the like". Not surprisingly, the invisible web contains about 500 times the information as the Surface Web. Which is compounded even more when you consider that people often do not look past the first screen of search engine results, making everything else pretty much invisible as well. (Devine and Egger-Sider, 2014). Anyone can browse the internet, using search engines such as Google, Bing, or Yahoo, for information that is "good enough". However, it takes knowledge and practice to preform serious searches of information that match you to the most relevant information on the web. (Sherman, C. & Price, G., 2001)

Academic institutions maintain much of what you can find on the invisible web. This information can be searched by typing "in this search string to your favorite search engine: site:.edu "subject I'm looking for"" (Boswell, 2016). Another way to search the invisible web is to add "database" to your search term or to use a website that is designed to search specific subjects in the invisible web. Purdue Online Writing Lab offers the following list of Resources to Search the Invisible Web:

- Alexa: A website that archives older websites that are no longer available on the Internet. For example, Alexa has about 87 million websites from the 2000 election that are for the most part no longer available on the Internet.
- Complete Planet: Provides an extensive listing of databases that cannot be searched by conventional search engine technology. It provides access to lists of databases which you can then search individually.
- The Directory of Open Access Journals: Another full-text journal searchable database.
- FindArticles: Indexes over 10 million articles from a variety of different publications.
- Find Law: A comprehensive site that provides information on legal

issues organized by category.

- HighWire: Brought to you by Stanford University, HighWire press provides access to one of the largest databases of free, full-text, scholarly content.
- Infomine: A research database created by librarians for use at the university level. It includes both a browsable catalogue and searching capabilities.
- MagPortal: A search engine that will allow you to search for free online magazine articles on a wide range of topics.

Site Search and Local Search

Site search is search activity performed on a website and not by a search engine. According to The Digital Marketing Glossary, "Site search is mainly done through internal search engines but may also be performed through navigation menus and tools."

Local search is trickier to define. Basically, it includes any search for something within a specific geographical area: i.e. "Thai restaurant in Norwalk, CT." Local search is what replaced the yellow pages (Bowling). Such searches are often performed on specialized search engines that utilize topical directories, such as BedandBreakfast.com.

Web Search Techniques

Whether searching the "Surface Web" or the "Invisible Web", or preforming a site search or local search, techniques are needed to gather the most relevant information. In Using Information Technology 11e, Brian Williams and Stacey Sawyer list the following techniques one can use to gain a more precise web search:

- Be specific and use correct spelling when searching.
- Typing words in lowercase will retrieve data that is lowercase and capitalized.

    - Using quotation marks around phrases will narrow your search. An example: college students' alcohol use is translated to: college and students' and alcohol and use will bring up hits that have the individual words in the texts. A better search would be "college students" AND "alcohol use" (LibGuides: Database Search Tips: Overview., n.d.).
- Putting unique words first will narrow your search.
- Utilizing Boolean operators will help narrow or expand your search.
    - "And" narrows the search results by connecting two or more words or phrases and only retrieves results which include all of them. "And" is often implied in searches, so using quotation marks to group phrases together and connect the phrases with "And" could be more effective for your search.
    - "Or" expands the search results by including two or more words or phrases and allowing for either to be in the search results.
    - "Not" must be used carefully because it will exclude any result which has that word or phrase in it.
- Utilizing wildcards – asterisks (*) or question marks (?) at the end of word will expand your search to include anything related to the word. For example, "Type dance (*) and you will get hits for dance, dances, dancers, dancing, dancewear, and so on" (Williams, Sawyer, pg 76).
- Using the search sites Help section could offer time saving tips on how to get more accurate results.
- Trying an alternate search site to get more general or specific information.

These techniques are very useful when applying them to the "Surface Web" or the "Invisible Web" and will help to increase precision of the search and decrease recall.

Precision and Recall

Precision and recall are calculations used to evaluate search strategies. Precision is the percentage of relevant records retrieved compared to the number of total retrieved. Recall is the percentage of relevant records retrieved compared to the total number of relevant records available. For example:

	Relevant	Nonrelevant	Tota l
Retrieved	10	80	90
Not Retrieved	2	8	10
Total	12	88	100

If a search engine has a total of 100 pages and retrieves 90 pages, of which 10 are relevant and 80 are nonrelevant, and does not retrieve 10 pages of which 2 are relevant and 8 are nonrelevant, the precision = (10/90) = 11%, and recall is = (10/12) = 83%. Precision and recall are usually inversely related, so as one percentage increases the other should decrease. The more documents are retrieved the less precise the search should be. (Manning, C. D., Raghavan, P., & Schütze, H., 2008)

Bib Essay Unit 06A: Management

Introduction

"I ask the staff to do only two things before opening a help desk ticket," says Dale Cates, Wilton Library Association's systems administrator. "One, make sure everything's plugged in. Two, try restarting the device." Do his colleagues follow these guidelines? "It never happens," says Cates, "Don't get me started."

Let's face it, not every library service professional is adept in (or even interested in) technology issues beyond their day-to-day responsibilities. Few of us joined the field for love of information technology management. Like web searching, it's something most of us prefer to take for granted… until things go wrong. Then we hope that someone with the right skill set is available.

But what if they aren't? What if you found yourself faced with an expectant patron and a balky 3D printer? What if you were asked for help in downloading an e-book? Or, never mind cutting-edge technology: could you troubleshoot a printer? A photocopier? A fax machine?

Even behind-the-scenes, one's knowledge base impacts one's authority and effectiveness across-the-board. Could you effectively advocate for the purchase of new equipment, or offer language for a job-listing that ensures that new hires will be able to hit the ground running?

These aren't just directors' concerns; they belong to us all.

So, how much do you need to know?

Make a Statement

It all starts with mission, vision and impact statements. "Technology provides the chance for librarians to innovate, boost quality, measure success, and align services with the priorities of their organizations" says librarian Susan Lessick. However, those priorities must be clear. Digital tools can help to fulfill vision, not substitute for it. A good example might be using Skype to make possible an author talk that could not otherwise have happened.

How does one evaluate new technology's place in the library? Ellyssa Kroski, Director of Information Technology at the New York Law Institute, uses these three questions:

- What is it?
- Why is it important?
- How can it help me better serve my users tomorrow?

When technology's incorporation is organic, "it's an opportunity for librarians to show how digital and analog skills can blend together using the same level of humanity" (Greenwalt).

Know the Equipment

Whether a librarian is a sole decision-maker or just one voice among many in the process, effective advocacy requires familiarity with hardware and software products. What do they do, and what do they cost? Information technology managers know that "it is necessary to make substantial investments in equipment, but the funds needed for this investment have to be squeezed out of budgets that have already been drastically cut" (Bengtson & Bunnett, 708).

Which brings us to a fundamental purchasing dilemma: "to position the library as a leader in introducing new technologies requires that we invest in promising but still unproven, and usually quite expensive, equipment" (Bengtson & Bunnett, 708). It's a nightmare scenario: bet big on new tech, only to see it fall flat. Maybe patrons don't use it, or its maker stops supporting it (remember the Microsoft PixelSense?), or perhaps technological leaps quickly render it obsolete.

How does a technology manager hedge this risk? One answer is to invest in versatile technology: easily repurposed equipment that can embed throughout the library. For example, a single iPad, in the course of a single day, could be checked out and used by patrons for in-house entertainment or learning, incorporated into a robotics program, and outfitted with a credit card reader for use at a fundraiser. The library in Wilton, CT, issues iPads to department heads for personal use so that they will remain comfortable, and current, in their use. Managers at Boise State University's Albertsons Library were so impressed by the iPad's usefulness as a staff training instrument (not to mention its ubiquity among the students) that they gave iPads to all staff members (Aagard). There's an abundance of articles with titles such as " 20 Coolest iPad Ideas for Your Library," and "Great Uses for an Old PC." In contrast, an investment in a less versatile instrument --say, a computerized sewing machine-- is a riskier bet.

A well-informed manager, will recognize that sometimes the wisest technology investment is made behind-the-scenes. Dale Cates reports that Wilton Library's new Wi-Fi system is used by 3200 discrete devices per month; in contrast, their Makerspace is used by 120 patrons per month. Although it was only the latter that debuted to a ribbon-cutting ceremony and front page press, the former was clearly the investment with greater benefit to the community.

Know the Law

Successful management requires current knowledge not only of technology, but also of relevant law. For instance, before accepting funds from the federal e-Rate program to improve telecommunications and Internet access, it is important to understand the Children's Internet Protection Act (CIPA) and the filtering requirements that all e-Rate-funded institutions must meet (Caldwell-Stone).

New technologies beget new laws, which in turn beget new technologies. Enter the world of Digital Rights Management (DRM). "Digital rights management (DRM) technology controls how digital information resources, including media, can be accessed, copied, distributed, reformatted, or otherwise changed. These software and hardware controls are usually embedded in the work or device, and can be protection schemes as basic as password protection" (ALA). DRM can involve complex technological, legal and even ethical issues. For example, applicable copyright law for digital works obtained under a license agreement may be completely different from that which governs a print collection's use. Furthermore, DRM is all about controlling access; it's easy to see how it may collide with a librarian's ethical mandate to maximize access.

Show Me the Money

Once mission is defined, it can be pursued, but at what cost? This evaluation requires a manager not only to understand budgets, but also to gather and intelligently interpret information that underlies the dollar amounts. After all, "You can't make responsible decisions without the right information" (Garvey).

Once a budget has been formulated, a manager can help to pursue funding. In these tough financial times, it behooves the responsible librarian to explore the full spectrum of financial resources. "Grants can be a library's best friend in terms of start-up money," (Balas), but one can also solicit donations from local businesses and community members. Librarians should also be conversant in crowdfunding resources, such as the creativity-oriented donation-based website Kickstarter, which allow libraries to fund projects through large numbers of small donors.

Make a Plan

Librarian John Burke recommends a framework for new technology rollouts:

- **Inventory your current technology** – Before making new purchases, see what hardware on hand can be re-purposed.
- **Conduct a needs assessment** – Survey patrons and analyze the results. However, remember that "relying on patron feedback as the gold standard for project goals can be an extraordinarily limiting prospect" (Bengtson & Bunnett, 701). Patron input "should not trump the expert opinion of the trained and experienced librarian" (Bengtson & Bunnett, 702).
- **Investigate your options and opportunities** – Take stock not only of the marketplace, but also of the community's resources. Perhaps local partnerships can reduce costs for items or even eliminate them entirely.
- **Set priorities and make justifications** – Do your homework: back up advocacy with data, and establish a process for ongoing measurement of the success or failure of the technology's implementation. Be prepared to defend your choices.
- **Create a budget** – Make certain you understand the costs, not only of the new technology's acquisition, but of its maintenance.
- **Develop a timeline** – Identify milestones through which to measure the endeavor's progress. Consider an incremental approach; projects should "start small and then expand (or be withdrawn) based on what was learned from this limited initial rollout" (Bengtson & Bunnett, 702).
- **Plan to evaluate** – Be clear about which measures will determine your endeavor's outcome. Survey patrons to find out which populations you are reaching and which you are not; consider how to better connect with the latter. Be cautious, but do not be paralyzed by fear of negative outcomes.

Follow Through

A responsible manager will want to give a new technology plan's implementation the greatest chance for success. That means managing people as well as technology. For example, library staff members must help promote new programs and services. What's more, they require training to do so effectively.

Marketing

"I am concerned about the constant demand to 'keep up with technology'," said one anxious librarian. "There will always be another device, another way to access the information, and I am now in a position where I am like a salesman, not a librarian" (ZIckuhr). This is precisely the attitude that Sunnydale Public Library's Rachel Schmidt is trying to shift. She advocates strong, retail-like advocacy by frontline staff for technological resources, what she calls the "Would you like fries with that?" approach (Mies). Unrelated interactions with staff, such as when a patron signs up for a library card, are in Schmidt's view an "upselling "opportunity: "Did you know that we have a 3D printer?"

Patrons can sense a library's commitment to technology. If the staff is abuzz, if programs and services are abundant and well-publicized, new initiatives are well-positioned to succeed.

Training

Many library service professionals' eyes glaze over at the thought of technology training. Fortunately, that needn't be the case.

While it is undoubtedly true that "Librarians need to be broad-based information professionals, engaging with digital data curation and digitization projects with the same enthusiasm that they might display toward more comfortable, traditional channels of information" (Bengtson & Bunnett, 705), it will comfort the less technologically-inclined to recall that the overwhelming majority of tech-related questions at reference desks involve very basic questions. "How do I print?" "Does the original go face up or face down?" "Where's the file I just scanned?" Familiarity with Microsoft Office and your operating system's file management structure goes a long way.

When more in-depth knowledge is required, its acquisition needn't evoke dread. Estes Valley Library's Diana Laughlin suggests four cornerstones of effective staff-wide training:

- Get buy in
- Take it slow
- Build Trust
- Be transparent

A fifth component might best be described as: fun. "As we started this tech training process, people were afraid," says Laughlin. What turned attitudes around? Hands-on-workshops, tech "scavenger hunts" and team-building group projects… even costumes! Similarly, Sunnyvale's Rachel Schmidt found that positive outcomes correlated with positive feelings. What's more, fun doesn't have to be expensive. Schmidt's staff responded positively to small but meaningful gestures by administrators at each training milestone: one baked a tray of homemade brownies; another played a song on her flute.

Who You Gonna Call?

Sometimes training isn't enough and it's time to call in the IT cavalry. When things go wrong, the right response is determined by your local environment's structure. Do you work in a large library with dedicated in-house support? Is yours a town library with an IT team spread thin across many municipal departments? Does your library have a contract with a Managed Service Provider (MSP), such as Bibliomation? Familiarity with your organization's structure will help you determine the kind of support available and the internal point of contact. A good manager will know both how to ask for help, and whom to ask for help.

Conclusion

Information technology no longer exists in its own separate cubbyhole. Technology pervades every aspect of librarianship: "Libraries, if they want to be seen as vital, relevant and positioned as key players in the information handling of the future, must actively engage with technology on every level" (Bengtson & Bunnett, 705). Management of digital assets is now a skill required of every library service professional.

Reference

50 Awesome Search Engines Every Librarian Should Know About - BestCollegesOnline.com (2014). Retrieved September 22, 2016, from http://www.bestcollegesonline.com/blog/50-awesome-search-engines-every-librarian-should-know-about/

Aagard, Mary; Armstrong, Michelle; Cooper, Peggy; Nuxoll; Rita (1 January 2013) "iPads for All: Experiencing the Unexpected."Boise State University Scholar Works.(scholarworks.boisestate.edu/cgi/viewcontent.cgi?article=1074&context=lib_facpubs). Accessed 26 September 2016.

ALA. "Digital Rights Management (DRM) & Libraries." ALA. (http://www.ala.org/advocacy/copyright/digitalrights) Accessed 1 October 2016.

Balas, Janet L. "Do Makerspaces Add Value to Libraries?" (teamhughmanatee.files. wordpress.com/2013/04/do-makerspaces-add-value-to-libraries.pdf) Computers In Libraries 32.9 (2012):33.

Bengtson, J. & Bunnett, B. (2012). Across the Table: Competing Perspectives for Managing Technology in a Library Setting, Journal of Library Administration, 52(8), 699-715.

Boswell, W. (2016, June 02). The Invisible Web: What It Is, How You Can Find It. Retrieved September 22, 2016, from http://websearch.about.com/od/invisibleweb/a/invisible_web.htm

Bowling, Mary (14 August 2008). "What Exactly Is Local Search?" ClickZ. (https://www.clickz.com/what-exactly-is-local-search/60390/). Accessed 2 October 2016.

Breeding, Marshall (2 May 2016) "Library Systems Report 2016" American Libraries Magazine. (https://americanlibrariesmagazine.org/2016/05/02/library-systems-report-2016/). Accessed 26 September 2016.

Burke, John J. "Chapter 17: Writing a Technology Plan." Neal-Schuman Library Technology Companion. New York: Neal-Schumn Publishers, Inc., 2009. 233-238.

Caldwell-Stone, Deborah (2 April 2013). "Filtering and the First Amendment." American Libraries. (https://americanlibrariesmagazine.org/2013/04/02/filtering-and-the-first-amendment/) Accessed 20 September 2016

Definition of: spider (n.d.). Retrieved September 23, 2016, from http://www.pcmag.com/encyclopedia/term/51860/spider

Devine, J., & Egger-Sider, F. (2014). Going Beyond Google Again: Strategies for Using and Teaching the Invisible Web. Chicago: ALA Neal-Schuman.

Digital Marketing Glossary, The (5 December 2014). "What is Site Search Definition?" (http://digitalmarketing-glossary.com/What-is-Site-search-definition). Accessed 2 October 2016.

Fallows, Deborah. (11 March 2016) "How Libraries Are Becoming Modern Makerspaces" The Atlantic. (http://www.theatlantic.com/technology/archive/2016/03/everyone-is-a-maker/473286/). Accessed 27 September 2016.

Garvey, Toni "10 Things I Know to be True about Budgeting for Libraries." ALA. www.ala.org/advocacy/advleg/advocacyuniversity/budgetpresentation/preparing/tenthings. Accessed 26 September 2016.

Griffith, Eric. (22 April 2016) "Avoid the Trash Heap: Great Uses for an Old PC." PCMag. (www.pcmag.com/article2/0,2817,2454182,00.asp). Accessed 1 October 2016.

Invisible or Deep Web: What it is, Why it exists, How to find it, and Its inherent ambiguity, 2006, Retrieved September 22, 2016, from http://yunus.hacettepe.edu.tr/~soydal/bby216_2011/4/InvisibleWebWhatitis.htm

Kroski, Ellyssa. (9 February 2010). "10 Technology Ideas Your Library Can Implement Next Week" American Libraries Magazine. (americanlibrariesmagazine.org/2010/02/09/10-technology-ideas-your-library-can-implement-next-week/) Accessed 27 September

2016.

Lessick, Susan (October 2015) "Enhancing Library Impact Through Technology." Journal of the Medical Library Association. (www.ncbi.nlm.nih.gov/pmc/articles/PMC4613389/). Accessed 27 September 2016.

LibGuides: Database Search Tips: Overview. (n.d.). Retrieved September 24, 2016, from http://libguides.mit.edu/c.php?g=175963

Manning, C. D., Raghavan, P., & Schütze, H. (2008). Introduction to information retrieval. New York: Cambridge University Press.

Mies, Ginny (3 March 2016) "How to Make Technology Training Fun for Your Library Staff." TechSoupForLibraries. (http://www.techsoupforlibraries.org/blog/make-library-staff-technology-training-fun). Accessed 26 September 2016.

Resources to Search the Invisible Web. (n.d.). Retrieved September 22, 2016, from https://owl.english.purdue.edu/owl/resource/558/07/

Sherman, C., & Price, G. (2001). The Invisible Web: Uncovering information sources search engines can't see. Medford, NJ: CyberAge Books.

Wikipedia, "Surface Web." Wikipedia. Wikimedia Foundation, n.d. Web. 22 Sept. 2016.

The Ultimate Guide to the Invisible Web (2013, November 11). The Ultimate Guide to the Invisible Web | OEDB.org. Retrieved September 22, 2016, from http://oedb.org/ilibrarian/invisible-web/

Zickuhr, Kathryn; Rainie, Lee; Purcell, Kristen (22 January 2013) "Part 5: the Present and Future of Libraries." Library Services in the Digital Age. (libraries.pewinternet.org/2013/01/22/part-5-the-present-and-future-of-libraries/). Accessed 27 September 2016.

Bib Essay Unit 06B: Management

Introduction

Management within a library setting can be looked at as having two very broad sections, the management of staff and the management of resources. Libraries are places of information. Libraries contain collections of materials such as books, periodicals, and electronic resources that are housed for the purposes of lending or sharing with users within a defined community. Libraries are also physical spaces where patrons can go to meet, study, browse, attend a meeting, use technology and seek information from librarians. "Libraries should do more than just inform, they should allow human beings access to the great continuum of human knowledge, experience, and creativity" (Bengtson, 2012). Libraries cannot exist without the staff who work there and they cannot exist without effective management of the resources contained within.

The managers of a library, the library director, department heads and even the board of directors, have the responsibility of instituting library policies, training and supervising staff, overseeing effective programming, and organizing and modifying the many resources both print and electronic that a library contains.

Management of Staff

Library Organizational Structure

Dependent upon the size of a library, some libraries have developed a structure that breaks staff up into divisions which in turn are often broken up into departments. According to Rubin, "three broad categories provide a general picture of library organization: user services, technical services and support services" (Rubin, 2016). The user service unit can include departments such as reference, circulation, audio visual, youth services, interlibrary loan, special collections, mobile library and even library branches. Often within each of these units, there is a hierarchy of staff that could include a department head or head librarian, librarians, library technical aids, and library pages. Technical services units can include positions such as catalogers, processers, digital resource managers and technical support. Support services divisions include staff and departments such as library director and administrative assistants, treasurer, human resources, marketing and public relations, and even maintenance and security.

It is important to note that not all libraries are structured in this manner. Small libraries may have staff that participate in one or all of the service unit areas. In a small local library there is often one central desk that handles all circulation, reference, interlibrary loans, public access computer area, and may also oversee the children's area. In a small library, the staff, including the cataloger and processor, all complete circulation and reference desk duties in addition to their technical services duties.

Policy Management and Strategic Goals within a Library

A library director and the board of directors have a responsibility to uphold the tenants of the profession of librarianship as defined by the American Library Association through the policies created. "The fundamental obligations of libraries and professionals are clearly defined by the central document of the ALA: The Library Bill of Rights" (Rubin, 2016). It is also the library managers' responsibility to make sure that the staff can enact those ideals on a daily basis through the work that is done. "A clear policy must be formulated, defining objectives, priorities and services in relation to the local community needs. The public library has to be organized effectively and professional standards of operation must be maintained" (IFLA/UNESCO, 2016).

In addition to upholding or creating policies, library managers should establish strategic goals. This as well can help a library grow and change in the future as innovations arise within the field. These goals "might take the form of identifying a number of traditional services or resources and then vowing to automate them in the next one or two years, or setting a goal for each unit within the library to automate several of its operations during that same period of time" (Bengtson, 2012). However, as libraries strive to move into the future, the structure of the library and skills required by library staff will likely change. "What is most interesting and challenging for the library administrator is managing this transition from a predominantly print oriented and lower-paid workforce to one that is equipped with technology and computer skills and demands higher salaries" (Bengtson, 2012). The way to ensure that the strategic goals that involve new technology are met is through appropriate training of current staff and the hiring of new staff that have technology skills.

Strategic goals within a library may also include providing programming suitable for the library population. Library managers must work with staff to meet the needs of the patrons through programs that are offered. Examples of this could be basic computer classes for adults, story times for children, creating a makerspace, hosting book discussions. According to a 2011 Harris poll, "They (library users) believed that such (library) programs provided educational support for family members, high-quality health and financial information, and opportunities for lifelong learning. A significant majority also valued the library as a community center, a place for cultural programming, and an aid for finding jobs" (Rubin, 2016) (Harris Interactive. 2011.) The staff who design and carry out the programming must be well trained and supervised.

Management of Library Staff and Continued Development

As stated previously, one of the most important components of a library are the staff who work there. The staff are the gatekeepers and disseminators of information but are also often the public face of the library. One of the most important qualities of the library staff is their ability to effectively assist patrons in their needs. This is embodied by good customer service. "The philosophy of exceptional customer service infuses service with a distinctive sense of purpose that connects with customers' lifestyles and self-images, further strengthening their identification with and loyalty to the library" (Harmon, 2013). Managers can provide appropriate in-service training for staff and regular supervision as a way of ensuring that good customer service is met.

The library managers have the responsibility of making sure that the staff are well qualified, trained and have regular staff development. An economical way for libraries to provide ongoing training of staff can also occur through local library consortiums such as the Connecticut Library Consortium (CLC). "The Connecticut Library Consortium is a statewide membership collaborative serving all types of libraries by helping them strengthen their ability to service their users. We achieve our mission by initiating and facilitation cost-effective services, creating and supporting educational and professional development and fostering innovation" (Connecticut Library Consortium, 2016).

Technological advances should not be overlooked when managers consider training options for staff. As noted by Bernstein, "While many libraries have orientation programs for new staff, it is equally important to ensure staff members have opportunities to attend professional development meetings and training sessions to that they can continue to be ahead of the curve" (Bernstein, 2010). This means that when a new concept, technology, or policy is implemented that all of the relevant staff are well versed in how to carry it out and transfer that information to the patrons.

The management and organization of the resources contained in the library are another area of continued staff development and training. Managers must create opportunities for staff to be trained on the newest related methodology and technology as libraries continue to implement electronic based resources, hardware, and software. "Employing a staff tablet to demonstrate how to check out an ebook, for example, makes more sense than walking a patron through the process on a different interface, notes Michelle McGraw, information services manager for Hennepin County Library (HCL), MN" (Enis, 2015).

One example of a new mobile technology would be a magazine lending program such as Zinio Magazines (http://www.zinio.com). Libraries are starting to offer programs such as Zinio that can be accessed by home library user's mobile devices (such as i-pad, i-phone, adroid, kindle) through library's home page. Users must navigate through a library's web page to locate the magazines they would like to read (those offered by that individual library contract), use their library card barcode, and even download the Zinio app including creating a password. Though this could be considered a great resource for library patrons, the process is often not streamlined nor simple. Staff need to have training on the technology by using a variety of devices in order to assist patrons. Training can also including having written instructions for staff to use as a resource.

Sometimes, managers will find that there is a pushback for the implementation of new technologies from staff or patrons. "Each time a library adopts a new technology, the function and culture of the library evolves in some way" (Rubin, 2016). One way to curb this resistance is through education and training of staff. After all, a major innovation and technology was created by a librarian when the Dewey Decimal Classification System was created.

Management of Resources

Librarians disseminate information. In order for that information (in the form of print and electronic materials) to be distributed, a degree of organization has to occur. It is the library managers' responsibility to make sure that the library is selecting appropriate information, using the most economical systems to organize the information, and continually training staff on the organization.

Physical Materials

Most libraries have a set system for organization of materials by sections such as Non-Fiction, Fiction, Mystery, AudioBook, CD, DVD, Magazines, Newspapers, among others. Areas designated for population such as the Children's Department and Young Adult also have their organizational systems. Each section has a set classification system whether by alphabetical by author or by Dewey decimal classification (as with Non-Fiction). There are two parts to this organization: physical (shelf location within the library) and virtual (how they can be located in the library catalog).

Machine Readable Cataloging (MARC) is a standard in most libraries as a way of organizing their material's bibliographic records. When it was created, "MARC allowed librarians to enter, store, and disseminate bibliographic data electronically on tapes" (Rubin, 2016). Most libraries' have cataloging systems that use MARC, however, the systems are created and tailored towards libraries and library networks by "library support agencies, known as bibliographic utilities" (Rubin, 2016). The catalogers and technical service staff are able to input new records, make modifications and delete records, but the database platforms are created and software updates are provided by service vendors. One example of a company that offers cataloging software to libraries is Innovative. Innovative offers specialized systems to public, academia, special, law and consortia libraries. Sierra is one of the systems that Innovative offers to libraries for purchase that offers to both an internal cataloging program and an Online Public Access Catalog (OPAC). "The Sierra library services platform offers the power of open system architecture and robust API support, with complete print and electronic resource management with intuitive staff workflows." (innovative, 2016). As a library manager, using the most efficient, economical program platform for the library and having the appropriate training and staff in place to present solutions when problems arise is an important duty.

Electronic Materials

Increasingly, libraries and library collaborative systems are offering Electronic Resources (ER) as part of their collections. """Electronic resources" refer to those materials that require computer access, whether through a personal computer, mainframe or handheld mobile device" (Johnson, 2012). The resources can include eBooks, eJournals, eMagazines, eImages, and several types of databases and are accessed via the internet or local network. Libraries will have ER cataloged in their OPAC for remote accessibility by patrons, but the library itself often contracts with other service vendors for patrons to access the material.

Examples of vendor software used for ER are Zinio Magazines and Overdrive, http://www.overdrive.com. Overdrive offers applications for home users to be able to download eBooks and eAudiobooks to use on personal devices. The system requires the use of a library card and is dependent upon the virtual availability of the item. Library catalog may have only a couple of titles of an eBook available for lending. Patrons can download an ER from Overdrive when it is available, but the item does not remain in the application longer than the lending period. When the item is "due", it is automatically removed from the Overdrive application. The addition of Electronic Materials to library collections comes with the need to have rules set to deal with the changes. "Electronic resources present a number of challenges not encountered with the selection and acquisition of traditional analog materials and it is advisable for the library to develop clear policies and processes for the selection and management of such resources" (Johnson, 2012). An implemented policy will assist staff in areas such as the organization of materials, licensing, and restrictions.

Hardware/Software

Another necessary function of library managers is the managing computers and software that the library uses. Hardware used within a library can include computers, printers, fax machines, copy machines and even mobile devices such as i-pads and kindles. All of this hardware needs to be managed. Often, technical services will be in charge of making sure that the machinery and the software installed on it is working properly.

Choosing appropriate hardware to meet the needs to the staff and patrons also may fall within the role of management. Part of this is meeting the needs to the population. For example, if a library manager may choose to remove desktop computers in the Children's Area of a library and replace them with i-Pad loaded with educational applications. The library managers have to research whether this is an appropriate choice by looking into what the computers were being used for. If the local school district requires that children use a math program as part of homework, yet the program is not supported by i-Pad applications, would replacing the computers be a good choice for that population?

Since many patrons visit the library for the use of public computers and printers, those devices along with Broadband internet connection and WiFi capability should be maintained. Public computers must allow for user privacy in that the software installed is set to erase "cookies" created by internet traffic by patrons. They should also have word processing programs installed.

Conclusion

Library managers have a dynamic role to play. Not only should a manager appropriately oversee all functions of the library, they must set strategic goals for the future, provide training for staff, offer services including programming and new technologies, and manage the information resources within the library. The staff that make up the user, technical and support divisions within a library assist managers in making sure that all of these things are possible.

Bib Essay Unit 07: The Internet

Introduction

Public and school libraries offer many services to meet patron needs. This may include reference assistance, readers' advisory, help locating an item at another library, or programs and technology classes. Public and school libraries also offer public access to the Internet, despite the fact that many have access from their home computers or smartphones. Free access to the Internet is still beneficial and important today despite some of the challenges that school and public libraries may face by offering it.

Library Internet Services

According to a report titled, "Library Services in the Digital Age," published by the PEW Research Center in 2013, "The availability of free computers and internet access now rivals book lending and reference expertise as a vital service of the nation's public libraries" with "fully 77% of those surveyed say that offering free access to computers and the internet is a "very important" service for public libraries to provide" (Zickuhr, Rainie, Purcell). Even smartphone users, which made up 82% of those surveyed, "are significantly more likely than Americans who do not own these devices (72%) to consider free access to computers and the internet "very important" (Zickuhr, Rainie, Purcell).

Library patrons consider computers and access to the Internet to be very important for a variety of reasons. Many patrons use the Internet, including but not limited to, research and information, email, the news, entertainment, shopping, banking, applying for jobs, distance learning, and social networking (Williams, B. K., & Sawyer, S. C.). Library patrons also use the Internet to access the school or public library's Online Public Access Catalog, also known as an OPAC, to see what materials are available and where. OPACs are more advantageous to using a traditional card catalog, because "online catalogs are the most flexible and current. They are compact and entries can be found quickly" (Taylor, 2009). OPACs also allow patrons to locate items like books, DVDs, Blu-Rays, music CDs, and ebooks within and beyond the library. Many libraries are part of consortiums, meaning they share a common OPAC and patrons can check out materials at other libraries. Connecticut has three major public library consortia that each share a catalog and some systems and support: Bibliomation; Library Connection, Inc.; and Libraries Online, Inc. Additionally, Connecticut academic libraries have consortia too: "the CTW Library Consortium consists of Connecticut College, Trinity College and Wesleyan University. ConnSCU consists of the Connecticut State Colleges & Universities (four state universities, twelve community colleges, and Charter Oak State College). The Connecticut State Universities and the State Library share a catalog called CONSULS" (Connecticut State Library, 2016). Library patrons can access these OPACS from home or by visiting the library.

Another online feature offered to library patrons through the Internet is virtual reference services including "Ask/Text a Librarian" service. This online service allows library patrons to contact librarians with reference questions without physically going to the library. This is especially helpful for students taking remote classes online or adults with mobility issues.

This service has also evolved to utilize texting options. For example, the University at Buffalo allows students to have a conversation with a librarian through AOL instant messaging by contacting the username, ublibrarian10, or through text messaging by contacting 716-304-0002 (University Libraries, 2016). Some libraries even make video conferencing reference assistance available for patrons. For example, "at the University of Michigan, the Shapiro Undergraduate Library and the Residence Hall Libraries collaborated to use a desktop videoconferencing program to provide reference service to students located in residence halls across the campus" (Folger, 1996). The program allowed residence students to connect with a campus librarian through an internet video conferencing program, CU-SeeMe. Although some K-12 school libraries may only offer an OPAC that can be accessed the library, all libraries serve their users by providing access to the Internet.

Library Internet Policies

Because the Internet is a vital service offered by all types of libraries, libraries must set policies with guidelines for its use. For example, Avon Free Public Library's Internet use policy states that, "The Avon Free Public Library does not control the information accessible through the Internet and does not accept responsibility for its content" and that "Internet workstations are located in public areas shared by library users of all ages, backgrounds and sensibilities, so individuals are expected to be considerate of others when accessing potentially offensive information and images" (Avon Free Public Library, 2015). The policy further states that, "Internet privileges and/or library privileges may be suspended for misuse, abuse, or illegal use of the Internet, behavior which is disruptive to the operation of the library and/or the quiet enjoyment of the library by others, or because of other violations of this policy" (Avon Free Public Library, 2015). These policies reflect the standards set by the American Library Association (ALA) Code of Ethics, which states that librarians "protect each library user's right to privacy and confidentiality with respect to information sought or received and resources consulted, borrowed, acquired or transmitted" for all sources, including the internet (ALA, 2008).

Effects of CIPA and Internet Over-Filtering in Schools

In 2000 the United States Congress passed CIPA, the Children's Internet Protection Act (57 U.S.C. 254), with the intention of protecting people under 17 years of age from exposure to "obscene" images, "child pornography," and otherwise "harmful" images. However, there is concern that the types of websites that are filtered have gone far beyond the mandate in libraries and schools that must adhere to the law to receive federal funding or discounts through the Library Services and Technology Act, Title III of the Elementary and Secondary Education Act, and the Universal Service discount program (E-rate), or to comply with state filtering requirements that may also be tied to state funding (American Library Association, 2015). According to the

American Library Association, Research shows that “filters consistently both over- and underblock the content they claim to filter. Filters often block adults and minors from access to a wide range of constitutionally protected speech” (American Library Association, 2015). Filters also have an adverse effect on teaching and learning in public schools resulting in valuable lost learning opportunities, because CIPA requirements are frequently misinterpreted. This misinterpretation results in overly restrictive filtering that prevents educators from using interactive websites and social media sites and blocks students from relevant content to complete school assignments like creating and sharing documents, videos, graphics, music and other original content with classmates. The American Library Association believes that “minor students, and the librarians and educators who are responsible for their learning experience, should not be blocked from accessing websites or web-based services that provide constitutionally protected content that meets educational needs or personal interests even though some may find that content objectionable or offensive. Minors and the adult educators who instruct them should be able to request the unblocking of websites that do not fall under the categories of images required to be filtered under the Children's Internet Protection Act” (American Library Association, 2015). The American Library Association also suggests four specific recommendations for improvement: increase awareness of the spectrum of filtering choices; develop a toolkit for school leaders; establish a digital repository of internet filtering studies; and conduct research to explore the educational uses of social media platforms and assess the impact of filtering in schools (Batch, 2014).

How Libraries are Helping to Bridge the Digital Divide

According to the report, “Toward Equality of Access: The Role of Public Libraries in Addressing the Digital Divide,” public libraries have helped close the digital divide by providing free, public access to computers and the Internet, particularly for people without access at home or work (Pew Research Center, 2004). The term digital divide has been around since the 1990s to describe unequal access to computers and the Internet based on income, ethnicity, geography, age, and other factors. When the report was published in 2004, more than 95% of libraries offered public access to computers and the Internet compared to only 28% of public library systems in 1996. This bridging of the digital divide has especially benefitted African Americans and Hispanics, who are twice as likely to use library computers as Asian Americans and whites, and families making less than $15,000 annually, who are two to three times more likely to rely on library computers than those earning more than $75,000 (Pew Research Center, 2004). According to the report, "Although Internet use has increased substantially in the United States, nearly half of all American households don't have computers or Internet access at home. Traditionally disadvantaged groups, including African Americans, Hispanics, Native Americans and those with lower income and educational levels, remain among the least connected" (Pew Research Center).

Conclusion

According to Williams and Sawyer, "the Internet has been the great leveler for communications – just as the personal computer was for computing" (Williams & Sawyer, 2015). In 2012, 2.4 billion people were using the Internet, with North Americans making up 11.4% of the world's total users. When Using Information Technology: A Practical Introduction to Computers and Communications was published in 2015, it was estimated that 5 billion people worldwide would be connected to the Internet (Williams & Sawyer, 2015).

Both school and public libraries continue to bridge the digital divide and remove boundaries to accessing digital information by providing patrons with free public access to the Internet. Free access to the Internet is still beneficial and important today despite some of the challenges that school and public libraries may face by offering it.

Bibliography

American Library Association. (2015, June 30). Internet Filtering: An Interpretation of the Library Bill of Rights. American Library

Association. Retrieved from http://www.ala.org/advocacy/intfreedom/librarybill/interpretations/internet-filtering

American Library Association. (2009). Public Library Funding and Technology Access: Internet Connectivity in U.S. Public Libraries. American Library Association. Retrieved from http://www.ala.org/research/sites/ala.org.research/files/content/initiatives/plftas/issuesbriefs/connectivitybrief_2009_10_final.pdf

American Library Association. (2008, January 22). Code of Ethics of the American Library Association. American Library Association. Retrieved from http://www.ala.org/advocacy/proethics/codeofethics/codeethics.

Avon Free Public Library. (2015). Policy on Public Access to the Internet. Retrieved from http://www.avonctlibrary.info/PDFS/INTERNETpolicyrevised10-15.pdf

Batch, K. R. (2014). Fencing out knowledge: Impacts of the Children's Internet Protection Act

ten years later." American Library Association. Retrieved from http://connect.ala.org/files/cipa_report.pdf

Bengtson, J. a. (2012). Across the Table: Competing Perspectives for Managing Technology in a Library Setting. Journal of Library Administration 52:8, 699-715.

Bernstein, M. P. (2010, August 16). American Association of Law Libraries. Retrieved from AALL - Spectrum Journal Volume 13: http://www.aallnet.org/mm/Publications/spectrum/archives/Vol-13/pub_sp0811/pub-sp0811-obsolete.pdf

Connecticut Library Consortium. (2016, 07 12). Connecticut Library Consortium. Retrieved from http://www.ctlibrarians.org/?page=WhatWeDo

Connecticut State Library. (2016). New Connecticut Librarians: Consortia. CT State Library:

Division of Library Development. Retrieved from http://libguides.ctstatelibrary.org/dld/newlibrarians/consortia.

Enis, M. (2015). Meet the Tabletarians: Mobile Services. Library Journal, found online at (http://lj.libraryjournal.com/2015/01/technology/meet-the-tabletarians-mobile-services/). Retrieved from Meet the Tabletarians: Mobile Services: http://lj.libraryjournal.com/2015/01/technology/meet-the-tabletarians-mobile-services/

Folger, K. M. (1996). The Virtual Librarian: Using Desktop Videoconferencing to Provide Interactive Reference Assistance. Association of College and Research Libraries. Retrieved from http://www.ala.org/acrl/publications/whitepapers/nashville/folger

Harmon, C. a. (2013). Customer Service in Libraries: best practices. Lanhan, Maryland: Scarecrow Press, Inc. .

Harris Interactive. 2011. (n.d.). www.ala.org. Retrieved from "January 2011 Harris Poll Quorum": www.ala.org/research/sites/ala.org.research/files/content/librarystats.

IFLA/UNESCO. (2016, 07 09). International Federation of Libraries Association. Retrieved from IFLA/UNESCO Public Library Manifesto 1994: http://www.ifla.org/publications/iflaunesco-public-library-manifesto-1994

innovative. (2016, 07 15). iii innovative. Retrieved from https://www.iii.com/solutions/public

Johnson, S. -A. (2012, January). IFLA, International Federation of Library Associations and Institutions. Retrieved from Key Issues for eResource Collection and Development: A Guide for Libraries: http://www.ifla.org/files/assets/acquisition-collection-development/publications/IFLA_ELECTRONIC_RESOURCE_GUIDE_DRAFT%20FOR%20COMMENT.pdf

Library Bill of Rights. (1996, January 23). Intellectual Freedom Manual, Eighth Edition. Retrieved from Intellectual Freedom Manual: http://ifmanual.org/lbor

Pew Research Center. (2004). Toward Equality of Access: The Role of Public Libraries in

Addressing the Digital Divide. Retrieved from https://docs.gatesfoundation.org/Documents/TowardEqualityofAccess.pdf

Rubin, R. E. (2016). Foundations of Library and Information Science, Fourth Edition. Chicago: Neal-Schuman.

Taylor, A. G. (2009). Introduction to cataloging and classification. Westport, CT: Libraries Unlimited.

University Libraries. (2016). Ask a Librarian. University of Buffalo Libraries. Retrieved from http://library.buffalo.edu/askalibrarian/

Velasquez, D. (2013). Library Management 101: A Practical Guide. Chicago: ALA Editions.

Williams, B. K., & Sawyer, S. C. (2015). Using information technology: A practical introduction
to computers & communications (11th ed.). New York, NY:
McGraw-Hill.

Zickuhr, K., Rainie, L. & Purcell K. (2013, January 22). Library services in the digital age.
Retrieved from http://libraries.pewinternet.org/2013/01/22/Library-services/

Bib Essay Unit 08: Local Area Networks

What is a LAN?

A local-area network (LAN) is a network of computers that share information, hardware or software within the span of a relatively small area like rooms, buildings, offices and small libraries. Traditional LANs are connected by wires and cables. LANs generally consist of workstations and personal computers, called nodes. The nodes have their own CPUs but are able to access data and devices within the LAN. Workstations are computers used for more advanced purposes such as "engineering applications, desktop publishing, software development, and other types of applications that require a moderate amount of computing power and relatively high quality graphics capabilities" (Beal, n.d.-a). A positive feature of LANs is that they can transmit data very quickly as the computers are all connected. They also allow the users within the LAN access to potentially expensive devices such as high quality printers, thus decreasing the need for purchasing multiple devices.

Local Area Network (LAN) - www.certiology.com

(Certiology, 2016)

Other Network Types

WANs

LANs can be connected via telephone lines and radio waves to broaden the range of the network. These expanded networks are called wide-area networks (WANs) (Beal, n.d.-b). The Internet is a WAN. It connects computers all around the world and allows them to communicate with each other because they exist on the same WAN. LANs are connected to WANs via routers allowing them to quickly and safely transfer information. WANs are generally owned collectively or, like the Internet, are publicly owned (Certiology, 2016).

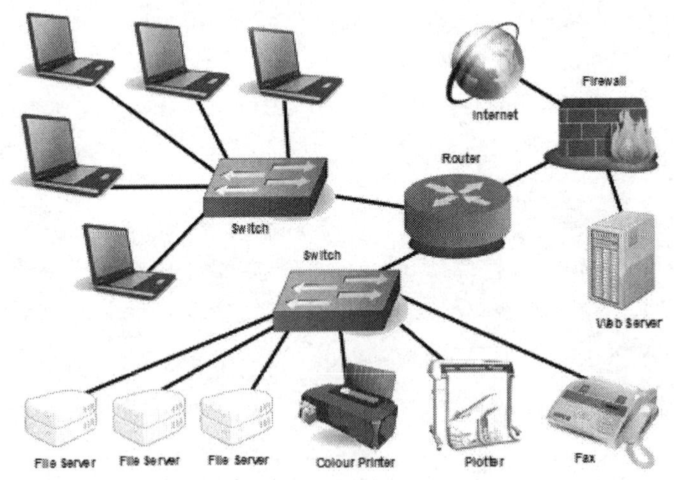

(Certiology, 2016)

WLANs

Wireless local-area networks (WLANs) are a becoming an increasingly popular option as the advancement of wireless technology continues. WLANs eliminate the need for physical cables and wires to be connected. Instead, the computers in the network are connected through wireless technology, like Wi-fi (Certiology, 2016).

WLANs are popular for libraries because they allow information to be shared among many people without physically having to use a library computer.

Patrons may bring their own devices and use the Wi-fi to perform tasks that they would on any library computer. In fact, according to the American Library Association, as of 2015 approximately 98% of public libraries offer Wi-fi to their patrons (2015). This popularity can be explained in the following quote from Shoreline Research which says: "A library's core business is to manage large amounts of information and make that information easily accessible to a wide range of people. So, a wireless network would seem to be a natural solution since it creates additional doorways and channels for that flow of information" (2006). Wireless networks greatly expand the number of patrons that can be reached and help to provide more services in a convenient way.

Client-Server Networks

Client-server networks consist of clients (microcomputers) and servers, which are powerful, central computers that supply data. The central servers control the security and file transactions. File servers are computers that store data and files shared by users on a LAN. Database servers store data, but do not store programs. Client-server networks require users to log in with valid usernames and passwords that are listed on the server. The server also has control of what a user on the LAN may access (Williams & Sawyer, 2015, p. 131).

Peer-to-Peer Networks

Peer-to-peer (P2P) networks connect computers together through the Internet. No server is needed for the connection. Files can be shared directly between the systems. To join this connection a connection to the Internet is needed as well as a P2P software. Through a P2P network one may search files on another person's computer. In turn, other people within the network may also access files on your computer, typically in a folder designated for sharing. Limewire is a popular example of a P2P network. P2P has made file sharing quick, easy and convenient, however, many there have been many issues with software piracy and illegal music downloads (Christensson, 2006). Security risks are more common in peer-to-peer networks; however, they are easy to set-up and less expensive than client-server networks. They can even work effectively for up to twenty-five computers (Williams & Sawyer, 2015, p. 132).

LAN Security in Libraries

In both wired and wireless LANs, information can be shared amongst users. A primary concern for library professionals is maintaining the privacy and security of library patrons within the LAN. "The key security concern for a library's public access wireless LAN involves isolation from the library's staff network" (Breeding, 2005). The information handled by libraries is required to stay private according to library privacy policies. Patron information such as names, addresses, phone numbers and items checked out need to remain confidential.

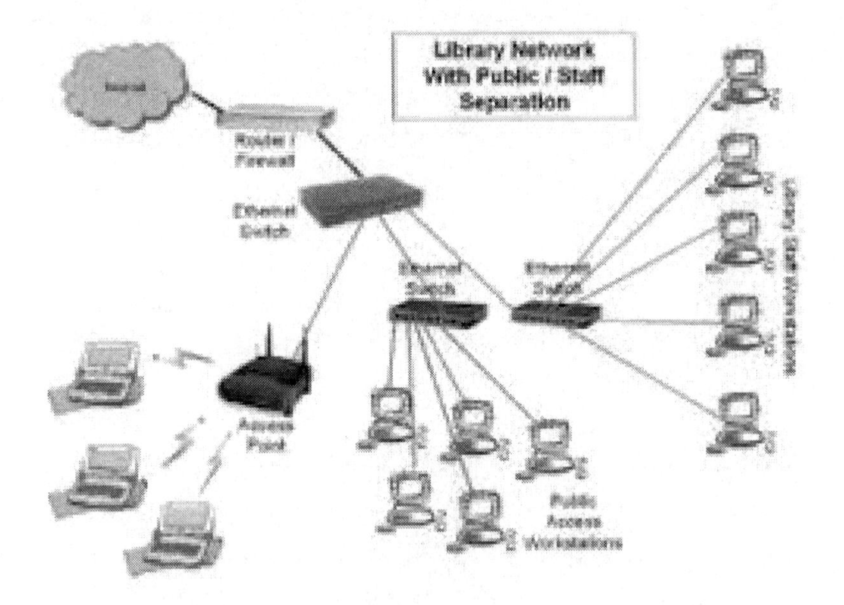

(Breeding, 2005)

In order for the information to remain private libraries may choose to have two separate LANs-one for patron use and one that is designated for library staff. The Internet is accessed through a router which is connected to two different Ethernet switches as well as a wireless access point. The access point allows those with laptops or other personal devices to access the Internet. The separate Ethernet switches allow public access workstations to be on their own LAN and library staff workstations to be on another.

In smaller libraries, it may be more practical to have one LAN and set up a virtual private network (VPN). This would protect patron information as well as ensure that library data, like budget information or business transactions remains amongst the library staff only (Breeding, 2005).

Web 2.0 and Library 2.0

Web 2.0 takes the World Wide Web from being a passive experience to one where interaction, collaboration, and conversation occur. Web 2.0 is often called the read/write web (O'Reilly, 2005), because it provides communication, reading, and writing rather than simply information and resource location. A key Web 2.0 principle is "the service automatically gets better the more people use it," and many, many people are using it (O'Reilly, 2005). Library 2.0 is when that concept is applied to library and literacy sharing websites. There are many websites dedicated to interactive book conversations.

Libraries can take advantage by creating their own Web 2.0 sites or having their staff participate in the online interactions, "These environments cry out for knowledgeable, reader-focused library workers to participate in them" (Wright and Bass, 2010). Library 2.0 sites give librarians a chance to "extend our reach to readers 24/7/365 and interact with our reading patrons in ways that were not possible just a few short years ago" (Harmon and Messina, 2013). Today, patrons want a more immediate and interactive library experience and Web 2.0 makes it possible for the library to go the patrons, rather than them going to the physical library (Harmon and Messina, 2013).

Libraries can use Web 2.0 for book groups, reader's advisory, and interaction among patrons. Many summer reading programs at public libraries use Web 2.0 by having children complete challenges rather than simply log books. Taking pictures of themselves reading, writing book reviews, and visiting the library to catch Pokémon characters through the Pokémon Go app are just a few ways libraries are integrating Web 2.0 technology. "Social media, even if the concept itself emphasizes the media aspect, is more about the social use of media than about the media itself" (Anttiroiko and Savolainen, 2011).

Library 2.0 allows librarians to interact with patrons local and otherwise. Comments, ideas, reviews, and suggestions can easily reach the library through virtual means. "There are many exciting ways for library workers to engage with patrons in these online social environments – as hosts, advisors, performers, referees, and resident smarty pants" (Wright and Bass, 2010).

Goodreads and LibraryThing

Goodreads is a networking site where over 50 million members, both readers and authors, have identified or "shelved" 1.5 billion books. Readers can review books (over 50 million reviews have been posted), make lists, and join groups based on myriad topics (goodreads.com). Libraries should participate since they are the equivalent of reading groups but with millions of members, compared with 10-12 members typically involved in person.

LibraryThing is another book lover's website where people can keep track of their reading, rate and review books, and participate in discussions. LibraryThing has several virtual book groups specifically for librarians with help in reader's advisory and engaging patrons using LibraryThing (Harmon & Messina, 2013). LibraryThing can also be used in integration with a library's catalog, which allows patrons to search, sort, and rate books based on the collection.

Libraries can integrate their services on Goodreads and LibraryThing. They can have pages on the review sites and link back to their own website, OPAC, or blog. Staff can review books, recommend books, and offer items available through their home library or through ILL.

Facebook

Facebook is one of the most popular social media websites to date. The New York Public Library has taken advantage of this Web 2.0 technology to earn over 250,000 likes. They regularly update the page with news updates, author interviews, recommendations, history, and book lists. Public libraries can get patrons to interact by asking questions about what they are reading and even sending selfies (pictures of themselves) reading. The New York Public Library asked its patrons to send photos of themselves reading while on vacation in different locations and posted them on the Facebook page. School libraries can also use Facebook to get students and parents involved. Even though Facebook's policies prohibit use under the age of 13, parents can still ask for recommendations, see what their children are doing in library, and gain expertise from the school librarian or teachers who interact with the page. An elementary school in West Virginia is even using Facebook to raise funds for a much needed library in their school (facebook.com/DunlowSchoolLibrary/).

Twitter

Twitter is another social networking site with very active participation, 310 million active users monthly (statista.com). Librarians can follow authors to read their posts and "retweet," quote their posts. They can answer direct messages from patrons local or otherwise. They can get involved in book talks and online Twitter book groups. Literary blog authors, book authors, and publishers hold book groups regularly on Twitter. The Seattle Public Library began a Twitter book group, 1book140, after a local librarian recommended everyone in the city read and discuss the same book (Harmon and Messina, 2013). Utilizing Twitter's hashtag (#) search method for keywords increases ability to focus on library or book related discussions. Bestselling authors use twitter to reach their target audience, and often participate in book discussions on the social networking site.

Blogs

Blogs today have RSS feeds, which make it possible for readers to subscribe,

"RSS allows someone to link not just to a page, but to subscribe to it, with notification every time that page changes" (O'Reilly, 2005). Blogs also use tags, hidden keywords based on subject material, which makes them appear in search engine results (Harmon and Messina, 2013). Book related blogs often offer giveaways, usually through the publisher, which increases readership, RSS subscriptions, and social media following.

The Bulldog Readers Blog is an example of using Library/Web 2.0 technology. An elementary librarian uses the blog to feature students, build a love of reading, and keep parents informed. The students make video trailers for books and post reviews and the librarian offers helpful tips and advice for peer school librarians. The comment section after each post allows blog readers to actively participate, fully utilizing Web 2.0 technology.

Libraries can utilize blogs to reach patrons near and far with little to no cost. Time management can be minimized by staff, board members, and even patrons rotating posting duties (Harmon and Messina, 2013).

Audio and Visual Media

YouTube is another Web 2.0 tool libraries can use to enhance their interaction with patrons. Author interviews, book trailers, book reviews, and recorded book discussions are all valuable assets to patrons and librarians. iTunes and Soundcloud are two of many sites where podcasts of similar information can be found.

Interactive OPACs and Reader's Advisory

Many libraries are starting to use catalogs with interactive features. Sections for "What should I read next?" can be found with links to books in the collection. Many of these are based off Amazon's very popular "Customers who viewed this item also viewed" (Harmon & Messina, 2013). Allowing patrons to comment, write reviews and interact with other patrons enhances the catalog. It creates "a more informative product for subsequent users"

(Anttiroiko & Savolainen, 2011).

Reader's advisory can be done completely online either with or without the help of a librarian. Rather than librarian's meeting with a patron to design a list of books they feel the patron would enjoy, sites have input pages with algorithms that calculate books to add to their list. "Offering an online version of this service is a very effective way to raise awareness about the value of libraries' personalized, reader-centered approach to book recommendations" (Wright & Bass, 2010).

Challenges

Using Library 2.0 may "require attitude and perception checks on the part of library staff, since most forms of informal and formal control simply do not exist on the read/write web" (Harmon & Messina, 2013, p. 46). Internet users are under very little legal stipulation and have the cover of anonymity to hide behind. Inappropriate or hurtful comments and offensive language are a few hurdles librarians may face.

Another challenge is adhering to library policies. Most school libraries have strict policies on which websites are deemed safe and on links to shopping sites. Any of the Web 2.0 sites discussed could contain offensive material for students or links to shopping which violate acceptable use policy.

To achieve a Library 2.0 presence, a library needs physical and virtual resources. A website, a Facebook page, a twitter account, a blog, etcetera, are required, as well as staff willing to dedicate time to update and interact online.

Web 3.0

Web 3.0 is a relatively new concept expected in the world of technology. Researchers feel Web 3.0 will be based off Web assistants which anticipate a user's preferences. These agents can then act on a user's behalf.

Conclusion

Library 2.0 makes it ubiquitous and free for libraries to "meet the needs of current patrons as well as patrons who may never walk through the door of the local library" (Harmon & Messina, 2013, p. 46).

> "Librarians who lament that the public seem to be forsaking libraries and going elsewhere for help fail to notice that many of those alternatives are just as public as the library, and are places where a practiced readers' advisory or reference librarian can really stand out from the crowd" (Wright and Bass).

There are many other social networking Web 2.0 sites that can be incorporated into library use. Galley sites, for example NetGalley.com, where people can request uncorrected proofs to read in advance then review, are becoming more popular. Oprah Winfrey started Oprah's Book Club 2.0, which is an interactive book group online making use of Web 2.0 technology, as seen in the title.

Librarians who participate in Library 2.0 sites will "get a much better sense of community needs and interests" (Harmon and Messina, 2013, p. 53). They can also use this information to aid in patron-driving acquisition, based on popular ratings and reviews, they can decide what is best to purchase for their patrons.

References

American Library Association. (2015). "Internet access and digital holdings in libraries". ALA Library Fact Sheet 26. Retrieved from http://www.ala.org/tools/libfactsheets/alalibraryfactsheet26

Anttiroiko, A. & Savolainen, R. (2011). Towards library 2.0: The adoption of web 2.0 technologies in public libraries. Libri, 61, 87-99.

Beal, Vangie. (n.d.-a). LAN-local-area network. In Webopedia. Retrieved from http://www.webopedia.com/TERM/L/local_area_network_LAN.html

Beal, Vangie. (n.d.-b). Workstation. In Webopedia. Retrieved from

http://www.webopedia.com/TERM/W/workstation.html
Breeding, Marshall. (2005). "The wireless library hotspot". Library Technology Reports, Sep/Oct2005, 41(5), 31-36.
Breeding, Marshall. (2009). Products and services for the library WLAN. Library Technology Reports. Retrieved from file:///C:/Users/Lauren/Downloads/4636-6910-1-PB.pdf
Certilogy. (2016). Different types of networks. Retrieved from http://www.certiology.com/computing/computer-networking/types-of-networks.html
Christensson, P. (2006). P2P Definition. Retrieved from http://techterms.com
Goodreads (2016). Retrieved July 23, 2016, from goodreads.com/about/us
Harmon, C., & Messina, M. (2013). Customer service in libraries: Best Practices. Lanham, MD: The Scarecrow Press, Inc. Ketheeswaren, S., Ashritha, S., Rosilinmary, S., & Visvanath, B. (2010). Wireless LAN for a Library: Issues and Challenges. Retrieved July 25, 2016, from https://www.researchgate.net/ O'Reilly, T. (2005). What is Web 2.0: Design patterns and business models for the next generation of software. Available online at oreilly.com/lpt/a/1
Shoreline Research. (2006). "Wireless LANs in libraries: from books to wireless broadband". National LAN Exchange. Retrieved from http://www.nle.com/literature/Bluesocket_wireless_LANs_in_libraries.pdf
Statista (2016). Retrieved July 21, 2016, from statista.com/statistics/282087/number-of-monthly-active-twitter-users/
Williams, B. K. & Sawyer, S.C. (2015). Using information technology: a practical introduction to computers & communications. 11th edition. New York: McGraw Hill Education.
Wright, d., & Bass, A. (2010). No reader is an island: New strategies for readers' advisory. Alki, 26(3), 9-10. Retrieved July 20, 2016 from http://0eds.b.ebscohost.com.www.consuls.org/ehost/pdfviewer/pdfviewer?sid=50deedf2-9784-4aa6-bc92-724ebd14a33a%40sessionmgr104&vid=3&hid=119

Bib Essay Unit 09A: Web 2.0 and Library 2.0

What is Web 2.0

When Web 2.0 first surfaced in the early 2000's it was an anomaly to most. There were several different definitions about what it was, and of course a great deal of skepticism. Many believed that it was just an opportunity for people to make more money. The phrase Web 2.0 was created by Tim O'Reilly in 2005, and has been defined as, "the emergence of Internet tools that foster collaboration and interaction" (Fox, 2009). Collaboration has been the major factor that differed from Web 1.0 to Web 2.0. Web 1.0 was primarily all about creating an environment where people could access information. Dan Zambonini said, "Web 1.0 was about connecting computers and making technology more efficient for computers. Web 2.0 is about connecting people and making technology more efficient for people" (Fox, 2009). Web 2.0 is not a separate entity, but an enhancement to 1.0, as it is using a space that was already provided as a place where people can connect to one another. One example to simplify this comparison would be the Encyclopedia Britannica Online and Wikipedia. Fox wrote, "If the Encyclopedia Britannica online represents Web 1.0, then Wikipedia represents Web 2.0 since it can be enhanced and edited by anyone" (Fox, 2009). O'Reilly explained that before Web 2.0 the internet was very passive, he used the example of it being like television, now users can participate in their internet use. A good example to showcase this is Amazon, "allowed visitors to create accounts and submit book reviews" (Struckland, 2007). Struckland wrote, "the Web 2.0 philosophy emphasizes the importance of people's interactions with the Internet" (Struckland, 2007).

What are its Capabilities?

Web 2.0 has revolutionized education and communication. It allows for real time updates that were not available in 1.0. One example is, during the 2007 San Diego fires, volunteers worked together to create a website that was linked to a my map Google map that highlighted areas that were affected by wildfires (Majchrzak & More, 2011). Blogging, creating videos, using social media; these things affect our lives every day. Studies have shown that younger people are are more attracted to Web 2.0 technologies because of the ease of being able to communicate and express themselves (Stern). One example of this is Pinterest. People create accounts and post everything and anything that can be thought of. All users have to do is search a topic and they are rewarded with hundreds of choices to choose from. Pinterest can link users to different links, blogs, and videos.

Today it is natural for us to type into Google any query we have, not only are we provided with information on the topic, but also answers from people part of the online community. Reading reviews of restaurants, liking something on Facebook, or posting a photo on Instagram are all examples of engaging in Web 2.0. Blogging and sharing our lives on the internet has become second hand nature to most. But how is this all relevant to the information community? Web 2.0 has created an environment that allows librarians to interact with their patrons and help connect their patrons through a wide variety of applications, web services, and software. We are no longer confined to sources only within our collection. We are easily able to consult online databases, connect people through skype, and easily reach out to other libraries

The Full Collaborative Experience

As mentioned earlier, Web 2.0 has had a tremendous impact on education, and has made the library media specialist's job go beyond checking out books. The e-learning environment is one example of how Web 2.0 has changed the face of education. Such things like Google Classroom and Wikispaces allow for, "a set of personalization functionalities such as personalised learning plans and learning materials, and is capable of initializing the interaction with learners by providing suggestions to online learners" (Juskeviciene & Kurilovas, 2014). Library media specialists are in charge of this learning and pilot most software for teachers in the building to use. This has allowed for students to get treated like individuals and be exposed to different learning styles. E-learning is also a gateway for collaboration as well as an opportunity for students to work independently and take charge of their learning (AlJeraisy, Mohammad, Fayyoumi, & Alrashideh, 2016). According to an article in Tojet, e-learning is allowing for students to work together, which is something that they crave. It also mentions that discussion boards, "are amongst the most frequently- and commonly- used tools" (AlJeraisy, Mohammad, Fayyoumi, & Alrashideh, 2016).

There are claims that e-learning environments create "asynchronous" interactions. Which means that students have time to mull over the discussion before answering each other's questions (What Do Synchronous and Asynchronous Mean?, 1999). This promotes higher thinking, independent research, and for every voice to be heard (AlJeraisy, Mohammad, Fayyoumi, & Alrashideh, 2016). This article also talks about Moodle Leaning Management Systems, this is very similar to Black Board. It allows discussions through threads. Unlike Blackboard, the discussion threads are not solely distributed through the instructor, users can also create discussion threads (Juskeviciene & Kurilovas, 2014).

There are issues with e-learning environments. For example, e-learning environments allow new learning challenges that may be geared towards a student centered classroom, however, the instructor has to drive instruction and student motivation. There is also the lack of personalization within an e-learning environment. With high levels of content being posted by users, not all voices will be heard. Although we are living in a technology driven society, we still need human contact and the opportunity for instructors to expand on topics and get to know students.

Library 2.0

Library 2.0 can be a complex idea. There seems to be some controversy as to the best definition to describe Library 2.0. A great example is 'Library 2.0' is the shorthand for a vast array of initiatives in all types of libraries to incorporate the tools for online collaboration into new ways to deliver

effective library services" (Library 2.0, 2016). Librarians have the difficult task of incorporating technology into the current library system. Another helpful definition of Library 2.0 is the application of interactive, collaborative and multimedia web-based technologies (Maness, 2006). Casey and Savastinuk (2006) noted that Library 2.0 should include three elements: constant change, giving library users control through user-driven services and implementing these ideas in order to improve all users. Library 2.0 in essence is adding in the
benefits of technology into a traditional library in order to benefit the community it serves. It is the next generation of our current library system. This is a necessary change for the public library users and the community the library serves.

What led to Library 2.0? The World Wide Web itself led to the transformation of Library 2.0. It changed the way people interacted and communicated with each other. We are able to share our thoughts, opinions, photos, information and many other aspects of our lives. Librarians then realized that it would advantageous to use this to create a user-centered environment. This helped people learn and fulfil their informational needs and allowed users to share their content and knowledge (Parker & Godwin, 2012). The library became a place where users could act on those needs of gaining information,, sharing thoughts and opinion, photos, and information. The public could rely on Library 2.0 to act on those needs.

Benefits of Library 2.0

Library 2.0 has quite a few benefits in a library setting. Library 2.0 is user-centered, provides a multimedia experience, is socially rich, and communally innovative (Maness, 2006). Library 2.0 is user-centered in that users can help create the content and services they see online. It is a multi-media experience because it contains video and audio components. Library 2.0 "continually change its services, to find new ways to allow communities, not just individuals to seek, find, and utilize information" (Maness, 2006). With technology continually changing, it is important to change services as the community and library leaders see fit for current demands.

With Library 2.0 comes the need for a "Librarian 2.0." Partridge (2011) conducted a research study and at one point asked participants what a Librarian 2.0 would need. "As one participant observed, "Openness and willing to learn are the heart of web 2.0." Librarians in a 2.0 world engage in reflective practice, they "have a knowledge of oneself ... they know their own strengths." "They are willing to grow with the job" (Partridge, 2011). This type of librarian must be willing to go above and beyond to have every aspect of Web 2.0 incorporated and done right in the library setting. A Librarian 2.0 would, in the participant's mind, be completed knowledgeable and fully engaged in his or her job. They are the ones who are willing to grow, learn and adapt to any changes that occur from year to year.

Library 2.0 brings forward the interaction between the library and its' users (Holberg et. al., 2009). This is an important piece of the library in today's society. In order for a library to be a well used place, users must feel the library provides the needed services for them. Users are much more driven by the use of technology. This technology aspect has allowed users to access information faster and more accurately. Library 2.0 is a necessary addition to the current library system in order to properly service all users in the 21st century.

The difference between Library 1.0 and Library 2.0 should be noted. Library 1.0 focuses on cataloging, traditional reference, text-based tutorials, and online communities via mailing lists. Library 2.0 includes Tagging in OPAC's, Online communities through Social Networks, Digital collection via YouTube, Podcast-based tutorials, References with blogs and Instant Messaging (Cho, 2013). Libraries are always adding new technologies because they believe that these services meet their users needs (Casey & Savastinuk, 2007).

Issues

With anything, sometimes there can be problems associated with implementing a new idea. Users' preferences and behavior toward Web 2.0 services differ among groups of users and their ability and willingness to use Library 2.0 services. (Anttiroiko & Savolainen, 2011). Not all users prefer to use the newest technology when using a library. This can cause a disconnect between the library and the users. A fair balance must be maintained between new technology and older practices in order to cater to all library users. An example of this can be seen with older library users. With technology changing so quickly, it can be more difficult for older users to access all the aspects and technology a library can offer. If a library can provide guidance, training or extra assistance to the older library users, this can open the door and allow more use of technology from people of all ages.

Another concern with Library and Web 2.0 is privacy. Parker & Godwin (2012) state, "The ability to use the web tools, to communicate and to share, promised so much. However, the apparently free tools have often come at the price of the invasion of privacy. We are the product that Facebook sells to its advertisers. Google continues to build up extensive information about us via its applications and our searches." Users must be aware that what they do online is not always secure whether it be at home or in a library setting. A way to protect users from some harmful malware or viruses, proper firewalls and antivirus software is needed.

Conclusion

Overall, there are many benefits to Library and Web 2.0. Web 2.0 allows access to information quickly, people to share their ideas with others, and has had a great impact on education through e-learning environments. Library 2.0 is not all that different. It uses social media to involve patrons in their library. It also allows for patrons to access new technologies and to be provided with convenient services.

References

AlJeraisy, M. n., Mohammad, H., Fayyoumi, A., & Alrashideh, W. (2016). Web 2.0 in
Education: the Impact of Disccussion Board on Student Performancs and Satisfaction. Tojet: The Turkish Online Journal of Educational Technology, 247-258.

Anttiroiko, A.-V., & Savolainen, R. (2011). Towards Library 2.0: The Adoption of Web 2.0
Technologies. Toward Library 2.0.

Casey, M. E., and L. C. Sevastinuk. 2006. "Library 2.0 service for the next-generation library."
Library Journal 131(14): 40– 42.

Casey, M. E., & Savastinuk, L. C. (2007). Library 2.0 : A Guide to Participatory Library
Service. Medford, N.J.: Information Today, Inc.

Fox, D. K. (2009). What is Web 2.0? AALL Spectrum Members' Briefing, 2.
Juskeviciene, A., & Kurilovas, E. (2014). On Recommending Web 2.0 Tools to Personalise Learning. Informatics in Education, 17-31.

Holmberg, K., I. Huvila, M. Kronqvist-Berg, and G. WidénWulff. 2009. "What is Library 2.0?"
Journal of Documentation 65(4): 668–681.

Library 2.0. (2016). Retrieved from ALA American Library Association:
http://www.ala.org/tools/atoz/library-20

Majchrzak, A., & More, P. H. (2011). Emergency! Web 2.0 to the Rescue! Communications of
the ACM, 125-132.

Maness, J. (2006). Library 2.0 Theory: Web 2.0 and Its Implications for Libraries . Webology.

Parker, J., & Godwin, P. (2012). Information Literacy Beyond Library 2.0. London: Facet
Publishing.

Partridge, H. (2011). Librarian 2.0: It's All in the Attitude! ACRL, 256-263.

Stern, Joshua. Introduction to Web 2.0.
http://www.wlac.edu/online/documents/Web_2.0%20v.02.pdf .

Jonathan Strickland "How Web 2.0 Works" 28 December 2007.

HowStuffWorks.com. <http://computer.howstuffworks.com/web-20.htm>

What Do Synchronous and Asynchronous Mean? (1999). Retrieved from World Wide Learn:

http://www.worldwidelearn.com/education-advisor/questions/synchronous-asynchronous-learning.php

Bib Essay Unit 09B: Web 2.0 and Library 2.0

Introduction

Our lecture notes and chapter work covered many issues related to Web 2.0, Library 2.0, and telecommunications. The goal of this piece is to synthesize that information and focus on the most salient issues that affect librarians today, as evidenced by the prominence of our chosen themes in recent literature.

Web 2.0

An unofficial definition of Web 2.0 is "the interactive, user-centered design of the World Widc Web where users not only access the web content but at the same time generate the web content" (Aquil, Ahmad, & Siddique, 2011, p. 395). Web 2.0 changes the experience of the Internet, because it allows information to be created and shared, rather than simply controlled (Zadeh, Veisi, & Zadeh, 2013). Some popular Web 2.0 technologies include blogs, wikis, social networks, tagging, and RSS feeds. Many have asked if Web 2.0 and social media are the same thing. Although they have overlapping features, and are often thought of synonymously, Web 2.0 is a more complex concept, because it focuses on more than just the social aspect of these sites (Anttiroiko & Savolainen, 2011). Social media can be included as a tool of Web 2.0, but Web 2.0 has many more facets.

Library 2.0

Library 2.0 can be 'defined' as "a big conceptual mashup of Web 2.0 tools adapted to library services" (Zadeh, Veisi, & Zadeh, 2013, p.370). Library 2.0 requires constant change, and encouraging participation and control to patrons through user-driven services (Anttiroiko & Savolainen, 2011). The four main reasons libraries use Web 2.0 is communication, content sharing, social networking, and crowdsourcing (Anttiroiko & Savolainen, 2011). Library 2.0

allows libraries to reach out to potential library patrons who do not visit the library, making information accessible to anyone, anytime (Miller, 2005). This allows patrons to become more aware of the services they can receive from their library, and to receive assistance at the time most convenient to them. Library 2.0 is a two way service, because it not only gives patrons access to information, but it also allows them to take a more involved role by using Web 2.0 technologies to provide feedback on the library's services (Curran, Murray, & Christian, 2007).

Archives 2.0

Archives 2.0 are "less about the integration of Web 2.0 technologies into online finding aids, and more related to a fundamental shift in perspective, to a philosophy that privileges the user and promotes an ethos of sharing, collaboration, and openness" (Palmer, 2009). Just making the archives digital is not what makes them archives 2.0. The change occurs when users are encouraged to give substance to the archive, and the role of the archivist lessens (Ramsey-Tobienne, 2012). One archive 2.0 example is the September 11 Digital Archive. Contributions from users included "more than 150,000 digital items, a tally that includes more than 40,000 emails and other electronic communications, more than 40,000 first-hand stories, and more than 15,000 digital images" (September 11 Digital Archive). This "participatory archive" made these items accessible to a wider audience, were given deeper contextualization, and "became the basis for interesting connections among collections and among users leading to new research opportunities" (Ramsey-Tobienne, 2012, p.7).

Wikis

A wiki is a "website which makes it possible for a user to work collaboratively to add and update information on a particular subject" (Zadeh, Veisi, & Zadeh, 2013, p. 369). Libraries use wikis to encourage interaction between patrons and staff, and to allow librarians to answer questions, give feedback, and give information. Wikis need to be used as a resource, rather than for specific research. One negative about wikis is that the user participation means that some of the information published could be inaccurate. The wiki exchange can be archived for future reference. (Zadeh, Veisi, & Zadeh, 2013). A wiki can be an easy way to improve customer service and receive feedback.

Facebook

With social media gaining more and more popularity, libraries have come to use Facebook as a tool to create library awareness and connect with their patrons. Librarians in academic libraries have found using a Facebook page as a beneficial method to answer reference questions posed by undergraduates. A Penn State librarian researched for a semester all of the reference questions he received. He found that undergraduate students sent a majority of their questions through Facebook, rather than phone, email, or in person inquiries. (Mack, Behler, Roberts, & Rimland, 2007). Facebook has also been used as a promotion tool, set up books clubs, increase visibility about the library, provide chat reference, make library announcements, and post photos. Facebook can also be used to search databases and catalogues, or to post videos as tutorials (Hendrix, et. al, 2009). It must also be noted that a library needs to commit to keeping their Facebook page up to date. If it is not frequently updated, at least once a week, the library's Facebook presence will not be a beneficial tool (Jacobson, 2010). Librarians that consider their audience can reach many more patrons through Facebook.

Blogs

Blogs are an effective tool to reach patrons and allow them to subscribe to an RSS feed. The benefit of an RSS feed is not having to check several pages to search for information, because many sources with regularly updated information are delivered at the same time. (Zadeh, Veisi, & Zadeh, 2013). A blog called "Learning 2.0" was created by librarians at the Public Library of Charlotte and Mecklenburg County for other librarians to learn about Web 2.0 and to get step by step instructions to try out the technologies themselves.Each blog post features a different Web 2.0 technology, such as Blogger, Flickr, PBWiki and Delicious. This program also offered an incentive by offering prizes for those that completed all of the activities, and wrote a blog entry about their success and challenges (http://plcmclearning.blogspot.com/). This blog was an effective tool to reach libraries all over the world. Blogs foster communication between users and librarians, allow feedback, present library issues, and provide links to relevant catalogs and resources (Anttiroiko & Savolainen, 2011).

Social Tagging

Social tagging, or social indexing allows users to assign a "tag" or description of a resource for the purpose of helping them find the resource later by entering the keyword. Some popular tagging applications are Delicious, LibraryThing and PennTag (Noorhidawati, Hanum, & Zohoorian-Fooladi, 2013). The benefit associated with using social tagging is that it allows users to organize information into ways that create meaning for them. These tags form a tag cloud, with the high frequency tags receiving a bigger and darker font. The tagging becomes social when folksonomies are produced, which help library users to "catalogue or tag the resources they use in their own way, and share the information by inviting others to view, comment, rate and give feedback" (Ram, Paul Anbu, & Kataria, 2011, p. 454). One drawback to libraries is that they lose control of authority because the tags are not assigned using controlled vocabulary in the normal cataloging scheme. Another benefit is that by observing how the users categorize information, they can learn about their information seeking behavior, and can tailor their services to meet the patron's needs (Noorhidawati, Hanum, & Zohoorian-Fooladi, 2013).

Conclusion

Although Web 2.0 brings many advancements in technology, it also brings some hurdles to overcome. Some of these challenges are technical difficulties, online vandalism and lack of training opportunities for the staff (Sawetrattanasatian, 2014). With technology constantly updating, librarians might have trouble updating all their new services. Libraries should consider the advice of Anttiroiko and Savolainen, "Public libraries should base their adoption of social media on their own natural context and learn the best way of applying its methods in their core processes" (Anttiroiko & Savolainen, 2011, p. 96).

Bib Essay Unit 10A: Telecommunication

Connecting to the Internet - The Basics

For Unit 10, "Telecommunication Issues," our lecture notes predominantly cover Internet communications technology. Similarly, for this part of the bibliographic essay, our primary focus will be on how individuals and organizations connect to the Internet.

Typically, to access to the Internet, people need network hardware such as modems, routers, and switches (Williams & Sawyer, 2015). A modem, short for MODulator dEModulator, is "a device that bridges the internet connection from a service provider to a computer or to a router" (Ngo, 2016) by converting "analog and digital data in real time for two-way network communication" (Mitchell, 2016). Analog signals can be sent over telephone lines and other transmission media (Roberts, 2015; Williams & Sawyer, 2015).

There are wired and wireless Internet connections (Williams & Sawyer, 2015). Both dial-up and digital subscriber line (DSL) connections work using telephone lines, but DSL is a high-speed way to connect to the "plain old telephone system" (POTS) (GCFLearnFree.org, 2012; Williams & Sawyer, 2015). Cable connections, as the name implies, work using company cable connections and are another high-speed option (GCFLearnFree.org, 2012; Williams & Sawyer, 2015). The above-named wired connections need the support of wired communications media (twisted-pair wire, coaxial cable, and fiber-optic cable) in order to transfer data (Williams & Sawyer, 2015). Wireless connections use electromagnetic waves, not wires or cables, to transfer data (Williams & Sawyer, 2015). Satellite connections are one type of wireless connection, and they work using radio waves called microwaves (Williams & Sawyer, 2015). Libraries, in order to connect many computers to the Internet at high speeds, typically use leased T-1 lines, which are high-speed phone lines made of fiber-optic or copper (Burke, 2013; Williams & Sawyer, 2015).

While this is a brief overview of connecting to the Internet, it lays the groundwork for understanding some of the other telecommunications issues presented in this bibliographic essay: bandwidth needs,Wi-Fi, utilizing mobile technology, and network security and privacy issues.

Bandwidth Needs

Bandwidth, or channel capacity, determines the speed of the Internet connection (Williams & Sawyer, 2015). To understand bandwidth, consider this analogy: "Think of bandwidth like a freeway. All cars (data) travel at the same speed, so to get more data from the internet to your computer faster, the freeway needs to be wider" ("The Guide to Internet Speed," n.d.). Adding more T-1 lines is one way to upgrade bandwidth (or widen the freeway) (Blowers, 2012). Bandwidth requirements in libraries have ballooned, in part, because Web 2.0 applications require more bandwidth (Blowers, 2012). Libraries can utilize bandwidth planners and calculators, as well as monitoring the current network (network load, workstation performance, peak usage periods and trends), to forecast the community's bandwidth needs (Blowers, 2012).

Wi-Fi

A simple database search illustrates the shift in scholarly writing from wired networks to wireless networks in recent times. Using the search terms "libraries AND wired networks" and limiting the results to the past six years generated five results, whereas the terms "libraries AND wireless networks" with the same limiter yielded 1,962 results. In schools, for example, where tests might be administered online only, using Ethernet cables and switches can be viewed as impractical ("County Schools Headed to Better Technology," 2015). Wireless networks allow people to easily connect to the Internet using their laptops and mobile devices (Williams & Sawyer, 2015).

Wi-Fi, or WIreless FIdelity, is a type of wireless connection (Williams & Sawyer, 2015). People use other terms, like "wireless network," "802.11 network," "wireless local access network (LAN)," and "WLAN," interchangeably (Peters & MaintainIT Project, 2008). The center of the wireless network is the access point (AP), which "connects to the Internet [on one side], usually through a standard Ethernet cable, and on the other side, it broadcasts a wireless signal" (Peters & MaintainIT Project, 2008). A wireless router in one kind of AP (Ngo, 2016). The devices that connect to the wireless signal, like laptops and mobile devices, are called Wi-Fi clients or WLAN clients (Ngo, 2016).

Mobile Technology

With the tremendous rise of smartphones and other mobile devices in the past decade, libraries have needed to adjust their services to accommodate this new crop of users (Harmon & Messina, 2013). Some approaches libraries have taken include: developing mobile websites and applications ("apps"); collecting more digital objects (electronic journals, books, and databases); and using mobile devices for programs like tours and scavenger hunts (Harmon & Messina, 2013). Typically, mobile websites and apps will give patrons the ability to search the catalog, access their accounts, view the library's hours and contact information, and connect to reference librarians (Harmon & Messina,

2013).

A growing trend in libraries is the use of quick response (QR) codes (Hampton, Peach, & Rawlins, 2012; Lamb & Johnson, 2013). Utilizing a QR app and a mobile device camera, a user can scan these two-dimensional barcodes and be linked to websites with "text, images, videos, audio, maps, [and] even surveys" (Lamb & Johnson, 2013). In libraries, QR codes can be used for tours and scavenger hunts (as previously mentioned), for reader's advisory services and links to ebooks, to market and promote the library, and for many other creative purposes (Hampton, Peach, & Rawlins, 2012; Lamb & Johnson, 2013).

Security & Privacy

When looking at electronic security in libraries, one must consider the need to protect workstations and servers against hackers and other cyberthreats, like viruses and spyware (Burke, 2013; Williams & Sawyer, 2015). Firewalls, which protect servers from unauthorized access, provide a base level of protection (Burke, 2013; Williams & Sawyer, 2015). Other methods to block intruders include antivirus software and password protection (Williams & Sawyer, 2015). Requiring a login is especially important for wireless networks, since wireless signals are not necessarily confined to the library's walls (Burke, 2013).

From a user's perspective, perhaps the best advice regarding connecting to a Wi-Fi hotspot is to install VPN (virtual private network) software, which secures your connection and hides your browsing activity from the wireless network (Andrés, 2010). Another tip is to use web addresses with HTTPS (as opposed to HTTP), which means the connection is encrypted or coded (Andrés, 2010).

In terms of patrons' privacy, libraries should be concerned with the data collection practices of their vendors. Multiple articles addressed an issue with Adobe Digital Editions, where Adobe allegedly failed to protect the privacy of its ebook users (Farkas, 2015; West, 2014). West (2014) went beyond admonishing Adobe; she advocated for basic security measures, like clearing caches, cookies, and saved passwords, and more advanced actions, like performing an internal security audit to see how staff members are complying with privacy-related institutional policies.

Concerning social networking, libraries are in a somewhat paradoxical situation: libraries value open and free access to information, but they also strive to protect patron privacy (Griffey, 2010; Zimmer, 2013). In an effort to preserve privacy and defend minors from the perceived ills of social networking (bullying, offensive content), some libraries (especially school libraries) have blocked access to social networking sites, which seems akin to censorship (Griffey, 2010, p. 35). Complicating the matter, libraries are actively involved with Web 2.0 technologies, as previously discussed, and must take a stance on "the tracking, collecting, and retaining of data about patron activities" for the sake of Library 2.0 tools (Zimmer, 2013, p. 31).

Conclusion

Computers in libraries can "communicate with others in the same library or across the world" (Burke, 2013, p. 65). This bibliographic essay has looked at some of the technology behind these connections, in particular the communications media from our lecture notes. Broadband Internet connections, like DSL and cable, are essentially replacing older, dial-up connections (Williams & Sawyer, 2015). People, including library patrons, want to access the Internet quickly, and from their preferred devices. Wi-Fi is making that possible, and is causing libraries to rethink the services they provide to mobile users. With the good comes the bad; security threats to networks and computers and concerns about people's privacy give libraries cause to evaluate their practices and their policies.

References

Andrés, S. (2010). How to stay safe on public Wi-Fi. PC World, 28(7), 94-96.

Anttiroiko, A., & Savolainen, R. (2011). Towards Library 2.0: The adoption of Web 2.0 technologies in public libraries. Libri, 61(2). doi:10.1515/libr.2011.008

Aquil, M., Ahmad, P., & Siddique, M. A. (2011). Web 2.0 and libraries: Facts or myths. Journal of Library and Information Technology, 31(5), 395-400.

Blowers, H. (2012). Bandwidth, broadband, and planning for public access. Computers in Libraries, 32(8), 24-26.

Burke, J. (2013). Neal-Schuman library technology companion: A basic guide for library staff. New York: Neal-Schuman.

County schools headed to better technology [Editorial]. (2015, January 15). Northeast Mississippi Daily Journal (Tupelo, MS).

Farkas, M. (2015). If not us, then who?. American Libraries, 46(3/4), 27.

GCFLearnFree.org. (2012, March 9). Computer basics: Connecting to the Internet [Video file]. Retrieved from https://www.youtube.com/watch?v=hMX6dVa61t0

Griffey, J. (2010). Chapter 5: Social networking and the library. Library Technology Reports, 46(8), 34-37.

Hampton, D., Peach, A., & Rawlins, B. (2012). Extending library services with QR codes. Reference Librarian, 53(4), 403-414. doi:10.1080/02763877.2012.704576

Harmon, C., & Messina, M. (2013). Mobile library services: Best practices. Lanham, Md: Scarecrow Press.

Jacobson, T. B. (2010). Facebook as a library tool: Perceived vs. actual use. College & Research Libraries, 72(1), 79-90. doi:10.5860/crl-88r1

Lamb, A., & Johnson, L. (2013). QR codes in the school library: A dozen practical uses. Teacher Librarian, 40(3), 63-67.

Mitchell, B. (2016, October 13). What is a modem in computer networking? Retrieved from https://www.lifewire.com/what-is-a-modem-817861

Ngo, D. (2016, October 20). Home networking: Everything you need to know.

Retrieved from https://www.cnet.com/how-to/home-networking-explained-part-1-heres-the-url-for-you/

Noorhidawati, A., Hanum, N. F., & Zohoorian-Fooladi, N. (2013). Social tagging in a scholarly digital library environment: Users' perspectives. Information Research: An International Electronic Journal, 18(3), n3.

Palmer, J. (2009). Archives 2.0: If we build it, will they come?. Ariadne, (60).

Peters, C., & MaintainIT Project. (2008). The joy of computing: Recipes for a 5-star library. United States: MaintainIT Project.

Ram, S., Paul Anbu K, J., & Kataria, S. (2011). Responding to user's expectation in the library: Innovative Web 2.0 applications at JUIT Library: A case study. Program, 45(4), 452-469.

Roberts, B. [thenewboston]. (2015, May 31). Computer networking tutorial - 18 - modem [Video file]. Retrieved from https://www.youtube.com/watch?v=9Fif9s7lCHY

Sawetrattanasatian, O. (2014). The implementation of Web 2.0 technology for information literacy instruction in Thai university libraries. International Association For Development of the Information Society.

Bib Essay Unit 10B: Telecommunication

Telecommunication Defined

Telecommunications refers to "the exchange of information by electronic and electrical means over a significant distance" (Techopedia, 2016). While there are many technologies that fall under the telecom category (i.e. telegraph, telephones, radio, satellite, etc.), today's most frequently used platform is the Internet. This innovation resulted from the combination of communications with computer technology, known as the digital convergence (Williams & Sawyer, 305). The advent of this technological climate change impacted information science dramatically, which in turn necessitated access to the Internet for libraries, their staff, and their patrons. The following is a brief overview of the types of telecommunications technologies utilized by libraries, as well as an outline of some issues posed by the use of these tools.

From Analog to Digital

Most Internet users are familiar with the term 'modem'. Short for modulate/demodulate, these devices configure digital signals into analog signals so that they might be transmitted (sending modems), and then translate those signals back to digital signals for use at their final destination (receiving modems). Signals were originally transferred using existing technologies (phone lines), but transmission has advanced over the years. Some of the newer methods include:

- High-speed phone lines - DSL modems and T1 and T3 lines
- Cable Modem
- Wireless Modem - For satellite and other through-the-air links

(Williams & Sawyer, 306-307).

Wireless Communications

Wireless communications are those telecommunications in which "electromagnetic waves (rather than wire or cable) carry the signal over part or all of the communication path" (Williams & Sawyer, 327). Today, Wi-Fi carries "more than 60% of the world's internet traffic" (Pullen, 2015). There are two radio frequencies utilized by Wi-Fi: 2.5 gigahertz, and the new standard, 5 gigahertz. "With Wi-Fi, 2.4 gigahertz is the lower frequency, so it can reach computers located farther away than the 5 gigahertz band can. But 5 gigahertz offers the capacity to carry more transmissions (Pullen, 2015)".

Wireless Communication Devices

Not only has the delivery method of the Internet changed, the devices used to access and utilize digital information have, as well. There are four generations of two-way wireless communications devices:

- 1G (First-Generation) Cellular Service: Analog Cellphones These tools allow users to communicate by voice through a system of ground-area transmitter-receiving towers.

- 2G (Second-Generation) Wireless Service: Digital Cellphones & PDAS Voice communications and data are sent digitally through a network of cell towers.
- 3G (Third-Generation) Wireless Services: Smartphones Often called broadband technology. Carries data at high speeds to devices that can display color video, access the Internet, email, video conferencing, etc.
- 4G (Fourth-Generation) Wireless Digital Services: Smarter Phones Enables faster Internet surfing. LTE (Long Term Evolution) supports data transfer rates of up to 100 megabits per second over cellular networks. (Williams & Sawyer, 336-338.)

As today's library patrons are well aware, mobile devices are hardly the only implements used to connect to the Internet. Desktop computers, laptop computers, tablets, eReaders, 3D printers and a host of other technologies also rely upon wireless Internet connectivity.

American Library Association - Telecommunications Issues

Given that one of the cornerstones of librarianship is to provide equal access to information for all patrons, the American Library Association (ALA) has been on the forefront of the push to ensure satisfactory Internet access for library users. According to the ALA, "Assured library access to affordable high-capacity broadband internet service is critical to meeting [the] extraordinary demand [for Internet access in libraries] . . . and to fully realizing the human, civic and economic potential of the digital age" (ALA, 2016). Some of the specific efforts undertaken by the American Library Association are detailed below:

LEGISLATIVE ACTION: ALA urges Members of the 114th Congress to . . .

- *SUPPORT* modernization of the FCC's 1980s-era *"Lifeline"* program to close the "homework gap" between students with ready access to high speed internet service at home (and on their own mobile devices) and the school children in an estimated 5 million US households whose economic circumstances require them to rely solely upon public access at their local libraries;
- *ASSURE* that any "network neutrality" legislation considered: prohibits internet service providers from blocking, degrading or requiring payment for the "prioritization" of any content delivered through their facilities; applies the same rules to fixed and mobile broadband providers; and requires public disclosure of network management practices and performance;
- *ENDORSE* efforts in Congress and at the FCC to increase the amount of unlicensed spectrum available to support critical 21st century library technology services in every library in America, as well as the emerging and rapidly evolving "Internet of Things;" and
- *ENCOURAGE* the FCC to heed public calls for it to preempt state laws that create artificial barriers to broadband infrastructure investment, deployment, competition and innovation, and to foster more competition in the provision of high-capacity broadband internet services.

(ALA, 2016)

Association of Research Libraries - Telecommunications Policies

Much like the American Library Association, the Association of Research Libraries (ARL) is concerned with telecommunications reform.

"Net neutrality' is the principle that Internet users should have the right to access and use services via the Internet as they wish, and that network operators should not be allowed to "discriminate" - slow, block, or charge fees - for Internet traffic based on the source or content of its message. (ARL, 2016)

In May 2010, the Federal Communications Commission (FCC) introduced protections which said that "internet service providers could not bock websites or impose limits on users" (whitehouse.gov, 2015). Weeks later, Verizon (an ISP) sued the FCC, overturning this order. In the years that followed, millions of Americans petitioned the President and the FCC, imploring them to protect net neutrality. Finally, in 2015, the FCC voted "in favor of a strong net neutrality rule to keep the Internet open and free" (whitehouse.gov, 2015).

Access for Rural Communities

In addition to the concerns surrounding the principle of net neutrality, access to users in remote locations is also a matter for concern. Research has shown that:

Disparities between rural and nonrural libraries are not merely a problem of weaker technological infrastructure. Instead, rural libraries cannot reach their full customer service potential because of lower staffing (but not lower staff dedication) and funding mechanisms that rely primarily on local monies. (Real et. al., 2014)

Given the existing digital divide, it is vitally important for libraries to strive to provide access to information via the Internet. When resources are unavailable, patrons are likely to suffer academically, intellectually, and socially. A 2014 study conducted by the ALA and Information Policy and Access Center revealed that "virtually all (98%) public libraries provide no-fee Wi-Fi access and an average of 20 computers" (Bertot et. al., 2014). That being said, there is still a disparity between the quality and speed of Internet connectivity in urban versus rural libraries, which is illustrated in the following table:

Figure 7: Public Library Outlet Subscribed Upload Speed Compared to Captured Device-Level Speed, by Locale Code

Locale Code	Subscribed Median Speed	Direct Connect Speed Test (median)	Wi-Fi Speed Test (median)
City	29.3 Mbps (n=1,048)	25.2 Mbps (n=977)	6.3 Mbps (n=495)
Suburban	20.0 Mbps (n=846)	8.9 Mbps (n=728)	5.9 Mbps (n=498)
Town	10.0 Mbps (n=784)	3.3 Mbps (n=781)	2.9 Mbps (n=478)
Rural	8.9 Mbps (n=961)	2.1 Mbps (n=972)	1.4 Mbps (n=689)
Overall	**15.0 Mbps (n=3,636)**	**7.5 Mbps (n=3,458)**	**4.1 Mbps (n=2,160)**

(Real et. al., 2014)

Though broadband speeds are improving nationwide, distribution is uneven throughout the country. Further steps must be taken to meet community digital inclusion needs.

Remote Users

While remote access to libraries is not a new phenomenon, telecommunications innovations have changed the expectations of remote users. Beyond the use of Online Public Access Catalogs (OPACS), remote users now also reserve, renew, and borrow content (such as eBooks) digitally. Distance learning has also impacted the digital services that libraries provide.

Decades ago, when many institutions of higher education offered correspondence classes, they simply mailed students easy-to-follow instructions. As the off- campus education programs became more sophisticated, the institutions sent packets of information that included lectures, photocopies of reading materials, and assignments. In order to complete many of these assignments, students needed to seek help at a nearby library. (Cooper & Dempsey, 1998)

Today, in addition to providing information to students in person, libraries offer access to materials online. "The librarian's professional role will no longer be that of intermediary between consumers and commodities but rather between learners and resources provided to expand their knowledge and skills" (Cooper & Dempsey, 1998). Connectivity to high-speed Internet is an essential component of providing this service.

Bib Essay Unit 11A: Telecommunication

Introduction

We are now in a digital age, able to remotely access and download information in a variety of formats to a multitude of devices. Digital information has grown exponentially and librarians are at the helm trying to effectively collect, manage, disseminate, and archive these digital resources; while also protecting copyright and honoring licensing agreements. Today's librarians need to be familiar with the current devices and access methods and advocate for both the users and content providers.

File Formats

All digital resources are files to be saved, opened, and sent through computerized devices via special software. Each file format serves the same purpose: to display digital content on a computer or mobile device. The table below organizes some of the file extensions you may encounter when interacting with digital content.

Format	Abbreviation	Description
Hypertext Markup Language	HTML	ccessed through a webpage via the internet
pen eBook Format	OEB	A legacy e-book format superseded by EPUB; ased on technology by SoftBook Press and XML.
ortable Document Format	PDF	file represents documents as flat, fixed-layout displays with text, fonts, graphics, and other information
Document	DOC	Microsoft Word Document

Document XML	DOCX	Microsoft Word Open XML Document
ιmerican Standard ode for Information Interchange	ASCII	· Code that represents text in ımputers (and other devices) that use text; encodes 128 specified haracters into seven-bit integers
Program Database	PDB	Stores debugging information about a program or program nodules such as a DLL or EXE
Amazon Word	AZW	Format exclusive to Amazon Kindle
Literature	LIT	Iicrosoft Reader format (expired 2012)
Déjà Vu [French]	DJVU	· Stores scanned documents ontaining a combination of text, line drawings, indexed color images, and photographs (Alternative to PDF)
Electronic Publication	EPUB	EPUB is the distribution and interchange format standard for digital publications and documents based on Web Standards.
Ioint Photographic Experts Group	JPEG	10:1 digital image compression
Auxiliary	MP3	PEG Layer III Audio is the most common sound file format
Audio Video Interleave	AVI	Multimedia container format for video-with-audio playback

(International Digital Publishing Forum, 2016) (CSU, 2011)

Devices: Ereaders and Tablets

Electronic devices are the vehicles used to display media formats and files. Their ability to run software, access the internet, and read (need words that address or imply encryption) files is essential to the process of sharing digital resources such as ebooks and ejournals. E-readers contain a variety of features and no two are the same. Models are competitively priced and their features include a long battery life (10 days), lightweight and ergonomic designs, use of "E ink", Wi-Fi and/or 3G compatible, and storage capabilities for thousands of books (CSU, 2011). Tablet and ereader ownership growth (in developed countries) was projected as 15-20% in 2015 (Behar, Colombani, & Krishnan, 2011). The growth in popularity of ereaders means its use in the library will become more prominent.

Librarians and Media Specialists are frequently expected to assist patrons with their electronic devices being used to access and read these files. The iOS and Android tablets, Kindles, Nooks, and smartphones are used to access digital content. The most popular are Nook and iPad, and Kindle which just announced a new model will be released.

Ereaders

·Kindle	· Icarus
· Nook	· Cybook Odyssey
· iPad	·Pyrus
·Jetbook	·BOOXS
· PocketBook	·Kobo
· Sony Reader	

DRM and Format Standards

The International Digital Publishing Forum (IDPF) has created a format standard for which eBooks can be accessed across a variety of software platforms. This standard is known as "EPUB," which a user would see as a format option when accessing their eBook (CSU, 2011).

Digital Rights Management, or DRM, are "access control technologies embedded within electronic documents to restrict copying, printing, and/or sharing of digital resources, protecting the rights of the copyright holder to control the distribution of the resource, and usually require users to license or purchase the resource" (CSU, 2011). Creating a copy of digital media is easy, quick, and does not degrade its content, herein lies the need for DRM in the issue of copyright and fair use. "EBooks in particular are licensed, and license terms trump fair use. DRM systems will not allow Interlibrary Loan" (CSU, 2011). The library looking to add to their collection of eBooks may find that DRM does not allow eBooks to behave the same way printed books behave within the collection.

Ebooks

In the past 3 years digital content usage, particularly ebooks, for school and library use has exploded. The growth of the e-book market in recent years is creating a monumental shift in how libraries loan their materials and what libraries add to their collection. With the popularity of ebooks on the rise, authors, publishers, and distributors are working to compete in this market and keep up with growing demand of ebook access offering perpetual access, subscription, or pay-per-view services (O'Brien, Gasser, & Palfrey, 2012). With the convenience and accessibility of e-books via the web, authors, publishers and distributors are concerned with the library's ability to offer access to ebooks for free. "A patron can 'check out' an e-book without entering the library, and an e-book copy automatically reverts to the library without patron intervention at the end of a loan period" (O'Brien, Gasser, & Palfrey, 2012). Why buy an e-book? For libraries this means options and pricing to fit their needs for popular titles, and a variety of fiction and nonfiction a-la carte, in packages, or a combination. "A survey of almost 3,000 consumers.... shows that readers tend to read more when equipped with digital readers....The vast majority of those readers will pay for their e-books" (Behar, Colombani, & Krishnan, 2011). Whether owners of ereaders buy, borrow, or engage in both buying and borrowing, the eBook is a rapidly expanding growing type of sharable media in the digital era.

Book Publishers

There are 5 major book publishers in the industry; they have not always made it easy for libraries to provide ebooks. In 2013 a best seller ebook title that sold to consumers for $13.00 cost a library $85.00. This is because from a publisher's perspective an ebook will never be lost or damaged, one purchased copy could last indefinitely and be shared repeatedly. (Digital Book World, 2013; Budler, J., & LeRue, J. 2013) This reasoning resulted in many publishers refusing to sell to libraries. The solution that evolved is that libraries subscribe to a third party host that negotiates licensing and usage parameters with the publishers.

Electronic Journals and Periodicals

E-journals are an edited package of articles that are distributed to most of its subscribers in electronic form. The term can include magazines, serials, or newsletters that are usually accessed via Web pages, and sometimes through email. In the last two decades there has been a rapid transition from print to e-journals, e-journal packages via aggregator services or subscriptions agents, and through Open Access (Bosch, 2014). In the 1990's e-journal packages first became available as CD-ROMS, and then over the Web. An E-journal's full-text articles are usually in HTML and/or PDF format. Some individual subscriptions for general interest e-magazines offer full-text, while others only allow access to a limited amount of text, such as the table of contents or an abstract, with the full text requiring a fee.

E-journals have become popular for many reasons: they save money over print journals, they save space, and they don't get lost, stolen, or damaged. Usage has created a new set of issues such as archiving, copyright, Internet access, hardware costs. A recent study of e-journal preservation at Columbia and Cornell university's found that "only 15 percent of e-journals are being preserved and that the responsibility for preservation is diffuse at best" (Kelley, 2012). Some universities are beginning to use private companies such as Lots of Copies Keeps Stuff Safe (LOCKSS) and Portico for digital archiving. Libraries have had to push publishers to consider archiving back issues, or give libraries access to do so themselves. Many libraries do not have a system in place to select materials to archive.

Journal aggregating companies negotiate copyright with the publishers, and they develop a uniform method of access to all titles. Obtaining copyright from many different publishers contributes greatly to the cost of the package. Graphics may not be included. Large bundled e-journal packages are problematic for some libraries. Many journals in these large packages are never used. Libraries need to consider that more staff time and resources may be needed to support the computer, printers, and remote access needed for e-serials. Some patron complaints about e-journals are that screens are not comfortable to read from, networks or server search engine may not be of high quality and are not always peer-reviewed. Librarians now have an opportunity to influence the development of e-journal access and preservation.

Accessing eBooks and eJournals

<u>Overdrive</u>

The industry leader for non-journal items is Overdrive, with the largest catalog of eBooks, audiobooks, streaming video and periodicals. Library circulation through Overdrive is projected to increase 30-40% in 2016 (Overdrive, 2016). Using Overdrive just got easier with OverDrive Read, which is browser-based allowing you to access your checked out media without downloading special software. This is a game changer, no need to register for Adobe Digital

Editions or other protection technologies, nor download various apps or software when using different devices. Simply type in your library card number and click. To find out if your local library uses Overdrive search here: https://www.overdrive.com/libraries.

One Click Digital (CT residents)

The CT State Library uses One Click Digital to provide Connecticut residents audio and ebooks. Authorized users can register for One Click Digital remotely using a CT public library card or from an onsite location such as a public library or school. The latter option is useful for students without a library card as they can still access the state library collection from within their school. Downloading ebooks and audiobooks for the first time will require some initial setup. Mobile devices will require an app and ebooks on a computer require Adobe Digital Editions; for audiobooks download OneClickDigital Media manager. You can explore the collection here: http://iconnct.oneclickdigital.com/

Open Access

While Open Access (OA) publication costs are lower than for print, there are costs involved. Often the publication costs are provided by the author, either personally, through a grant, or by their research institution or university. Some OA coalitions raise funds from print version subscriptions, volunteer labor, and advertising to cover publishing costs. (Chan, 2012). With OA, authors retain all or some of their copyright, giving them more control over their work. There are also hybrid journals that have OA and subscriber only content. With the average cost of serial subscriptions for libraries continuing to increase from year to year, open access to a variety of digital resources seems necessary for libraries and schools to provide both quality and quantity of information to its users and patrons. "What is Open Access?" (n.d.) believes that, "Open access is a means of taking advantage of the global reach and relative inexpense of internet publishing to make peer-reviewed scholarly materials freely available.". Some perceived drawbacks of OA is less quality control due to the overwhelming volume of material submitted to the peer review process. Traditional book publishers have been moving to producing e-books, including e-textbooks as well as producing an OA online edition and a print for purchase edition, which has increased their sales of the print edition, as browsing customers find interest enough to purchase a hard copy (Swan, 2012).

Open Access Initiatives and Depositories:

- Directory of Open Access Journals (DOAJ) - https://doaj.org/
- Open eBooks Project - Federal repository for students in need - http://openebooks.net/faq.html
- Library of Congress Digital Collections - https://www.loc.gov/library/libarch-digital.html
- Librivox - Free public domain audiobooks - https://librivox.org/
- CK-12 Foundation - Open Educational Resources including FlexBooks - http://www.ck12.org/
- Coursera - Free online courses from the world's best universities - https://www.coursera.org/
- Learning Ally - Free audio books for learning or visually impaired - http://www.learningally.org/

Epic! for Educators (in school use)

Epic! offers unlimited use ebooks for children 12 and under and is often referred to as "Netflix for Books". The service is offered free to school teachers and school librarians in hopes that their students will purchase a subscription to the service for home. The books are web based and can be viewed from a computer, Chromebook, iOS and Android devices, and some Kindle Fires. The books look identical to their print version and can be read offline. There is also a read to me feature and Spanish texts. Unique to Epic! is the ability to create student profiles and preferences to make searching more customized. There is also a reading log and reward system to track progress. Sign up here: https://www.getepic.com/educators

Open eBooks Initiative (for Title 1 eligible)

This free ebook program is an extension of First Book (https://www.firstbook.org/) and provides free eBooks to children in need. The ebooks are accessible with iOS and Android devices only at this time. Any adult working with eligible students must first register with First Book (https://register.firstbook.org/?rgst=openebooks). Some examples of eligibility are: at least 70% of students from low-income families, a Title 1 eligible school, an eRate of 90%. (FirstBook, 2016) Learn more at http://www.openebooks.net/index.html

Bookshare (for Print Disabled)

Bookshare is a free service available to the "print disabled" that provides audio books, audio supported text and digital braille. According to their website Bookshare "operates in the U.S. under a copyright exemption—the Chafee Amendment—which grants nonprofit organizations the ability to make books available to people with print disabilities without publisher permission." (Bookshare, 2016) Membership is free to qualifying U.S. students who are deemed print disabled must by a competent authority. Free access is funded by the Department of Education and Office of Special Education Programs. "The Bookshare site does not provide access to copyrighted works for the general public."(Bookshare, 2016) Learning Ally is a similar site requiring membership and they extend their services to students with dyslexia.
To learn more visit: https://www.bookshare.org/cms and http://www.learningally.org/

Some additional issues when working with digital media.

In a public library, children could potentially download movies and ebooks from the management systems with inappropriate content. This is why schools prefer their own service providers with an age appropriate collection. SLMS also need to be aware that if they opt to circulate e-readers the ADA requires

that they provide access to e-readers that students with disabilities can navigate(Acedo, S., & Leverkus, C. 2014).
Lastly, publishers and vendors have an understanding that while an individual is able to read and store a purchased ebook on up six devices that is not true for libraries. They can not "buy one ebook, load it on six different devices, and circulate those devices to six different people" (Acedo, S., & Leverkus, C. 2014).

Discussion Question 1 (Shonya, Kaitlyn, & Lorraine) Which devices and media formats do you use? And what and how does your school or library use?
Discussion Question 2 (Shonya, Kaitlyn, & Lorraine) Some publishers allow their books to be used for the blind, disabled, poor etc but it would be easy for a librarian abuse this specialized access and share these resources with populations they were not intended for. How would you handle a teacher using a BookShare account for a child that did not qualify?
Discussion Question 3 (Shonya, Kaitlyn, & Lorraine)Why can't you purchase an ebook from Amazon and put it on multiple Kindles in your library?

References

Acedo, S., & Leverkus, C. (2014). UPDATES ON EBOOKS Challenges & Changes. Knowledge Quest, 43(1), 44-52.

Behar, P., Colombani, L., & Krishnan, S. (2011). Publishing in the Digital Era: A Bain & Company study for the Forum d'Avignon. Bain & Company Inc.

Bookshare. (2016). Beneficent Technology, Inc. Retrieved from https://www.bookshare.org/cms/

Bosch, S. (2014, April 11). Steps Down the Evolutionary Road. Periodicals Price Survey 2014. Retrieved from: http://lj.libraryjournal.com/2014/04/publishing/steps-down-the-evolutionary-road-periodicals-price-survey-2014/

Budler, J., & LeRue, J. (2013, August 5). E-Books Strain Relations Between Libraries, Publishing Houses [Interview by L. Neary]. In Morning Edition. Washington: NPR.

Chan C. & Swan, A. (2012, Sept. 12). Why Librarians Should Be Concerned with Open Access. Open Access Scholarly Information Sourcebook. Retrieved from: http://www.openoasis.org/index.php%3Foption%3Dcom_content%26view%3Darticle%2 6id%3D254%26Itemid%3D256

CT State Library. (2016.). ResearchIt CT. Retrieved from http://libguides.ctstatelibrary.org/researchIT_CT/about-researchIT_CT

Colorado State University, Front Range Community College, Poudre River Public Library District. (2011). eBooks and eReaders in Public and Academic Libraries. 2-55.

Digital Book World. (2013, February 5). The Real Cost of Ebooks for Libraries. Retrieved from http://www.digitalbookworld.com/2013/the-real-cost-of-ebooks-for-libraries/

Epic for Educators (n.d.) https://www.getepic.com/educators

First Book. (n.d.) https://www.firstbook.org/

International Digital Publishing Forum (IDPF). (2016). EPUB. Retrieved from http://idpf.org/epub.

O'Brien, D. R., Gasser, U., & Palfrey, J. (2012). E-BOOKS IN LIBRARIES: A Briefing Document developed in preparation. The Berkman Center for Internet & Society at Harvard University.

Overdrive. (2016, April 6). OverDrive Reports 2016 Digital Library Trends for Public Libraries [Press release]. Retrieved from http://www.msn.com/en-us/money/topstories/overdrive-reports-2016-digital-library-trends-for-public-libraries/ar-BBrqGuf

Bib Essay Unit 11B: Media Formats

Media Resources

According to the Association of College and Research Libraries(ACRL), "Technology used in teaching, learning, and research has created new challenges and opportunities for managers of college and university library media resource collections and services" (ACRL, 2012). Much like telecommunication, media formats have changed drastically over time. The two main format categories are print, and electronic. Examples of print media formats are:

- Books
- Periodicals
- Pamphlets
- Maps
- Government Documents, etc.

Some electronic media formats are:

- Web pages
- PDFs
- CD-ROMs
- DVDs
- eBooks
- eJournals/Periodicals
- Open Source Publications

Though not as popular today, a third medium housed by many library collections is the microform. The term microform "refers to various books, journals, and other materials that have been photographed in a reduced - sized print" (Bloomsburg University of Pennsylvania, 2015). Microfilms and Microfiche fall into this category.

eBooks

The first eBooks were created in the 1970's, as part of the Project Gutenberg's efforts to "digitiz[e] cultural works to encourage the creation and dissemination of e-books" (O'Brien et. al., 2012). It wasn't until 2007, however, when Amazon released their Kindle eBook reader, that this format exploded in the mass market. By 2008:

A little more than $1 out of every $100 in total publishing trade revenue went to eBook sales. Just four short years later, it had jumped to $23 of every $100. The 2014 data—from the Association of American Publishers (AAP)—also shows that the eBook market share continues to hover around a quarter of total trade sales. (Inouye, 2016)

Given the massive popularity of this new format, it comes as no surprise that libraries have become some of the biggest distributors of eBooks. Libraries are key to the reading ecosystem. Their importance cannot be overstated…The large majority of people are not early adopters, so having a place where anyone can walk in and try out and learn about new technologies—accessing ebooks on smartphones, preloaded iPads or Kindles, and the like—is enormously useful. What's more, librarians also learn about the newest services and technologies and provide information and objective feedback about them. (Inouye, 2016)

eReaders

EBooks can be accessed on many different devices. Users can access eBooks on desktop and laptop computers, on their tablets and smartphones with eReader applications, or through eReaders, which are "mobile electronic devices that are designed primarily for the purpose or reading digital e-books and periodicals" (Wikipedia, 2016). While similar to tablet computers, eReaders typically have more readable screens, and longer battery life (Wikipedia, 2016). There are several manufacturers of eReaders, including:

Apple iPad	Bookeen Cybook

Ectaco JetBook	Entourage eDGe
Hanvon E-Book Reader	Iriver Story
Kindle	Kobo
Nook	Sony
Velocity Micro Cruz Reader	

Most of these readers are comparable in size (about 6 inch screens, weight approximately 7 ounces) and storage capacity (4GB) (Colon & Lendino, 2016). In addition to the different eReader devices, eBooks are published in a number of different digital file types. Some of these are:

Format	Abbreviation	Description
Broadband eBooks	BBeB	Propriety format developed by Sony, now replaced by EPUB.
Digital Accessible Information System	DAISY	Developed for people with print disabilities. Has support with features for multimedia, navigation & synchronization.
DejaVu	DjVu	Specialized format for storing scanned documents. Used as an alternative to PDF.
Document File Format	.DOC	Created by Microsoft word, supported by a few eReaders. Enables editing.
Electronic Publication	EPUB	The open standard for eBooks created by International Digital Publishing Forum.
FictionBook	Fb2	Popular XML-based eBook format, available on 'free readers' such as Okular
Hypertext Markup Language	HTML	Can be read using a web browser.
Portable Document	PDF	Developed by Adobe, provides platform-independent way to

Format		exchange fixed-layout documents.
Rich Text Format	RTF	This format can be easily edited, and easily converted into other eBook formats.

Challenges

Though libraries have embraced eReader technology, it has also created some challenges. In "Ebooks on Fire: Controversies surrounding Ebooks in Libraries", Charles Hamaker outlines the following issues raised by the advent of eBooks:

- Revocable Rights -Publishers can, and often do, provide limited and impermanent access to materials. A book that is available after purchase one day, may not still be there on the next.
- Protecting the Text - The eBook format is easily adjustable. Therefore, authors can change the text in previous editions without notifying the reader.
- Library Issues - The costs and challenges in acquiring and cataloging eBooks are many. Keeping up with the changing landscape makes long-term acquisition and maintenance next to impossible.
- Confidentiality - Some eBook lending services "automatically use the patron's library account to create the supporting accounts needed on its own platform and in the DRM environment" (Breeding, 2011).
- Paying a Premium - Some publishers impose additional fees to libraries once eBooks reach a certain circulation number, arguing that it is no different than 'wear out' on traditional print texts.

(Hamaker, 2011)

Conclusion

The famous architect Henry Bergman once said, "Each and every problem we face today is the direct and inevitable result of yesterday's brilliant solutions"

(Information Ethics, 2008). Never has this sentiment been truer than it is now, in the height of the information age. Technological innovations have accelerated the creation of information exponentially. As a result, the provision of access to this information has become more challenging for library staff. Ensuring access to the latest telecommunication innovations comes at a cost, but also has extraordinary benefits.

Likewise, the transition of print media to digital formats has created obstacles, both technical and financial. Despite this, demand for access to digital media formats is increasing. As the debate continues between publishers and libraries, The myth that when a library buys a book the publisher loses future sales [is being debunked]. Instead, [studies confirm] that the public library does not only incubate and support literacy, as is well understood in our culture, but it is an active partner with the publishing industry in building the book market, not to mention the burgeoning e-book market.

References

American Library Association (2016). 2016 Telecommunications Fact Sheet. Retrieved July 16, 2016, from http://www.ala.org/advocacy/sites/ala.org.advocacy/files/content/advleg/federallegislation/03-23-16%20FINAL%20TELECOM%20One-Pager%20SJM.pdf

Association of College and Research Libraries (2012). Guidelines for Media Resources in Academic Libraries. Retrieved July 18, 2016, from http://www.ala.org/acrl/standards/mediaresources

Association of Research Libraries (2016, March 31). Telecommunications Policies. Retrieved July 12, 2016, from http://www.arl.org/focus-areas/telecommunications-policies#.V5zuFiMrLJyBertot, J. P., Lee, J., Pawar, N., & Jaeger, P.T. (2015, April 11).

Broadband Quality in Public Libraries. ALA / IPAC, April 2015. Retrieved 21 July, 2016, from http://www.ala.org/offices/sites/ala.org.offices/files/content/Speed_Te

st_FINAL_0.pdf

Media Types. Retrieved July 19, 2016, from http://guides.library.bloomu.edu/c.php?g=318498&p=2128737 Breeding, Marshall. (2011). Smarter Libraries through Technology: Developments in E-books and RFID. Smart Libraries Newsletter 31 (7), 1-2.Colon, A., & Lendino, J. The Best eReaders of 2016. PCWorld Online. Retrieved July 19, 2016, from http://www.pcmag.com/roundup/294182/the-best-ebook-readers

Comparison of e-book formats. (2016, July 20). In Wikipedia, The Free Encyclopedia. Retrieved 20:09, July 31, 2016, from https://en.wikipedia.org/w/index.php?title=Comparison_of_ebook_formats&oldid=730626951

Cooper, R., & Dempsey, P.R. (1998). Remote Library Users: Needs and Expectations. Library Trends, 47 (1), 42-65. Retrieved July 30, 2016, from http://www.lib.pu.edu.tw/~jiang/articals/Remote%20Library%20Users--Needs%20and%20Expectations.htm

E-reader. (2016, April 26). In Wikipedia, The Free Encyclopedia. Retrieved July 28, 2016, from https://en.wikipedia.org/w/index.php?title=E-reader&oldid=717236747

eReader Resources. (2016, January 2). In ipl2.org. Retrieved July 30, 2016, from http://www.ipl.org/div/ereader/Hamaker, C. (2011, December 17).

Ebooks on Fire: Controversies Surrounding Ebooks in Libraries. Information Today Online, 19(10). Retrieved July 30, 2016, from http://www.infotoday.com/searcher/dec11/Hamaker.shtml Information Ethics (2008).

Unintended Consequences [blog post]. Retrieved from http://infowarethics.org/quotes.techno-ethics.html Inouye, A. S. (2016, January 4).

What's in Store for Ebooks? Looking at the digital future of libraries in 2016 and beyond. American Libraries Online. Retrieved July 30, 2016, from https://americanlibrariesmagazine.org/2016/01/04/whats-store-ebooks/O'Brien, D.R., Gasser, U., & Palfrey, J. (2012, July 1).

E-Books in Libraries: A Briefing Document Developed in Preparation for a Workshop on E-Lending in Libraries. Berkman Center Research Publication 2012(15). Retrieved 28 July, 2016, from http://papers.ssrn.com/sol3/papers.cfm?abstract_id=2111396##

Here's How Wi-Fi Actually Works. Time Magazine Online.Retrieved July 12, 2016, from http://time.com/3834259/wifi-how-works/Real, B., Bertot, J. C., & Jaeger, P.T. (2014, March 13).

Rural Public Libraries and Digital Inclusion: Issues and Challenges Information Technology and Libraries Online, 33(1), 6-24. Retrieved July 20, 2016, from https://ejournals.bc.edu/ojs/index.php/ital/article/viewFile/5141/pdf

Techopedia (2016). Telecommunications. Retrieved July 30, 2016, from https://www.techopedia.com/definition/5570/telecommunications

Whitehouse.gov (2015, February 26). Net Neutrality: President Obama's Plan for a Free and Open Internet. Retrieved July 10, 2016, from https://www.whitehouse.gov/net-neutrality

Williams, B. K., & Sawyer, S. C. (2015). Using information technology: A practical Introduction to computers & communications (11th ed.). New York, NY: McGraw-Hill.

Zickuhr, K., Lee, R., Purcell, K., Madden, M., & Brenner, J. (2012, June 22). Libraries, patrons, and e-books. Pew Internet & American Life Project. Retrieved 29 July, 2016, from http://libraries.pewinternet.org/2012/06/22/part-1-an-introduction-to-the-issues-surrounding-libraries-and-e-books/

Questions for Discussion:

1. As a distance learner, what are your expectations for library media services? Are there any services that you wish were offered that are not?
2. Are you an eReader? If so, what advantages do you feel that this platform provides for library patriots? If not, why not?

Bib Essay Unit 12: The Future of Libraries

Introduction

Libraries face a number of challenges from the new forms of Media mentioned above, not the least of which is that much of it is available at relatively low cost to anyone with a computer and internet access. Websites like Project Gutenberg even offer free E-Books of books in the Public Domain, making it seem superfluous for most libraries to maintain older books.

With E-Books available online and the ability of the average person to research almost any topic via the internet from their home, libraries are quickly evolving from what they were only two decades ago. The first change is obvious to anyone who has patronized libraries steadily over the past couple decades: there are less books. As the internet has become more commonplace, libraries have been cutting back on their non-fiction collections in particular. Reference materials such as Encyclopedias and Dictionaries have become almost obsolete. The University of California, Santa Barbara (UCSB) recently renovated their Library. Their goal was to "add 60,000 square feet of new library space and renovate 92,000 square feet of existing library space." The goal included such features as "expanded wireless access," "additional and enhanced group study and collaboration spaces," and a "faculty collaboration studio (Barclay, 2015)." One will notice that "additional space for books" is not included in the newly expanded library.

Further contributing to the changes in libraries is the fact that governments have continued to cut funding for them, forcing them to find places to cut expenses. 2012 marked the third straight year that almost half of the States in the United States cut funding to libraries. In 2009, The Free Library of Philadelphia, one of the oldest Libraries in the country, was almost closed by the Pennsylvania State legislature (Agresta, 2014).

As technology changes, and the way we access information with it, it is clear that libraries will have to change as well. Some have even already started, anticipating their impending obsolescence. Most of these libraries have simply changed their focus from being a repository of knowledge to being a place where ideas and skills are shared and practiced. They do this through a simple process that starts with adopting new technology and equipment.

Adopting New Technology and Equipment

The past couple decades, with the emergence of personal computers and internet use as common and essential elements of our civilization, has seen a small preview of what lies in store for the libraries of the future. During the 1990s and early 2000s, Libraries became places where new technology and guidance in using that new technology were made available to patrons. Instead of simply being a place where people could go to look up information in books or borrow a book for reading pleasure, libraries became the place where people could go to use computers and internet, which were not, at that time, something most people had in their homes. As technology continues to progress and computers and internet access become only more widespread, libraries will need to adopt even newer technology.

Some new technologies that will be adopted or have already begun to be adopted include:

Tablets – A Tablet is a "is a thin, flat mobile computer with a touchscreen display…processing circuitry, and a rechargeable battery in a single device (Tablet Computer, 2017)." Tablets offer a wealth of opportunities for libraries and their patrons. They are a portable device that patrons and librarians can use to carry the library's catalog with them in their search for books or other materials without continually returning to the reference desk or a desktop computer (Troknya, 2015).

3D Printers – A 3D Printer is a machine that creates a Three Dimensional object “in which successive layers of material are formed under computer control to create an object (3D Printing, 2017).” The most common material 3D printers work with is plastic polymers, however 3D Printers do exist that can work with almost any material including woods and metals. 3D Printers can be used for a number of functions in Libraries, from teaching patrons the skills required to use them in a workplace to allowing patrons to construct whatever their minds can imagine. 3D printers are already becoming a major part of many industries and many people are using them to create inexpensive models and prototypes of inventions. As 3D Printers are still relatively expensive, costing anywhere from a couple hundred to several thousand dollars, the ability of libraries to provide this emerging technology to their patrons is valuable.

Augmented Reality – Augmented Reality “is a live direct or indirect view of a physical, real-world environment whose elements are *augmented* (or supplemented) by computer-generated sensory input such as sound, video, graphics or GPS data (Augmented Reality, 2017).” Augmented Reality is generally used via a smartphone, Tablet, or other mobile electronic device. Augmented reality is already available on many smartphones and tablets in photo applications that allow users to place objects such as sunglasses or bunny ears on the heads of people in the picture. Less frivolous uses of Augmented Reality include educational programs where users can look at the world around them and have supplemental background information available regarding what they see. Augmented Reality is also useful to learners of another language, as it can not only translate spoken and written words for users, but also can superimpose words on real world objects so that users can find the word for an object (Aggarwal). The applications are endless, and as augmented reality becomes a larger part of our lives, libraries will need to incorporate it into their offerings.

Virtual Reality – Virtual Reality is a step above Augmented Reality. Instead of taking in information from the real world, Virtual Reality completely replaces the real world with a computer simulated one. Virtual Reality is already quickly finding uses in everything from training surgeons to helping

Ikea customers design their kitchens (Wakefield, 2016). Virtual reality has the ability to be endlessly useful in education and the acquisition of information as it could be used to allow library patrons to *experience* information rather than just acquire it.

Social Media – Social Media allows people to communicate and socialize via the internet using smartphones and computers. It also changes how public institutions such as libraries function in their community. From blogs to YouTube Videos and Facebook campaigns, Social Media has been essential to helping Libraries across the United States raise awareness of their services and connect with patrons and advocates. Some Libraries, such as New York Public Library, have even been able to use Social Media to offer social events with authors via the internet, making such offerings available to anyone with an internet connection (Dankowski, 2013). As Social Media becomes an ever-increasing part of people's lives, it will play a crucial role in how Libraries connect to their communities.

Artificial Intelligence – Artificial Intelligence is "an area of computer science that deals with giving machines the ability to seem like they have human intelligence (Whitehair, 2016)." Artificial Intelligence is already available to many consumers in the form of software such as Apple's Siri, Amazon Echo, and IBM's Watson. Such programs "learn" from user input to provide more personalized and, hopefully, accurate search results and information. The applications in libraries is obvious – imagine each patron having a personalized account that searched for information and recommended books based on their individual preferences and interests. The voice recognition software these programs use could make access to information much faster and would be useful in accommodating patrons with disabilities.

Focusing on Skills and Equipment

Many libraries, as they adopt new technologies, are focusing less on traditional information acquisition and turning to teaching skills involving some of this technologically advanced equipment. These libraries are serving their patrons by "offering programs in technology, career and college readiness and also in innovation and entrepreneurship – all 21st-century skills, essential for success in today's economy (Martin, 2015)."

For example, in 2014, the San Diego Public Library Central Library opened what they call an "IDEA Lab," where students can explore new technology. The lab hires teenage interns to run workshops about their interests. "These range from Photoshop to stop-motion animation and skill-building technology projects (Martin, 2015)." These internships not only teach necessary career skills to participants, but also allow the interns running them to acquire experience relating to potential career goals (Martin, 2015).

Another way in which Libraries are embracing this new role is with "Maker Spaces." A Maker Space is an area where libraries "collect old and new technologies, from sewing machines to 3-D printers, and encourage patrons to develop and share skills that cannot be practiced over the Internet (Agresta, 2014)." The skills practiced in Maker Spaces can either be related to 21st century career skills or can embrace skills used in old and new hobbies. As stated above, these spaces allow patrons to practice skills that are not possible to practice over electronic media such as the internet. While traditional information acquisition through books and E-Books is limited to theoretical knowledge, Maker Spaces expand the ability of individuals to gain practical information and experience.

A Center of Local Creativity and Culture

Libraries have long been places where the works of local people are held and displayed, but as the role of the library changes, many libraries are beginning to focus even more on this role.

One organization that is encouraging Libraries to further embrace local creativity is the Library As Incubator Project (LAIP). The LAIP "highlights the ways that libraries and artists can work together, and works to strengthen these partnerships…The Library as Incubator Project calls attention to one of the many reasons libraries are important to our communities and our culture, and provides a dynamic online forum for sharing ideas (LAIP, 2011)." Some projects that the LAIP has contributed to "include the Local Music Project at the Iowa City Public Library, where librarians lease recordings from local artists and offer them online to cardholders for free, and the Brooklyn Art Library's Sketchbook Project, a traveling bookmobile that accumulates donated 32-page sketchbooks from both professional and amateur artists and displays them around the country (Agresta, 2014)."

Libraries have always been places where local artists display their work, where local authors have their books available, and where local history resources can be utilized for research. New technologies, however, allow these resources to be accessed electronically, making them more available to a wider community of people. As the library's role as a place of general information fades, libraries will undoubtedly come to put more emphasis on sharing local treasures.

Libraries Remain Unchanged

Libraries may be a case of how the more things change, the more they stay the same. The fear that libraries will be made obsolete and eventually go extinct because of the technological advancements of the Information Age is largely unfounded. A recent Pew Internet & American Life Project study "found that 73% of patrons visit libraries to browse, and personalized recommendations are still an important service to the library-goer (Dankowski, 2013)." And if you are concerned that new, electronic media will replace old print media, consider that "Research in the relatively new discipline of book history has demonstrated that new modes of communication do not displace old ones… Radio did not destroy the newspaper; television did not kill radio; and the Internet did not make TV extinct. In each case, the information environment became richer and more complex (Darnton, 2011)."

The fact that print media will remain is a fact that many libraries seem to recognize. Many are reducing their print collections, but are far from eliminating them altogether. Many are in fact using new technology to make print storage and retrieval more efficient. In 2011, the University of Chicago opened a newly renovated library building that stored most of its print materials in the library's basement. The collection of 3.5 Million books are accessible through an automated retrieval system (Barclay, 2015). Such automated systems are quickly being installed in Academic Libraries across the country and one day may be the main way that print materials are stored and retrieved in libraries, meaning that the rest of the library can focus on providing access to new technologies and Maker Spaces.

The roles that libraries are beginning to embrace and will embrace more in the future are not new roles. Libraries have been exhibiting local creativity and providing skills based information for a long time. They have often been places where people can access new technologies before such technologies become commonplace in the home. None of this is new. All that will change is that they will increase their focus in these areas, and libraries will become places where information is not just accessed, but where it can be experienced.

Bibliography:

Aggarwal, Vineet. Augmented Reality – Introduction and its Real World Uses. Retrieved from https://www.3pillarglobal.com/insights/augmented-reality-introduction-and-its-real- world-uses

Agresta, Michael. (2014, April 22). What Will Become of the Library? Retrieved from http://www.slate.com/articles/life/design/2014/04/the_future_of_the_library_how_they_ll _evolve_for_the_digital_age.html

Angell, Brian D., & Smith, Gabie E. (1998) Print Versus Electronic: Editors' Insights on the Costs and Benefits of Online Journals. *The Journal of Technology Studies, Volume 24.* Retrieved from http://scholar.lib.vt.edu/ejournals/JOTS/Winter-Spring-1998/angell.html

Augmented Reality. (2017, April 8). Retrieved from

https://en.wikipedia.org/wiki/Augmented_reality

Barclay, Donald A. (2015, August 19). Turning a Page: Downsizing the Campus Book Collections. Retrieved from https://theconversation.com/turning-a-page-downsizing-the- campus-book-collections

Dankowski, Terra. (2013, July 16). How Libraries are Using Social Media. Retrieved from https://americanlibrariesmagazine.org/2013/07/16/how-libraries-are-using-social-media/

Darnton, Robert. (2011, April 17). 5 Myths About the 'Information Age'. Retrieved from http://www.chronicle.com/article/5-Myths-About-the-Information/127105/

Directory of Open Access Journals. About DOAJ. Retrieved from https://doaj.org/about

Inouye, Alan S. (2016, January 4). What's In Store for E-Books: Looking at the Digital Future of Libraries in 2016v and Beyond. Retrieved from https://americanlibrariesmagazine.org/2016/01/04/whats-store-ebooks/

Library As Incubator Project. (2011, May 25). About. Retrieved from http://www.libraryasincubatorproject.org/?page_id=9

Martin, Crystle. (2015, August 19). Who Says Libraries are Dying? They are Evolving Into Spaces for Innovation) Retrieved from https://theconversation.com/who-says-libraries- are-dying-they-are-evolving-into-spaces-for-innovation

Perrin, Andrew. (2016, September 1). Book Reading 2016. Retrieved from http://www.pewinternet.org/2016/09/01/book-reading-2016/

Tablet Computer. (2017, April 6). Retrieved from https://en.wikipedia.org/wiki/Tablet_computer

Troknya, Mark. (2015, April 1). Tablets: Are They Right for Your Library? Retrieved from http://publiclibrariesonline.org/2015/04/tablets-are-they-right-for-your-library/

United States Census Bureau. (2014, February 3). Table 4. Households with a Computer and Internet Use: 1984 – 2012. Retrieved from https://www.census.gov/data/tables/2012/demo/computer-internet/computer-use-2012.html

Vaccaro, Adam. (2014, June 27). Why it's Difficult for your Library to Lend E-Books. Retrieved from https://www.boston.com/news/technology/2014/06/27/why-its-difficult-for-your-library-to-lend-ebooks

Wakefield, Jane. (2016, October 24). The Real-World Uses of Virtual Reality. Retrieved from http://www.bbc.com/news/technology-37576755

Whitehair, Kristin. (2016, February 11). Libraries in an Artificially Intelligent World. Retrieved from http://publiclibrariesonline.org/2016/02/libraries-in-an-artificially-intelligent-world/

3D Printing. (2017, April 6). Retrieved from https://en.wikipedia.org/wiki/3D_printing#Printers

Acknowledgement

This is a course pack for students in an information and library science program, or anyone who are interested in learning information and library science.

The lecture notes were originally developed by Dr. James Kusak. Contributions also include Dr. Hok Joon Kima and other faculty members in the Department of Information and Library Science, Southern Connecticut State University.

Dr. Yan Quan Liu
2017

Made in the USA
Middletown, DE
29 August 2017